人文社科
高校学术研究论著丛刊

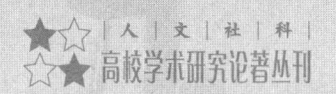

商务导论

刘胡蝶 主编

中国书籍出版社
China Book Press

图书在版编目(CIP)数据

商务导论/刘胡蝶主编. -- 北京：中国书籍出版社, 2020.10

ISBN 978-7-5068-8051-0

Ⅰ.①商… Ⅱ.①刘… Ⅲ.①商业经营 – 高等学校 – 教材 Ⅳ.① F715

中国版本图书馆 CIP 数据核字（2020）第 213556 号

商务导论

刘胡蝶　主编

丛书策划	谭　鹏　武　斌
责任编辑	刘建华　成晓春
责任印制	孙马飞　马　芝
封面设计	东方美迪
出版发行	中国书籍出版社
地　　址	北京市丰台区三路居路 97 号(邮编：100073)
电　　话	（010）52257143（总编室）　（010）52257140（发行部）
电子邮箱	eo@chinabp.com.cn
经　　销	全国新华书店
印　　厂	三河市德贤弘印务有限公司
开　　本	710 毫米 × 1000 毫米 1/16
字　　数	270 千字
印　　张	12.25
版　　次	2022 年 1 月第 1 版
印　　次	2022 年 1 月第 1 次印刷
书　　号	ISBN 978-7-5068-8051-0
定　　价	62.00 元

版权所有　翻印必究

目 录

Part I Getting Business Perspectives 1
    Chapter 1 Business Environment and Ethics ················· 1
    Chapter 2 Forms of Business ································· 12

Part II Managing the Business 24
    Chapter 3 Management and Leadership ····················· 24
    Chapter 4 Organizing the Enterprise ························ 33

Part III Understanding People in Organizations 42
    Chapter 5 Managing Human Resources ····················· 42
    Chapter 6 Motivating People ·································· 51

Part IV Understanding Marketing 64
    Chapter 7 Marketing and Product Developing ············· 64
    Chapter 8 Pricing, Distributing and Promoting ············ 82
    Chapter 9 International E-commerce and Logistics ········· 94

Part V Managing Financial Resources 105
    Chapter 10 Principles of Accounting ························ 105
    Chapter 11 Money and Banking ······························ 119

Part VI Dealing with Crisis and Risks 127
    Chapter 12 Financing and Investment ······················ 127
    Chapter 13 Risk Management ································ 139

Part VII Doing Business Globally 148
    Chapter 14 Intercultural Communication ··················· 148
    Chapter 15 International Business Practices ··············· 159

Part VIII Understanding Principles of Economy ·················· **171**
    Chapter 16 Micro Economics ·· 171
    Chapter 17 Macro Economy ·· 179
Reference ··· **187**

Part I Getting Business Perspectives

Chapter 1 Business Environment and Ethics

Business Environment

Economic Environment	Technological Environment	Competitive Environment
•Freedom of ownership •Exchange rate policy •Trade cycle (business cycle) •National income and living standard	•Information technology •Production technology •Database •Bar codes •Internet	•Customer service •Stakeholder recognition •Employee service

Political Environment	Legal Environment	Social Environment
•Government intervention •Taxes and regulation •Government spending •Government monopoly	•Contract laws •Employment laws •Restrictive trade practices •Tort laws •Property laws •Industrial regulations •Elimination of corruption •Price control	•Diversity •Demographic changes, e.g. aging population •Birth rate •Family changes •Growing concern for the environment •Growing interest in health and fitness

Factors of Production

Land	Land and other natural resources are used to make homes, cars and others.
Labor	Human resources, including the physical and intellectual capabilities of people, have always been an important resource in producing goods and services, but many people are now being replaced by technology.
Capital	Capital includes funds, machines, tools, buildings, and other means of manufacturing.

商务导论

Entrepreneurship	All the resources in the world have little value unless entrepreneurs are willing to take the risk of starting businesses to use those resources.
Knowledge	Modern technology has revolutionized business, increasing productivity, making it possible to quickly determine wants and needs and to respond with desired goods and services.

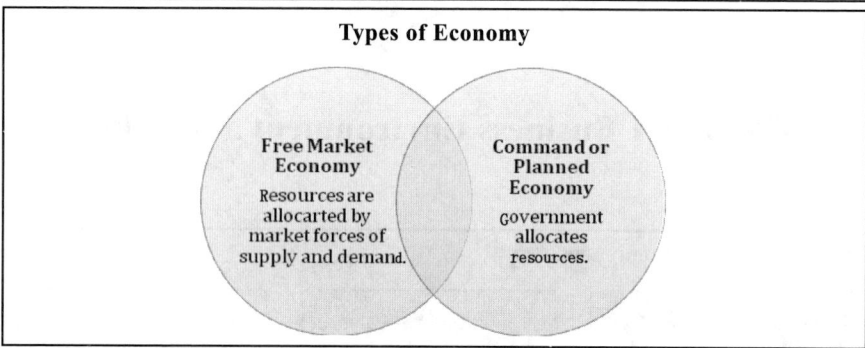

Types of Economy

- **Free Market Economy**: Resources are allocarted by market forces of supply and demand.
- **Command or Planned Economy**: Government allocates resources.

TYPES OF SYSTEM	WHO OWNS	WHO DECIDES
Pure Capitalism	Private ownership	The market system
Pure Socialism	Government ownership	Centralized decision-making
Mixed Economy	Some private, some government	Both market and government
Communism	The people	The government

Economic Goals

Stability	Condition in which the balance between the money available in an economy and the goods produced in it remains about the same
Growth	Increase in the amount of goods and services produced by a nation's resources
Full Employment	A state when everyone is willing to look for employment can find it within a reasonable amount of time and effort, which means full utilization of a country's human resources
Healthy Balance of Payments	Increase exports and create trade surplus

Stability

The fluctuation is measured with CPI (consumer price index). The greatest enemy to stability may be inflation, however, prolonged stability may cause stagnation or deflation, which may lead to recession. And a severe and long-lasting recession is called a depression.

Inflation → Stagnation → Deflation → Recession → Depression

Growth

GDP and GNP are most common measures to judge the economic growth.

GDP (Gross Domestic Product)	GNP (Gross National Product)	Real GDP/GNP
• Total market value of all final goods and services produced within the territory of a country in a year.	• Total value of all the goods and services produced by the residents of a country in a year.	• GDP/GNP adjusted for inflation and changes in the value of a country's currency.

Full Employment

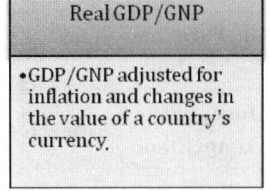

Full employment does not mean zero unemployment, as a compromise between different opinions, the unemployment rate of 4% ~ 6% is considered to be acceptable as full employment.

Frictional Unemployment	Seasonal Unemployment
Incessant movement of people between jobs or through different stages of lifecycle	A seasonal variation in the structure of jobs and labor offered

Unemployment

Cyclical Unemployment	Structural Unemployment
The overall demand for labor is low	Mismatch between the supply of and demand for workers

Forms of competition

	Number of competitors	Similarity of products	Control over price	Ease of market entry
Pure Competition	Enormous	Identical	None	Easy
Monopolistic Competition	Many	Similar	Some	Fairly easy
Oligopoly	Few	Similar or identical	Some	Difficult
Monopoly	None	No directly competing products	Considerable	Regulated by government

Competition in industries

	Typical industries (esp. in China)
Pure Competition	grain, vegetable, newspaper, milk, bottled water ...
Monopolistic Competition	garment, electric and electronic appliances, furniture, housing ...
Oligopoly	steel, automobile, civil aviation, telecommunications, banks ...
Monopoly	tobacco, salt, power, water supply, express way, rail transportation...

Social Responsibilities

How companies behave will affect the society and their stakeholders?

Stakeholders are people or groups who supply a company its productive resources and hereby have an interest in how the company behaves.

Ethics: a view about what is right and wrong, what is moral.
If a company behaves in an ethical way, how does this benefit people and society do?
Conversely, how are people harmed by a company's unethical actions?

Why should companies behave ethically?	Why should companies not behave ethically?
· because their owners want them to	· they do not have to provided they behave legally
· to attract ethical investors	· it can impose extra costs
· to attract ethical customers	· there is no agreement on what is ethical
· to attract employees	· there is a conflict of interest
· to avoid unfavorable media attention	

在中国

市场经济地位

市场经济地位是反倾销调查确定倾销幅度时使用的一个重要概念。反倾销案发起国如果认定被调查商品的出口国为"市场经济"国家，那么在进行反倾销调查时，就必须根据该产品在生产国的实际成本和价格来计算其正常价格；如果认定被调查商品的出口国为"非市场经济"国家，将引用与出口国经济发展水平大致相当的市场经济国家（即替代国）的成本数据来计算所谓的正常价值，并进而确定倾销幅度，而不使用出口国的原始数据。例如，20世纪90年代，欧盟对中国的彩电反倾销，就是将新加坡作为替代国来计算我国彩电的生产成本。当时，新加坡劳动力成本高出中国20多倍，中国的产品自然被计算成倾销。

中国加入世贸组织时，主要贸易伙伴因多种原因，在中国加入世贸组织文件中坚持加入了几项对中国贸易不利的条款。文件第15条规定："如接受调查的生产者不能明确证明生产该同类产品的产业在制造、生产和销售该产品方面具备市场经济条件，则该世贸组织进口成员可使用不依据与中国国内价格或成本进行严格比较的方法"，但"无论如何，(a)项(ii)目的规定应在加入之日后15年终止"。自加入世贸组织以来，中国政府一直在努力争取各国际贸易伙伴国承认中国的完全市场经济地位，在建立市场经济体制方面取得了重要进展。但是，中国加入世贸组织15年到期后，印度、美国、欧盟等70余个国家和地区仍拒绝承认中国的市场经济地位，并以此为理由用"替代国"价格判断反倾销。数据显示，1995—2016年，中国遭受的反倾销案件占全球案件的近1/4，总共1217起，为世界之最。由于其他世贸组织成员不承认中国的市场经济地位，使得中国企业在应诉国外反倾销调查时处境极为不利，不但败诉率高，而且被裁定的倾销税率也让很多企业难以承受。最重要的是，不承认中国为市场经

商务导论

济国家的规定严重背离了中国经济发展的现实,是不公平的。

失业率

关于失业率各国有不同的定义,更有不同的统计方法。中国官方采用的失业率为"城镇登记失业率",是指在当地就业服务机构进行求职登记的、非农业户口人员、一定年龄范围内(男:16～50岁,女:16～45岁)人员占城镇劳动人口比例,这一数据十几年来一直稳定地维持在4%～4.3%之间,虽然有一定参考价值,但被认为严重低估了真实的失业情况。

垄断

垄断行业分为两种:技术垄断和政府垄断。

Key Terms	
Capital 资本	Frictional unemployment 摩擦性失业
Entrepreneurship 企业家	Seasonal unemployment 季节性失业
Free market economy 自由市场经济	Cyclical unemployment 周期性失业
Command or planned economy 计划经济	Structural unemployment 结构性失业
Mixed economy 混合经济	Pure competition 完全竞争
Capitalism 资本主义	Monopolistic competition 垄断性竞争
Socialism 社会主义	Oligopoly 寡头垄断
Communism 共产主义	Monopoly 完全垄断
Full employment 完全就业	Stakeholders 利益相关者
Balance of payments 国际收支(平衡表)	Ethics 伦理
Inflation 通货膨胀	Business ethics 商业伦理
Stagnation 通货滞涨	Occupational ethics 职业伦理;职业道德
Deflation 通货紧缩	Social ethics 社会伦理;社会道德
Recession 经济衰退	Individual ethics 个人伦理;个人道德
Depression 经济萧条	Organizational ethics 组织伦理;组织道德
GDP 国内生产总值	Utilitarian rule 功利规则
GNP 国民生产总值	Justice rule 正义规则
Real GDP/GNP 实际国内生产总值/国民生产总值	Practical rule 实用规则
	Moral rights rule 道德权利规则

Brainstorming

Why entrepreneur is an important factor of production in modern economy?
Do you think China is a free market economy? Why?
Choose some common products in life and think about the competition status of its industry.
Compare and analyze unemployment rates of different countries.
Exemplify enterprises' social responsibilities seen in our daily life.

Part I Getting Business Perspectives

Read More

Global Business Environment and Business Ethics

The global business environment can be defined as the environment in different sovereign countries, with factors exogenous to the home environment of the organization, influencing decision making on resource use and capabilities. To function effectively and efficiently, companies operating internationally must understand the social environment of the host country they are operating in. Today there are thousands of MNCs which operate in many parts of the globe. Such companies should acquaint themselves with the language and culture of the country in which they are operating. As firms have no control over the external environment, their success depends upon how well they adapt to the external environment. A firm's ability to design and adjust its internal variables to take advantage of opportunities offered by the external environment, and its ability to control threats posed by the same environment, determine its success.

Business ethics considers the ethical relationship between businesses and consumers, between businesses and their employees. It also considers the impact of globalization on the environment, and on society at large. It can simply be defined in terms of social and ecological responsibility of business. It requires that business decisions should not be made exclusively from the narrow, economical perspective, but also the social and ecological concerns should be taken into account. This means that people who work in the business life should consider how their economic decisions affect other people, environment or the society on the whole. In other words, it means that the interests of all the relevant parties or stakeholders are acknowledged and weighed.

Times have changed, however, and ethics in business and corporate social responsibility are becoming crucial. There are many reasons for this, driven by the social, political and economic developments in the world. With the emergence of multinational corporations and increasing economic globalization has come a greater concern about the ethics of businesses in a global environment. In the wake of globalization and liberalization policy, business ethics in globalized business environment has become a critical issue that has attracted business and management research scholars to engage on crucial debates and discussions at both local as well as international forum. This is because globalization policy, as it were, has brought about business uncertainties, changing demographics, and a push for diversity that has resulted into corporate business cultures that are less homogeneous and increasingly competitive. Consumers have shown their dissatisfaction through taking to the streets, and bring together many different types of activists and protestors campaigning on a variety of business related issues from globalization and human rights to third world debt. Stakeholders, and especially consumers, are becoming increasingly empowered and vocal, forcing businesses to review their strategies. Consumers now expect businesses to be socially responsible, and businesses are increasingly thought about what they can achieve by putting the power of their marketing behind some key social issues so that they can help make a positive social difference.

That's the reason why many corporates are looking to integrate business ethics with global business and led the way to bring business ethics and social responsibility into the public eye and onto the business agenda, championing key issues such as human and animal rights, fair trade and environmental impact. However, business ethics is not as simple as it looks as there is no longer a universal moral code and multinationals operate in different parts of the world, employing and serving people from different cultures. Profit will still be the main motivating factor for businesses and this affects all the people who work there, generating its own culture with its own standards, so it becomes difficult for individuals to stand up against any attitudes and decisions they disagree with.

(616)

https://www.myassignmenthelp.net/global-business-environment

What You Can Do: 10 Important Issues to Consider

Now that we have covered what environmental ethics means and how it relates to your business, let's get practical. What can you do to put environmental ethics into practice at your company?

The specifics may vary depending on what kind of company it is and what industry you're in, but there are some common threads. Here are ten important issues for you to consider, with ideas on what you could do to improve your environmental practices.

1. Full Cost Accounting

The main idea of environmental ethics is that nature has intrinsic value and shouldn't be treated merely as a resource to be used up. But traditional accounting doesn't match up with that vision. It only measures direct monetary costs, with no accounting for things like pollution and environmental waste, which are sometimes referred to as "negative externalities" in economic theory.

2. Energy Efficiency

Use this *Better Business Guide to Energy Saving* to help you walk through the steps. Basically, you just need to check your office, shop, factory or other workplace for compliance with basic energy common sense. For example:

Are you using energy-efficient lighting?

Are your heating and cooling systems properly controlled by thermostats?

Are windows and doors insulated to stop all that expensive cooling/heating from escaping?

Is your computer equipment operating efficiently?

Are you and your employees regularly switching things off when not in use?

3. Energy Sources

As well as looking at energy usage, you could evaluate the sources of that energy. There are plenty of alternatives to fossil fuels these days, and you could switch to an energy supplier that generates its energy from renewable sources.

4.The Supply Chain

When businesses look at their environmental impact, they often focus on their own direct contributions. But, as we've seen, environmental ethics demands a more holistic approach.

So, examine your entire supply chain: all of the companies that provide all of the components for your final products. Ask yourself:

How are those components built?

How are they transported?

How were the original materials obtained?

What does the entire process look like from the mining of the raw materials through to the finished item reaching the consumer?

5. Packaging

This year's Earth Day has a particular focus on ending plastic pollution. The majority of the world's plastic ends up in oceans, where it breaks up into small pieces that kill marine life. There are 51 trillion microplastic particles in the ocean today—500 times more than the number of stars in our galaxy.

6. Animal Welfare

The main idea of environmental ethics—that nature has intrinsic value—applies to animals too. Other species are not put on earth for our exploitation; they have a right to fair treatment.

What that means in practice is for you to work out according to your own ethical framework. Some people will want to avoid any and all uses of animal products, while others may prefer to insist that animals are treated humanely.

7. Pollution

It's likely that your business creates pollution in multiple ways, from the energy you use to direct pollution from manufacturing processes. So, examine ways to reduce that.

For example, you could look at ways to manufacture your products with fewer emissions, or reduce your overall carbon footprint by implementing the energy changes we talked about earlier or changing your transportation policies.

8. Transportation

Transportation is a major source of pollution and other negative environmental effects, so examine the way people and products are transported within your company. Can you reduce the need for transportation (for example, by switching to a local supplier) or switch to more eco-friendly transportation (e.g. train instead of plane)?

9. Resource Usage

We have talked about packaging already, but businesses use a lot of other resources. So, examine your practices and see where you can make improvements. For example:

Can you recycle more?

Can you use less to begin with?

Can you go paper free in your office, or at least reduce unnecessary paperwork?

10. Putting It Into Practice

All of the things we've talked about are important, but you can't do them on your own. In order to be successful, you'll need to get your staff on board, ensuring that they understand the importance of environmental ethics and know what they need to do to support it.

Conclusion

In this article, you've learned all about environmental ethical issues in business. We've looked at what environmental ethics means and how it can be applied to the business world, and we've covered ten things you can do to put environmental ethics into practice in your business.

As I mentioned, the specifics can vary a lot for different companies in different industries, but I hope this post has given you a useful framework with which to think about environmental ethics and to construct environmental policies that make sense for your particular business.

(819)

https://business.tutsplus.com/tutorials/what-is-environmental-ethics-for-business-cms-30933

Chapter 2 Forms of Business

Basic Forms of Business
Sole Proprietorship   • A business that is owned and usually manegd by one person.   **Partnership**   • A legal form of business with two or more owners.   **Corporation**   • A legal entity (legally a person) with authority to act and have liability apart from its owners.

Unlimited Liability	Limited Liability
There is no limit for the responsibility to pay for the business's losses, with the risk of sacrificing the owners' personal property.	The responsibility of a business's owners for losses is limited, only up to the amount they invest.

Note:
Owners of a corporation, i.e. shareholders, have limited liability;
Owners of sole proprietorship have unlimited liability;
And the responsibility of partnerships' owners depends on their types.

Sole Proprietorship
A sole proprietorship, also known as the sole trader, is a type of enterprise that is owned and run by one natural person and in which there is no legal distinction between the owner and the business entity.

Advantages	Disadvantages
· Freedom · Privacy · Low startup costs · Ease of starting and ending	· Unlimited liability · Limited resources · Lack of continuity · Overwhelming commitment

Partnership

Two or more people collaboratively operate a business. Same to the sole proprietorship, partnerships are non-incorporated businesses.

Advantages	Disadvantages
· Improved access to resources	· Unlimited liability
· Better prospect for growth	· Shared profit
· Definite legal framework	· Potential lack of continuity
· No special taxes	· Internal conflict

General partner is an owner who is active in managing the firm and thus have unlimited liability.

Limited partner is an owner who invests money in the business but stays away from its management and thus bears limited liability for the losses.

Partner and partnership

General partnership is a partnership in which all owners share in operating the business and in assuming liability for all its losses.

Limited partnership is a partnership with one or more general partners and one or more limited partners.

Note: *any partnership should have at least one general partner.*

Corporation

Corporations, also incorporated companies, are legal persons, who can sue and be sued, sign contracts, possess assets. The owners, i.e., shareholders or stockholders, are not personally responsible for the companies' losses. Their responsibility to pay the debt is limited to their investment, which is called limited liability.

Corporations come in many different types but are usually divided by the law of the jurisdiction where they are chartered into two kinds: by whether they can issue stock or not, or by whether they are formed to make profit or not.

- Stock corporations
- Non-stock corporations
- For-profit corporations
- Non-profit corporations

The common type of corporation is a **Conventional (C) Corporation**, a legal entity with liability separates from its owners, having the right to issue stocks.

A **limited liability company (LLC)** is the United States-specific form of a private limited company. It is a business structure that combines the pass-through taxation of a partnership or sole proprietorship with the limited liability of a corporation. An LLC is not a corporation in itself; it is a legal form of a company that provides limited liability to its owners in many jurisdictions. LLCs are well-known for the flexibility that they provide to business owners; depending on the situation, an LLC may elect to use corporate tax rules instead of being…

Advantages	Disadvantages
· Limited liability	· Double taxation
· Ease of raising money	· High start-up cost
· Long life and large size	· High organizing fee
· Separation of ownership from management	· Lack of secrecy

Separate Ownership and Management of a Conventional Corporation

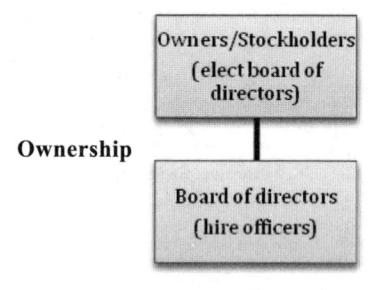

Ownership

Owners/Stockholders (elect board of directors)

Board of directors (hire officers)

Management

Chairman of the Board
President/CEO
Other Officers/Middle Managers
Line Managers/Supervisors
Employees

Branch, Subsidiary, Affiliate and Group

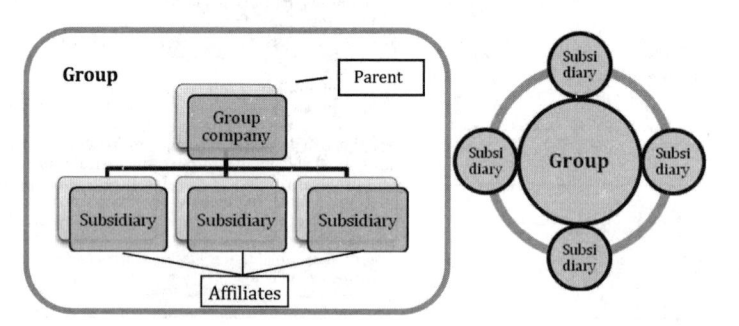

Subsidiaries under one parent company are affiliates. Parent company can be called a group company. The term "group company" is just showing its scale, not a legal term. They jointly compose a corporate group, which may also consist of collaborative members with equal status.

Part I Getting Business Perspectives

Subsidiaries are independent separate legal entities | Branches are not independent legal entities

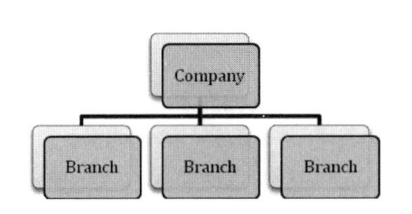

Branching is particularly widespread in banking and other financial institutions, where the products' complexity requires local offices to act more like an agency than as a separate company. A branch structure exposes the owning company to full taxability and legal liability in regard to the branch office's operations.

A branch office is an outlet of a company or, more generally, an organization that does not constitute a separate legal entity, while being physically separated from the organization's main office.

A Special Form: Franchising

Franchising

- Franchising is a special way of doing business, practicing the right to use a firm's business model and brand for a prescribed period of time under a franchise agreement.

*A franchise can be formed as a sole proprietorship, a partnership, or a corporation.

For franchisees

Advantages	Disadvantages
Easy start-up	Less independence/freedom
Instant recognition	High franchise fee
Low risk	Shared profit
Training and guidance	Coattail effects
Personal ownership	Fraudulent franchisors

For franchisors

Advantages	Disadvantages
Quick growth	Difficulty in management
Low cost	Shared profit
Raise funds	Coattail effects

Franchise agreement is an arrangement whereby someone with a good idea for a business sells the rights to use the business name and sell a product or service to others in a given territory.

> **Franchisor/-er** is a company that develops a product concept and sells others the rights to make and sell the products.
>
> **Franchisee** is a person or a business who buys a franchise.

Types of franchises

Distributorship	a dealer allowed to sell a product made by a manufacturer, e.g. car dealers
Chain-style business	a firm allowed to use the trade name of a company and follows guidelines related to the pricing and sale of the product, e.g. McDonald's
Manufacturing arrangement	a firm allowed to manufacture a product using the formula, technology or patent provided by another company, e.g. Microsoft

Language tip:
The word "franchise" is of Anglo-French derivation—from franc, meaning free—and is used both as a noun and as a (transitive) verb. As a noun, it refers to the permission given by the franchisor to the franchisee, e.g. a franchise holder, a franchise agreement. As a verb, it means to give or sell the permission to someone.

在中国

Sole proprietorship（商个人）

在中国 Sole proprietorship 分为两种形式：一种是个体工商户（依据国务院 2011 年分布的《个体工商户条例》登记），另一种是个人独资企业（依据《中华人民共和国个人独资企业法》注册）。

个体工商户	个人独资企业
·可以不起字号名称，也可以没有固定的生产经营场所而流动经营。 ·投资者与经营者是同一人，都必须是投资设立个体工商户的自然人。	·必须要有固定的生产经营场所和合法的企业名称。 ·投资者与经营者可以是不同的人。 ·个人独资企业可以设立分支机构。
个人独资企业的总体规模一般大于个体工商户。个人独资企业与个体工商户的法律地位和在财务制度和税收政策上的要求也不尽相同。	

Language tip

"个人独资企业"更接近 sole proprietorship 的含义，"个体工商户"是中国特有的一种形式，可译为 individually owned business。

Corporation（公司）

Corporation 根据现行中国《公司法》规定，分为有限责任公司和股份有限公司。	
有限责任公司即"有限公司" · 不能公开招股。只能向发起人募资，出资人数 1~50。股东间关系亲密，兼有合伙制的优点。 · 股东的股权证明为"出资证明"，是不能转让的。 · 最低注册资金为 3 万，不划分为等额股份。	**股份有限公司即"股份公司"** · 可以向社会公开招股。股东人数 2~200 人。（注：上市公司必须是股份公司，但股份公司不一定是上市公司。） · 股东的股权证明是股票，可以转让。 · 最低注册资金为 500 万，划分为等额股份。

Language tip

有限责任公司类似于美国的 LLC，可保留英文说法。股份有限公司实际上就是美国的 conventional corporation，可采用 joint-stock company 这一说法，根据维基百科，在现代公司法的体系下，这一说法被默认为包含"公司制"和"有限责任"两层含义，与股份公司含义一致。

中国企业的划分还可根据所有者的主体性质分为国有企业(state-owned enterprises) 和三资企业。"三资"是指含有外资的三种形式：中外合资企业、中外合作企业、外商独资企业。

根据以上定义，"三资企业"可以翻译为：Foreign-invested enterprises (Including "Sino-foreign joint ventures, Sino-foreign cooperative enterprises, solely foreign-owned enterprises"）。

拓展阅读：
中国企业大中小微划分标准及相关政策
政府鼓励个体户转企业的原因及优惠政策

Key Terms	
Sole proprietorship 个体工商户；个人独资企业	General partnership 普通合伙企业
Partnership 合伙企业	Limited partnership 有限合伙企业
Corporation 公司	Limited liability company 有限责任公司
Franchise/franchising 特许经营	Double taxation 双重税收
Franchising agreement 特许经营协议	Group Corporation 集团公司
Franchisor/franchiser 经销商；特许权授予方	Subsidiary 附属公司 / 子公司
Franchisee 特许经销商；特许权使用方	Affiliate 联属公司；关联公司
Limited liability 有限责任	Branch 分公司
Unlimited liability 无限责任	Joint-stock company 股份有限公司
General partner 普通合伙人	State-owned enterprises 国有企业
Limited partner 有限合伙人	Foreign-invested enterprises 三资企业

> **Brainstorming**
>
> Why do people set up businesses?
> Why do firms fail?
> How do small firms survive?
> What are alternatives to starting up a business if you want to be your own boss?

Read More

The Changing Forms of Business Organization

A business organization is a tool created to give owners and managers the power they need to shape and control the behavior of workers or employees to produce goods and services. Choosing the right form of organization is important because this determines how productively and profitably resources will be used to create the most wealth for their owners.

Perhaps the first type of business organization was the tribe or clan. Composed of family groups united by ties of blood and kinship, it was usually organized into some kind of hierarchy. Tribal leaders owed their positions to their membership of a particular family, or to particular qualities such as prowess in hunting or the ability to settle disputed and negotiate exchanges between families and maintain the tribal organization as an effective unit.

The tribal organization can function effectively when the property rights and obligations of all its individual members and the rights of different tribes are 3 Types of Business.

There are three major types of businesses.

1. Service Business

A service type of business provides intangible products (products with no physical form). Service type firms offer professional skills, expertise, advice, and other similar products.

Examples of service businesses are: salons, repair shops, schools, banks, accounting firms, and law firms.

2. Merchandising Business

This type of business buys products at wholesale price and sells the same at retail price. They are known as "buy and sell" businesses. They make profit by selling the products at prices higher than their purchase costs.

A merchandising business sells a product without changing its form. Examples are grocery stores, convenience stores, distributors, and other resellers.

3. Manufacturing Business

Unlike a merchandising business, a manufacturing business buys products with the intention of using them as materials in making a new product. Thus, there is a transformation of the products purchased.

A manufacturing business combines raw materials, labor, and factory overhead in its production process. The manufactured goods will then be sold to customers.

Hybrid Business

Hybrid businesses are companies that may be classified in more than one type of business. A restaurant, for example, combines ingredients in making a fine meal (manufacturing), sells a cold bottle of wine (merchandising), and fills customer orders (service).

Nonetheless, these companies may be classified according to their major business interest. In that case, restaurants are more of the service type—they provide dining services.

(396)

http://www.accountingverse.com/accounting-basics/types-of-businesses.html

The Business and Legal Considerations of Incorporating Your Business

Business considerations play a crucial role in deciding which form of organization is best for your enterprise. Balance the tax benefits of incorporating with various business and legal needs.

Ability to Raise Capital

If your new venture has a pressing need to raise capital from outside investors, forming a C-corporation is likely the easiest way to satisfy the demands of investors. C-corporations can have an unlimited number of shareholders, can have different classes of stock, and do not need to be dissolved if a shareholder leaves.

Partnerships, by contrast, must terminate whenever more than 50% of the partnership interest changes hands. Raising capital in a partnership is consequently more involved. S-corporations are limited to 100 shareholders, which can sometimes limit the ability of an S-corporation to raise capital. Schedule C for sole proprietors are limited to only one owner, so sole proprietors have no ability to raise capital from outside investors.

Ability to Transfer Ownership

At some point in time, you may need to transfer ownership of a business to someone else. You could be selling your business, transferring some of the ownership to your children, or bringing in a new business partner. With C-corporations and S-corporations you can add new shareholders and transfer shares with relative ease. Transferring a significant portion of a partnership, by contrast, may require that the partnership terminate and a new partnership be formed.

Finally, sole proprietors cannot transfer ownership of their business. If they want out, they can sell all the assets and liabilities of the business to someone else, but the buyer would have to form his own business.

Separation of Ownership & Management

In Corporations, Limited Liability Companies, and Limited Partnerships, owners are separate from management.

Owners do not necessarily take on any management responsibilities, and managers do not necessarily shoulder any ownership responsibilities. This separation is crucial for keeping liabilities from bad management decisions and from depleting the shareholder's personal assets. By contrast, general partners in a partnership and sole proprietors are not separate from management. They actively engage in management decisions and daily business activities and might become responsible for the consequences of management decisions.

Limited Liability Protection

The major legal consideration in choosing a form of business is limited liability protection. Limited liability means the owners of the business are only liable for the capital they have invested. Let's say my company is sued for $1 million, but as a shareholder, I have invested only $10,000. With limited liability, the most I can lose is the $10,000 I have invested. My personal assets (house, car, bank account) cannot be touched. Limited liability is available for C-corporations, S-corporations, Limited Liability Companies, and limited partners in a Limited Partnership or

Limited Liability Partnership.

General partners in a partnership and sole proprietors, however, have unlimited liability.

Creditors and lawsuits can go after the owner's personal assets (real estate, bank accounts, etc.). As such, general partnerships and sole proprietorships are appropriate for businesses with small risk for liability exposure. If you are at risk of being sued for accidents, bad decisions, or property damage, you should consider whether the limited liability features of different business entities offer the level protection you desire.

Ease of Incorporation

Setting up a sole proprietor business is the easiest thing to do. You actually don't need to do anything until you file your first business tax return on your Schedule C. This is also the easiest business to shut down—you just stop being in business. All the other forms of organization, however, require filing various papers with your state government and with the Internal Revenue Service.

To incorporate your business, you will need to write up your Articles of Incorporation, By laws, file various documents with your state government, obtain an Employer Identification Number from the IRS, and once approved, submit these documents to your bank to set up a business bank account.

You can incorporate a business yourself, or you can hire a professional incorporation service. You may also need the services of an attorney. State governments charge filing fees for processing your incorporation documents. Fees vary by state and can vary by the type of organization you want to form. You may need to register a fictitious business name with your county government, and this requires a filing fee and newspaper costs for announcing your business name to the public. These fees can quickly add up, so have solid reasons for incorporating, and understand how your form of organization will achieve your business, legal, and tax needs.

(759)

https://www.thebalance.com/business-legal-considerations-of-incorporating-4058138

How to create a successful online business startup while keeping your day job

I remember the day the business model began to take shape in my mind; I was ready to ditch my full-time job.

Top tips

Don't rush in on the wave of excitement—set aside the time to develop your idea properly.

Get in touch with your customers. Know who they are and engage them early and often.

Be clear about the skills you're looking for before you start recruiting staff.

The business

GoDaddy External link (opens in the same window) (formally known as Tweaky.com) is a web-based service business dedicated to helping customers improve their websites—one tweak at a time. Customers submit work requests using forms on the Elto.com website, and the job is broken down into bite-sized chunks and completed by an experienced web developer at an affordable fixed price. The service even walks customers through the tricky process of providing an effective brief and adds a layer of expert project management.

Starting a business while also working full-time

"I knew this was going to be a good idea from the beginning." Despite being sure, co-founder of the business Ned Dwyer says, getting it up and running took time. "I remember the day the business model began to take shape in my mind; I was ready to ditch my full-time job."

Taking advice from a colleague, he opted instead to work on the project a couple of days a week and one weekend a month, while the idea matured.

This approach also meant that the project cost very little to get started. Funding became a priority when it came time go live and officially launch the site. The budding business received an injection of funding from 99Designs founders Leni Mayo and Mark Harbottle. Ned and business partner Peter (PJ) Morgan had already developed a kind of mentoring relationship with the guys from 99Designs, so the investment was a perfect fit.

"Their experience building a marketplace has been invaluable, and they've been very willing to share what they know."

Friends, workmates and customers can be a good resource

Recruiting the right web developers has been fundamental to the site's success.

"At first we worked with friends, and people in the agency I was with at the time. They were 'test pilots' who helped us understand the skills we needed in our workforce."

When it came time to hire, Tweaky.com looked carefully at the LinkedIn profiles and recent projects of new applicants. "That gave us an idea of how they communicated and the quality of their work."

Make sure that you've created a service that people will want to pay for.

"It sounds obvious, but find out what your market really wants. Engage your customers early and often, and ask for feedback. Keep it low-key at first so you have a chance to iron out any wrinkles; work with a friendly group of customers while the business is crystallising. If you get it right, they'll also do a great job of getting the word out when you launch."

Group decisions can be tough

With a small team, there were some intense discussions about approach. "We were doing something that hadn't been done before and we had different backgrounds, different ideas about how to make this work. Even though the meetings became quite heated sometimes, we found a way through with mutual respect for each other's skills."

The result

Elto.com reached profitability just nine months after the site went live. During that time, the site also served over 1,500 customers and won Best Online Business at the 2012 Anthill Cool Company awards and the Best Startup Idea at the 2013 Startup Smart awards.

The team stayed motivated by taking a vow of sobriety until the business reached profitability. "We were working hard to get to the point where we could break out the bubble!"

(645)

http://www.business.vic.gov.au/case-studies/how-to-create-a-successful-online-business-startup-while-keeping-your-day-job#

Part II Managing the Business

Chapter 3 Management and Leadership

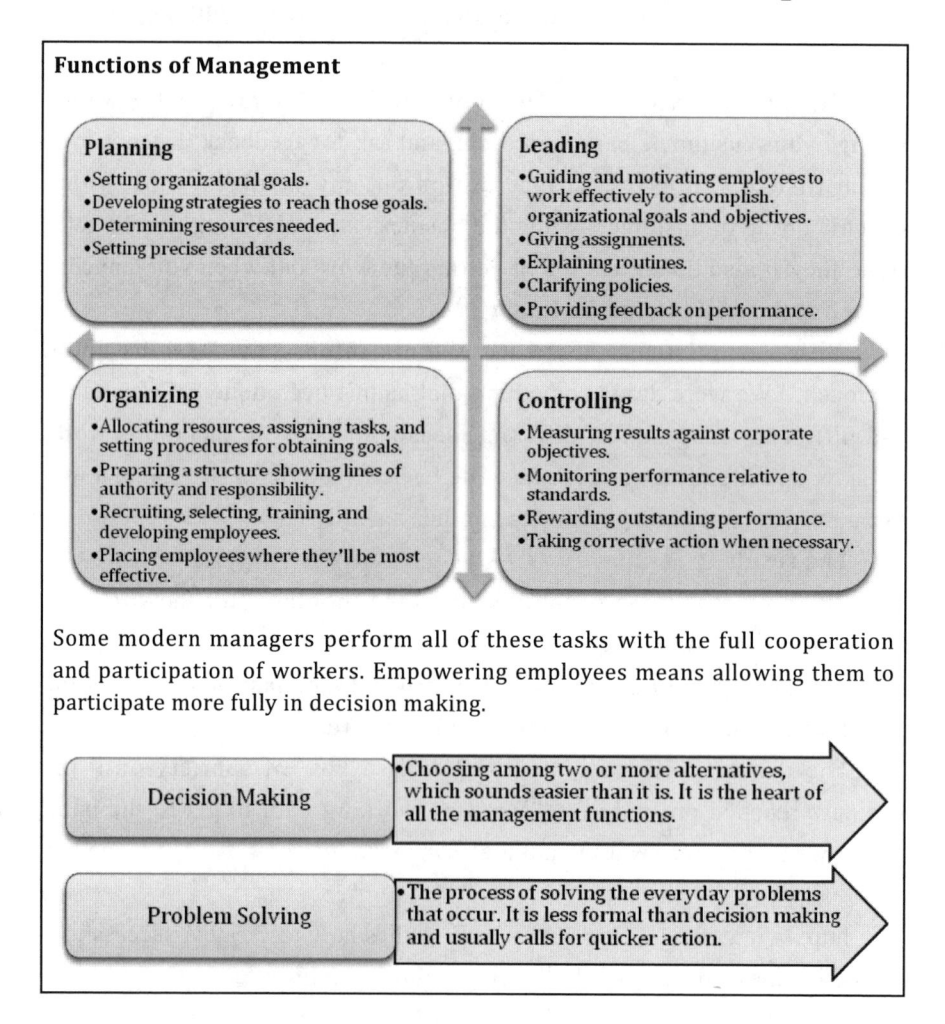

Functions of Management

Planning
- Setting organizatonal goals.
- Developing strategies to reach those goals.
- Determining resources needed.
- Setting precise standards.

Leading
- Guiding and motivating employees to work effectively to accomplish. organizational goals and objectives.
- Giving assignments.
- Explaining routines.
- Clarifying policies.
- Providing feedback on performance.

Organizing
- Allocating resources, assigning tasks, and setting procedures for obtaining goals.
- Preparing a structure showing lines of authority and responsibility.
- Recruiting, selecting, training, and developing employees.
- Placing employees where they'll be most effective.

Controlling
- Measuring results against corporate objectives.
- Monitoring performance relative to standards.
- Rewarding outstanding performance.
- Taking corrective action when necessary.

Some modern managers perform all of these tasks with the full cooperation and participation of workers. Empowering employees means allowing them to participate more fully in decision making.

Decision Making
- Choosing among two or more alternatives, which sounds easier than it is. It is the heart of all the management functions.

Problem Solving
- The process of solving the everyday problems that occur. It is less formal than decision making and usually calls for quicker action.

Part II Managing the Business

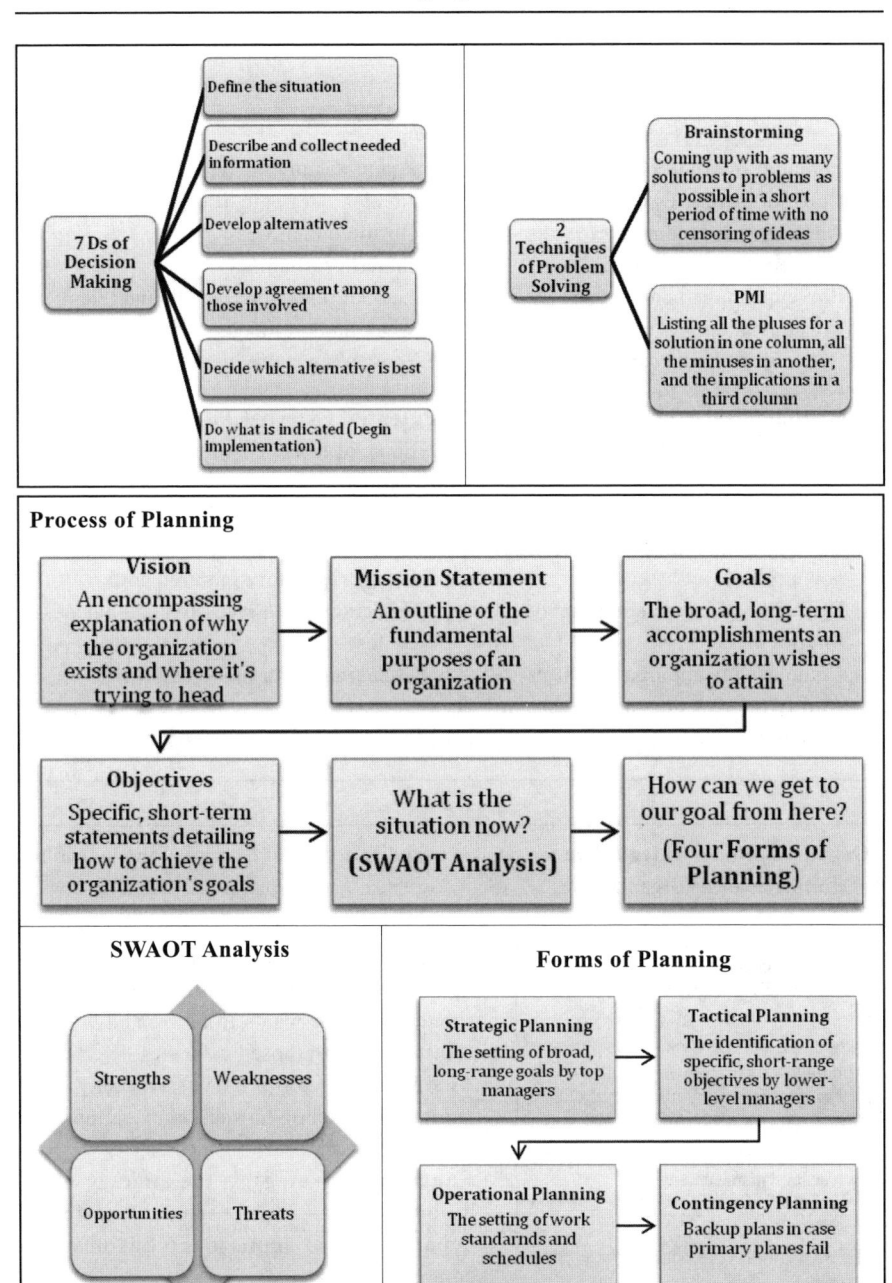

7 Ds of Decision Making
- Define the situation
- Describe and collect needed information
- Develop alternatives
- Develop agreement among those involved
- Decide which alternative is best
- Do what is indicated (begin implementation)

2 Techniques of Problem Solving

Brainstorming
Coming up with as many solutions to problems as possible in a short period of time with no censoring of ideas

PMI
Listing all the pluses for a solution in one column, all the minuses in another, and the implications in a third column

Process of Planning

Vision
An encompassing explanation of why the organization exists and where it's trying to head

→ **Mission Statement**
An outline of the fundamental purposes of an organization

→ **Goals**
The broad, long-term accomplishments an organization wishes to attain

Objectives
Specific, short-term statements detailing how to achieve the organization's goals

→ **What is the situation now?**
(SWAOT Analysis)

→ **How can we get to our goal from here?**
(Four Forms of Planning)

SWAOT Analysis
- Strengths
- Weaknesses
- Opportunities
- Threats

Forms of Planning

Strategic Planning
The setting of broad, long-range goals by top managers

→ **Tactical Planning**
The identification of specific, short-range objectives by lower-level managers

Operational Planning
The setting of work standarnds and schedules

→ **Contingency Planning**
Backup plans in case primary planes fail

SWAOT Analysis	
· Potential Internal STRENGTHS · Core competencies in key areas · An acknowledged market leader · Well-conceived strategies · Proven management · Cost advantages · Better advertising campaigns	· Potential Internal WEAKNESSES · No clear strategic direction · Obsolete facilities · subpar profitability · Lack of managerial depth and talent · Weak market image · Too narrow a product line
Potential External OPPORTUNITIES · Ability to serve additional customer groups · Expand product lines · Ability to transfer skills/technology to new products · Failing trade barriers in attractive foreign markets · Complacency among rival firms · Ability to grow due to increases in market demand	**Potential External THREATS** · Entry of lower-cost foreign competitors · Rising sales of substitute products · Slower market growth · Costly regulatory requirements · Vulnerability to recession and business cycles · Changing buyer needs and tastes

Organizational Strategies are the decisions and actions that determine the long-run performance of an organization.

Top Level management
[Corporate Strategy]

Middle-level management
[Business (or Competitive) Strategy]

Lower-level management
[Functional Strategy]

Corporate strategy is a strategy that determines what businesses a company is in, should be in, or wants to be in, and what it wants to do with those businesses.
Business (or competitive) strategy is a strategy focused on how an organization will compete in each of its businesses.
Functional strategy is the strategy used by an organization's various functional departments to support the business or competitive strategies.

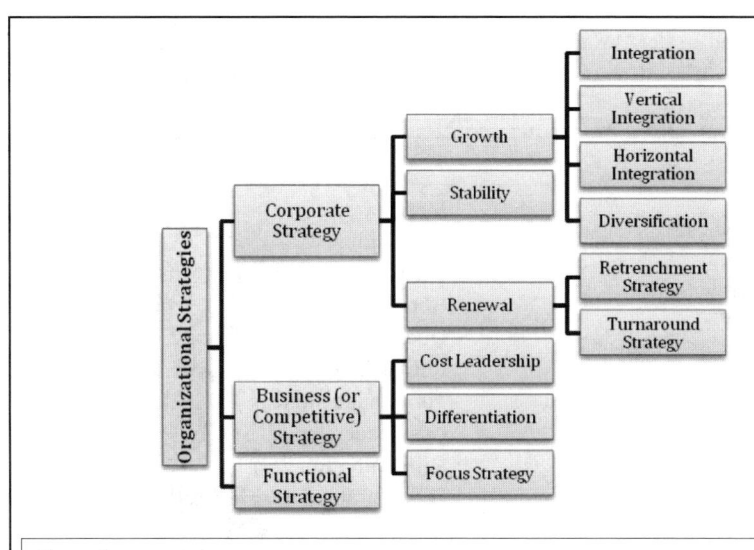

Part II Managing the Business

```
Organizational Strategies
├── Corporate Strategy
│   ├── Growth
│   │   ├── Integration
│   │   ├── Vertical Integration
│   │   ├── Horizontal Integration
│   │   └── Diversification
│   ├── Stability
│   └── Renewal
│       ├── Retrenchment Strategy
│       └── Turnaround Strategy
├── Business (or Competitive) Strategy
│   ├── Cost Leadership
│   ├── Differentiation
│   └── Focus Strategy
└── Functional Strategy
```

Growth strategy

Integration (or concentration): expanding the number of products offered or markets served either through its current business or through new business, i.e. merger or acquisition	**Merger:** the result of two firms forming one company
	Acquisition: one company's purchase of the property and obligations of another company

They all can do vertically, horizontally and diversely.

Vertical: involving different stages of related business	**Horizontal:** involving business in the same industry.

Diversified: involving different, either related or unrelated, industries

Managers can analyzea a corporate portfolio of businesses using the BCG matrix, a first portfolio developed by the Boston Consulting Group, introducing the idea that an organization's various businesses should be evaluated and plotted using a 2 × 2 matrix to identify which ones offered high potential and which were a drain on organizational resources.

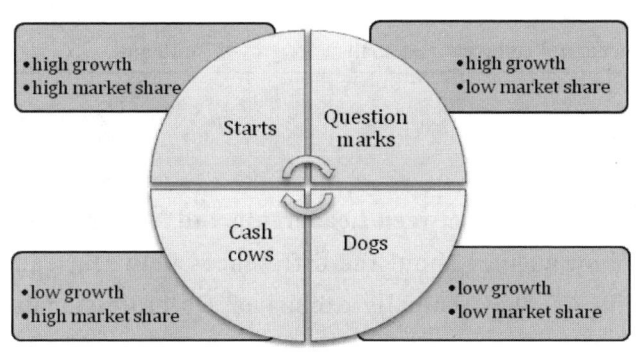

	Starts • high growth • high market share	**Question marks** • high growth • low market share
	Cash cows • low growth • high market share	**Dogs** • low growth • low market share

Managers need to determine a competitive advantage and then determine the best competitive strategy. Competitive advantage is what sets an organization apart, that is, its distinctive edge.

Key Terms

Planning 规划 Leading 领导 Organizing 组织 Controlling 控制 Decision making 制定决策 Problem solving 解决问题 Brainstorming 头脑风暴 Vision 愿景 Mission 使命 Mission statement 使命宣言 Goals/Objectives 目标 SWOT analysis 四点分析；SWOT 分析 Strategic planning 战略规划 Tactical planning 战术规划 Operational planning 执行规划 Contingency planning 权宜规划 Corporate strategy 企业战略 Business/Competitive strategy 经营/竞争战略 Functional strategy 职能战略 Growth 增长 Stability 稳定 Renewal 复兴 Integration/Concentration 集中	Merger 兼并 Acquisition 收购 Vertical integration 垂直整合 Horizontal integration 水平整合 Diversification 多元化 Retrenchment strategy 紧缩战略 Turnaround strategy 转向战略 Cost leadership 成本领先 Differentiation 差异化 Focus strategy 专一化/集中化战略 BCG matrix 波士顿矩阵 Competitive advantage 竞争优势 Leadership style 领导风格 Directive approach 命令式 Supportive approach 支持式 Participative approach 参与式 Achievement-oriented approach 结果导向式 Boss-centered/Autocratic 领导为中心的/独裁的 Democratic 民主的 Subordinate-centered/free-rein 员工为中心的 Conceptual skills 抽象概括能力 Human relations skills 人际关系能力 Technical skills 技术能力

Brainstorming

What are the characteristics of Chinese model of management?
Do you think leadership skills are born with or can be acquired through learning or practice?
Choose a successful company and analyze its growth strategies.

Read More

Differences between Leadership and Management

The many wonder about the differences between leadership and management. Are they mutually exclusive? Do professionals have both

Part II Managing the Business

qualities—or do they learn one or the other over a long period of time? These questions are just the tip of the iceberg. In this article, we will take a look at both.

What is Leadership? What is Management?

The words "leader" and "manager" are among the most commonly used words in business and are often used interchangeably. But have you ever wondered what the terms actually mean?

What Do Managers Do?

A manager is the member of an organization with the responsibility of carrying out the four important functions of management: planning, organizing, leading, and controlling. But are all managers leaders?

Most managers also tend to be leaders, but only IF they also adequately carry out the leadership responsibilities of management, which include communication, motivation, providing inspiration and guidance, and encouraging employees to rise to a higher level of productivity.

Unfortunately, not all managers are leaders. Some managers have poor leadership qualities, and employees follow orders from their managers because they are obligated to do so—not necessarily because they are influenced or inspired by the leader.

Managerial duties are usually a formal part of a job description; subordinates follow as a result of the professional title or designation. A manager's chief focus is to meet organizational goals and objectives; they typically do not take much else into consideration. Managers are held responsible for their actions, as well as for the actions of their subordinates. With the title comes the authority and the privilege to promote, hire, fire, discipline, or reward employees based on their performance and behavior.

What Do Leaders Do?

The primary difference between management and leadership is that leaders don't necessarily hold or occupy a management position. Simply put, a leader doesn't have to be an authority figure in the organization; a leader can be anyone.

Unlike managers, leaders are followed because of their personality, behavior, and beliefs. A leader personally invests in tasks and projects and demonstrates a high level of passion for work. Leaders take a great deal of interest in the success of their followers, enabling them to reach their goals to satisfaction—these are not necessarily organizational goals.

There isn't always tangible or formal power that a leader possesses over his followers. Temporary power is awarded to a leader and can be conditional based on the ability of the leader to continually inspire and motivate their followers.

Subordinates of a manager are required to obey orders while following is optional when it comes to leadership. Leadership works on inspiration and trust among employees; those who do wish to follow their leader may stop at any time. Generally, leaders are people who challenge the status quo. Leadership is change-savvy, visionary, agile, creative, and adaptive.

What are the traits of a manager possesses? Below are four important traits of a manager.

1. **The ability to execute a Vision:** Managers build a strategic vision and break it down into a roadmap for their team to follow.

2. **The ability to Direct:** Managers are responsible for day-to-day efforts while reviewing necessary resources and anticipating needs to make changes along the way.

3. **Process Management:** Managers have the authority to establish work rules, processes, standards, and operating procedures.

4. **People Focused:** Managers are known to look after and cater to the needs of the people they are responsible for: listening to them, involving them in certain key decisions, and accommodating reasonable requests for change to contribute to increased productivity.

What are the traits of a leader possesses? Below are five important traits of a leader.

1. **Vision:** A leader knows where they stand, where they want to go and tend to involve the team in charting a future path and direction.

2. **Honesty and Integrity:** Leaders have people who believe them and walk by their side down the path the leader sets.

3. **Inspiration:** Leaders are usually inspirational—and help their team understand their own roles in a bigger context.

4. **Communication Skills:** Leaders always keep their team informed about what's happening, both present and the future—along with any

obstacles that stand in their way.

5 **Ability to Challenge:** Leaders are those that challenge the status quo. They have their own style of doing things and problem-solving and are usually the ones who think outside the box.

The Three Important Differences

Being a manager and a leader at the same time is a viable concept. But remember, just because someone is a phenomenal leader it does not necessarily guarantee that the person will be an exceptional manager as well, and vice versa. So, what are the standout differences between the two roles?

1. A leader invents or innovates while a manager organizes. The leader of the team comes up with the new ideas and kickstarts the organization's shift or transition to a forward-thinking phase. A leader always has his or her eyes set on the horizon, developing new techniques and strategies for the organization. A leader has immense knowledge of all the current trends, advancements, and skillsets—and has clarity of purpose and vision. By contrast, a manager is someone who generally only maintains what is already established. A manager needs to watch the bottom line while controlling employees and workflow in the organization and preventing any kind of chaos.

In his book, *The Wall Street Journal Essential Guide to Management: Lasting Lessons from the Best Leadership Minds of Our Time*, Alan Murray cites that a manager is someone who "establishes appropriate targets and yardsticks, and analyzes, appraises and interprets performance." Managers understand the people they work with and know which person is the best fit for a specific task.

2. A manager relies on control whereas a leader inspires trust. A leader is a person who pushes employees to do their best and knows how to set an appropriate pace and tempo for the rest of the group. Managers, on the other hand, are required by their job description to establish control over employees which, in turn, help them develop their own assets to bring out their best. Thus, managers have to understand their subordinates well to do their job effectively.

3. A leader asks the questions "what" and "why" whereas a manager

leans more towards the questions "how" and "when." To be able to do justice to their role as leader, some may question and challenge authority to modify or even reverse decisions that may not have the team's best interests in mind.

Good leadership requires a great deal of good judgment, especially when it comes to the ability to stand up to senior management over a point of concern or if there is an aspect in need of improvement. If a company goes through a rough patch, a leader will be the one who will stand up and ask the question: "What did we learn from this?"

Managers, however, are not required to assess and analyze failures. Their job description emphasizes asking the questions "how" and "when", which usually helps them make sure that plans are properly executed. They tend to accept the status quo exactly the way it is and do not attempt a change.

(1102)

https://www.simplilearn.com/leadership-vs-management-difference-article

Part II Managing the Business

Chapter 4 Organizing the Enterprise

Allocating Authority

Authority: power to make the decisions necessary to compelete a task
Responsibility: duty to perform an assigned task

Chain of Command: the lines of authority that moves from the top of a hierarchy to the lowest level

Unity of Command: the principle that no subordinate in an organization should report to more than one boss.

Hierarchy of Authority: pyramidal organizational structure with ranked management levels

Tall Hierarchy	Low/Flat Herarchy

Minimum Chain-of-Command Principle (Minimum Hierarchical Levels): the principle that a company's structure should be designed with as few managerial levles as possible.

Note: *Though minimum levels of hierarchy are preferred, it will lead to broader span of control. If a manger has to supervise too many subordinates, efficiency may also suffer.*

Centralization and Decentralization

Centralized Organization: organization in which most decision-making authority is held by upper-level management	**Decentralized Organization:** an organization structure in which decision-making authority is delegated to lower-level management

Advantages:

· greater top-management control · more efficiency · simpler distribution system · stronger bran/corporate image	· better adaptation to customer wants · more empowerment of workers · faster decision making · higher morale

Disadvantages:

· less responsiveness to customers · less empowerment · inter-organizational conflict · lower morale	· less efficiency · complex distribution system · less top-management control · weakened corporate image

Note: Decentralization can be used to minimalize a company's hierarchy. When managers and employees at lower levels are given the authority to make important decisions, the problems of slow and distorted communication are avoided.

Division of Labor

> **Job Specializaiton**: the process of identifying the specific jobs that need to be done and designating the people who will perform them

> **Departmentalization**: the process of grouping jobs into logical units

by function	by product	by customer	by geographic location	by production process

If jobs are grouped by functions, the company adopts a functional structure. When companies grow larger, expanding geographically, or with wide range of products or different groups of customers, they would overlay their functional groupings with divisional groupings and develop to a divisional structure.

Formal vs. Informal Structure

Formal Organization
The structure that details lines of responsibility, authority, and position; that is, the structure shown on organization charts.

All the organizational structures illustrated above are formal structures

⬇

Informal Organization
The system that develops spontaneously as employees meet and form cliques, relationships, and lines of authority outside the formal organization.

It reflects the human relations within a company.

⬇

The Importance of Informal Structure

Effective in generating creative solutions to short-term problems	Creating camaraderie and teamwork among employees	The grapevine is quick in spreading unofficial information

Organizational culture is the shared company values and norms that influence how people and groups behave and interact with one another.

Company Values	Company Norms
• The shared standards a company's members use to evaluate whether or not they have helped the company achieve its goals.	• Beliefs, attitudes, and behaviors that specify how a company's members should behave.

Factors influencing Organizational Culture:
- Values of the founder
- Organizational socialization
- Ceremonies and rites
- Stories and language

Organizational socialization: The process by which newcomers learn and absorb a company's values and norms and acquire the work behaviors and attitudes necessary to perform their jobs effectively

商务导论

Key Terms	
Authority 职权 Responsibility 职责 Chain of command 命令链 Unity of command 统一指挥 Hierarchy of authority 命令层级 Tall hierarchy 高耸式层级 Low/Flat hierarchy 扁平式层级 Minimum chain-of-command 最短命令链 Minimum hierarchical levels 最小层级 Span of control 管理跨度 / 幅度 Centralized organization 集权制组织 Decentralized organization 分权制组织 Division of labor 分工 Job specification 工作专门化 Departmentalization 部门化	Functional structure 职能型结构 Operational structure 事业型结构 Line authority 直线职权 Staff authority 职能职权 Committee and team authority 委员会与工作组职权 Line and staff organization 垂直与参谋组织 Line personnel 直线员工 Staff personnel 职能员工 Matrix structure 矩阵结构 Formal organization 正式结构 Informal organization 非正式结构 Organizational culture 企业文化 Company values 公司价值观 Company norms 公司准则

Brainstorming

Analyze the organizational structure of the business you are working with or the school you are studying at.

Choose a famous company and analyze its organizational culture and how it is formed.

Read More

GOOGLE: a reflection of culture, leader, and management
(Abridged)

Company culture

Researching Google's culture, we would know Laszlo Bock, Head of People Operations at Google, the equivalence of Human Resources (HR) Director at other companies. "People operation" is a combination of science and human resources where Google looks at everything from a perspective of data. As a result, Google is always in the top companies throughout the last time.

Operating HR is obviously a field of science at Google. They are constantly experimenting and innovating to find the best way to satisfy employees and to help them work effectively. They do everything based on collecting and processing of collected data, using data to evaluate staff and to help them improve their work efficiency. If an organization wants to hire talented people who cannot be recruited in cash, they must focus on building a great working culture. This includes working environment, meaningful work, and employees' freedom.

Google is really touched by this philosophy, not just planning it out loud. They constantly experiment it, then improve it because it is paramount to the success of the company. For whichever company, all things start with people. A great company needs great people. One way to attract and retain such people is to make their work interesting. Mark Twain said, "Work and play are words used to describe the same thing under differing conditions."

Before heading to know about the culture, as well as subcultures, it is necessary to understand explicitly what cultures and subcultures are. ... "culture is a pattern of shared tacit assumptions learned or developed by a group as it solves its problems of external adaptation and internal integration that have worked well enough to be considered valid and, therefore, to be taught to new members as the correct way to perceive, think, and feel in relation to those problems." How about subcultures? The author, Schein claimed that the bigger an organization is, the more subcultures it contains because it is explained that "when organizations grow and mature, they not only develop their own overall cultures, but they also differentiate themselves in many subcultures based on occupations, product lines, functions, geographie and echelons in the hierarchy". According to ..., needless to say, that Google exists with a special culture and a wide variety of subculture because of its non-stop development. Thanks to the video clips (see at "Culture inside Google" ; "Google Culture" ; "Google's organizational culture"), as well as a myriad of websites on the Internet mentioning the culture of Google, it facilitates us to understand more about Google's culture and learn more lessons about the different ways to manage this company by the establishers.

Predominant culture at Google

The dominant culture in the organization depends on the environment in which the company operates the organization's objectives, the belief system of the employee and the company's management style. Therefore, there are many organizational cultures. For example, employee follows a standard procedure with a strict adherence to hierarchy and well-defined individual roles and responsibilities. Those in competitive environments, such as sales may forget strict hierarchies and follow a competitive culture where the focus is on maintaining strong relationships with external parties. In this instance, the strategy is to attain competitive advantages over the competition. The collaborative culture is yet another organizational way of life. This culture presents a decentralized workforce with integrated units working together to find solutions to problems or failure.

Why do many large companies buy its innovation? Because its dominant culture of 99% defect-free operational excellence squashes any attempts at innovation, just like a Sumo wrestler sitting on a small gymnast. They cannot accept failures. In fact, failure is a necessary part of innovation and Google took this change by Oxygen Project to measure the abilities of their multicultural managers. This means that Google itself possesses multiple different cultures. Like Zappos, Google has established a common, organizational culture for the whole offices that are distinctive from the others. The predominant culture aimed at Google is an open culture, where everybody and customer can freely contribute their ideas and opinions to create more comfortable and friendly working environment.

... provide us three levels of culture which are Artifacts, Espoused values and Underlying assumptions helping us to understand the culture at Google. The "artifacts" are identified such as dress codes, level of formality in authority relationships, working hours, meeting (how often, how run, timing), how are decisions made, communication, social events, jargon, uniforms, identity symbols, rites and rituals, disagreements and conflicts, balance between work and family. It seems that Google is quite open in these artifacts by showing a respect for uniform and national culture of each staff individually and giving them the right to wear traditional clothes.

Working at Google, employees enjoy free food served throughout the day, a volleyball court, a swimming pool, a car wash, an oil change, a haircut, free health care, and many other benefits. The biggest benefit for the staff is to be picked up on the day of work. As assessed by many

Part II Managing the Business

traffic experts, the system set up by Google is considered to be a great transport network. Tad Widby, a project manager and a traffic system researcher throughout the United States, said, "I have not seen any larger projects in the Bay Area as well as in urban areas across the country". Of course, it is impossible for Google to "cover up the sky", so Yahoo also started implementing the bus project for employees in 2005. On peak days, Yahoo's bus also took off. Pick up about 350 employees in San Francisco, as well as Berkeley, Oakland, etc. These buses run on biofuels and have Wi-Fi coverage. Yet, Danielle Bricker, the Yahoo bus coordinator of Yahoo, has also admitted that the program is "indirectly" inspired by Google's initiative. Along with that, eBay recently also piloted shuttle bus transfers at five points in San Francisco. Some other corporations are also emerging ideas for treatment of staff is equally unique. Facebook is an example, instead of facilitating employees far from the workplace; it helps people in the immediate neighborhood by offering an additional $10,000 for an employee to live close to the pillar within 10 miles, nearby the Palo Alto Department.

Tolerate with mistakes and help staff correct

At Google, paying attention to how employees work and helping them correct mistakes is critical. Instead of pointing out the damage and blaming a person who caused the mistake, the company would be interested in what the cause of the problem was and how to fix it as quickly and efficiently as possible.

Also as its culture, we understand that if we want to make breakthroughs in the workplace, we need to have experimentation, failure and repeat the test. Therefore, mistakes and failures are not terrible there. We have the right to be wrong and have the opportunity to overcome failure in the support of our superiors and colleagues. Good ideas are always encouraged at Google. However, before it is accepted and put into use, there is a clear procedure to confirm whether it is a real new idea and practical or not?

Exponential thought

Google developed in the direction of a holding company—a company that does not directly produce products or provide services but simply invest in capital by buying back capital. In the company, the criteria for setting the ten exponential function in lieu of focusing only on the change in the general increase. This approach helps Google improve its technology and deliver great products to consumers continuously.

The talent

Of course, every company wants to hire talented people to work for them. However, being talented is an art in which there must be voluntary work and enthusiasm for the work of the devotees. ... illustrated that distinctive cultures dramatically influencing performance do exist. Likewise, Google, Apple, Netflix, and Dell are 40% more productive than the average company which attracts top-tier employees and high performers. Recognizing this impact, Google created a distinctive corporate culture when the company attracted people from prestigious colleges around the world.

Build a stimulating work environment

When it comes to the elements that create creativity and innovation, we can easily recognize that the working environment is one of the most important things. Google has succeeded in building an image of a creative working environment. Google offices are individually designed, not duplicated in any type of office. In fact, working environment at Google is so comfortable so that employees will not think of it as a working room, with a full area of work, relaxation, exercise, reading, and watching movies. Is the orientation of Google's corporate culture to stimulate creativity and to show interest in the lives of employees so that volunteers can contribute freely?

Subculture is also a culture, but for a smaller group or community in a big organization. Google, known as the global company with many more offices, so there are many subcultures created among groups of people who work together, from subcultures among work groups to subcultures among ethnic groups and nations, multi-national groups, as well as multiple occupations, functions, geographies, echelons in the hierarchy and product lines. For example, six years ago, when it bought 100 Huffys for employees to use around the sprawling campus, has since exploded into its own subculture. Google now has a seven-person staff of bicycle mechanics that maintains a fleet of about 1,300 brightly-colored Google bikes. The company also encourages employees to cycle to work by providing locker rooms, showers and places to securely park bikes during working hours.

And, for those who want to combine meetings with bike-riding, Googlers can use one of several seven-person.

Leadership influences on the culture at Google

From the definition of leadership and its influence on culture, what does leader directly influence the culture existed? According to Schein, "culture and leadership are two sides of the same coin and one cannot understand one without the other". It breaks the notion that managers have no change. The manager really makes a difference. In fact, a leader has a massive impact on the culture of the company, and Google is not an exception. The leaders of Google concerned more about the demands and abilities of each individual, the study of the nature of human being, an appreciation of their employees as their customers. At Google, the founders thought they could create a company that people would want to work at when creating a home-like environment. It is real that they focus on the workplace brings the comfort to staff creatively and freely.

In my opinion, a successful business cannot be attributed solely from a single star; that needs the brightness of all employees. It depends very much on the capacity and ability to attract talented people. It is the way in which the leader manages these talents, is the cornerstone of corporate culture. One thing that no one can deny is that a good leader must be a creator of a corporate culture so that the employees can maximize capabilities themselves.

(1954)

https://doi.org/10.1186/s40991-017-0021-0

Part III Understanding People in Organizations

Chapter 5 Managing Human Resources

HR Process		
Foundation	Job Relatedness	
	Person-job Match	
Planning	Job Analysis	
	Forecasting	
Staffing	Recruitment	
	Selection	
Developing	Training	
	Development	
Performance management	Evaluation	
	Compensation & benefits	
Motivating	Motivation	
	Scheduling	
Other	Career management	
	Employee-union relations	

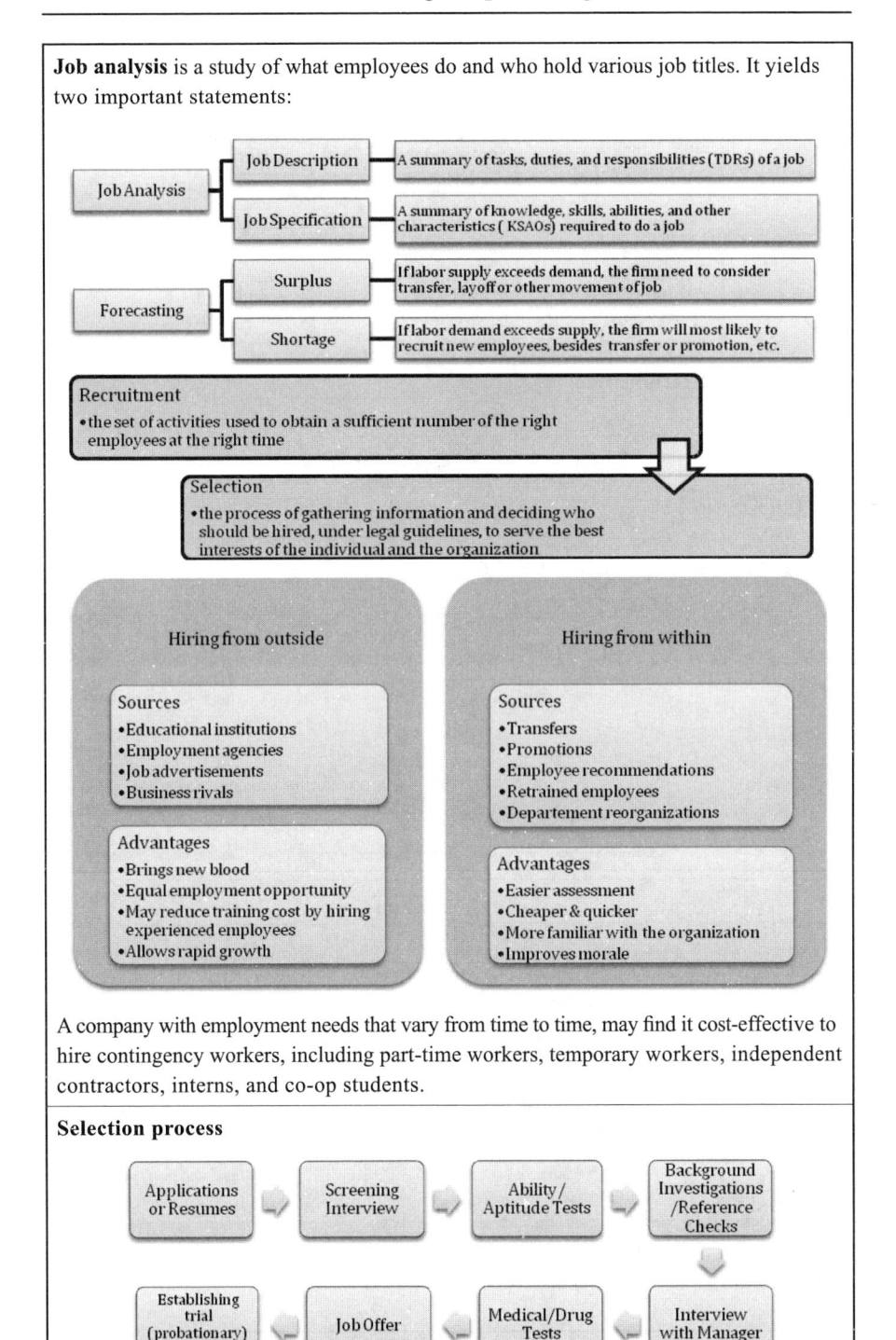

Job analysis is a study of what employees do and who hold various job titles. It yields two important statements:

```
Job Analysis ─┬─ Job Description ─── A summary of tasks, duties, and responsibilities (TDRs) of a job
              └─ Job Specification ── A summary of knowledge, skills, abilities, and other
                                      characteristics (KSAOs) required to do a job

Forecasting ─┬─ Surplus ── If labor supply exceeds demand, the firm need to consider
             │             transfer, layoff or other movement of job
             └─ Shortage ─ If labor demand exceeds supply, the firm will most likely to
                           recruit new employees, besides transfer or promotion, etc.
```

Recruitment
- the set of activities used to obtain a sufficient number of the right employees at the right time

Selection
- the process of gathering information and deciding who should be hired, under legal guidelines, to serve the best interests of the individual and the organization

Hiring from outside

Sources
- Educational institutions
- Employment agencies
- Job advertisements
- Business rivals

Advantages
- Brings new blood
- Equal employment opportunity
- May reduce training cost by hiring experienced employees
- Allows rapid growth

Hiring from within

Sources
- Transfers
- Promotions
- Employee recommendations
- Retrained employees
- Departement reorganizations

Advantages
- Easier assessment
- Cheaper & quicker
- More familiar with the organization
- Improves morale

A company with employment needs that vary from time to time, may find it cost-effective to hire contingency workers, including part-time workers, temporary workers, independent contractors, interns, and co-op students.

Selection process

Applications or Resumes → Screening Interview → Ability/Aptitude Tests → Background Investigations/Reference Checks

↓

Establishing trial (probationary) Periods ← Job Offer ← Medical/Drug Tests ← Interview with Manager

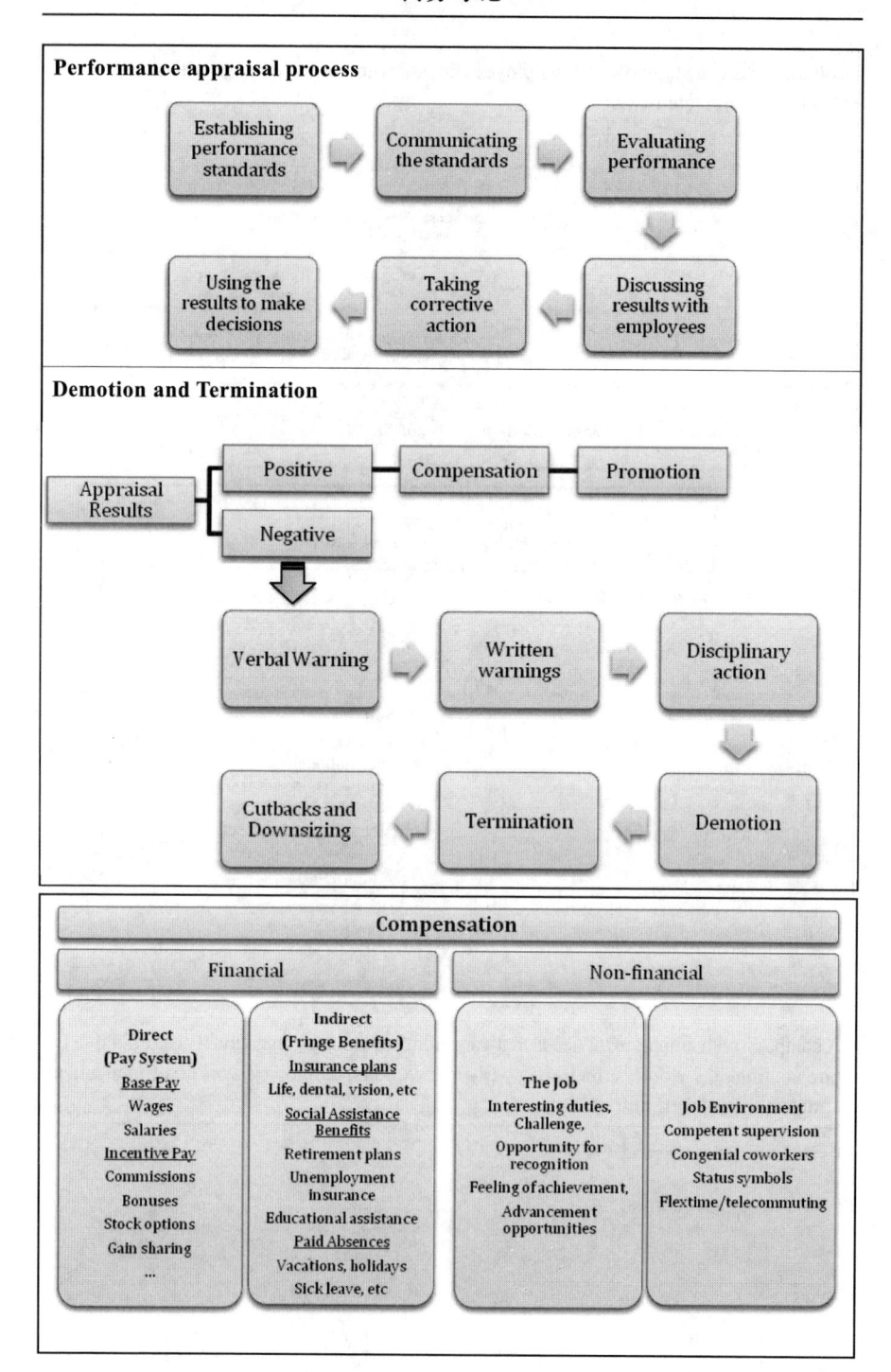

Performance appraisal process

Establishing performance standards → Communicating the standards → Evaluating performance → Discussing results with employees → Taking corrective action → Using the results to make decisions

Demotion and Termination

Appraisal Results → Positive → Compensation → Promotion

Appraisal Results → Negative → Verbal Warning → Written warnings → Disciplinary action → Demotion → Termination → Cutbacks and Downsizing

Compensation

Financial

Direct (Pay System)
- Base Pay
- Wages
- Salaries
- Incentive Pay
- Commissions
- Bonuses
- Stock options
- Gain sharing
- ...

Indirect (Fringe Benefits)
- Insurance plans
  - Life, dental, vision, etc
- Social Assistance Benefits
  - Retirement plans
  - Unemployment insurance
  - Educational assistance
- Paid Absences
  - Vacations, holidays
  - Sick leave, etc

Non-financial

The Job
- Interesting duties, Challenge,
- Opportunity for recognition
- Feeling of achievement,
- Advancement opportunities

Job Environment
- Competent supervision
- Congenial coworkers
- Status symbols
- Flextime/telecommuting

Labor Union and management relations

Workers unionize to force management to listen to the complaints of all their workers rather than to just the few who were brave (or foolish) enough to speak out. The power of unions, then, comes from collective action. Collective bargaining is the process by which union leaders and managers negotiate common terms and conditions of employment for the workers represented by unions.

When bargaining fails, each side can use several tactics to support its cause until the impasse is resolved.

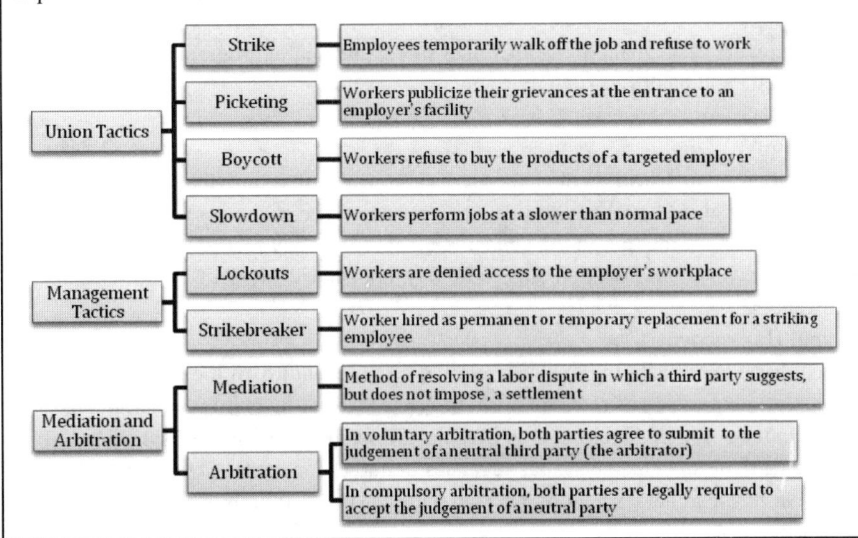

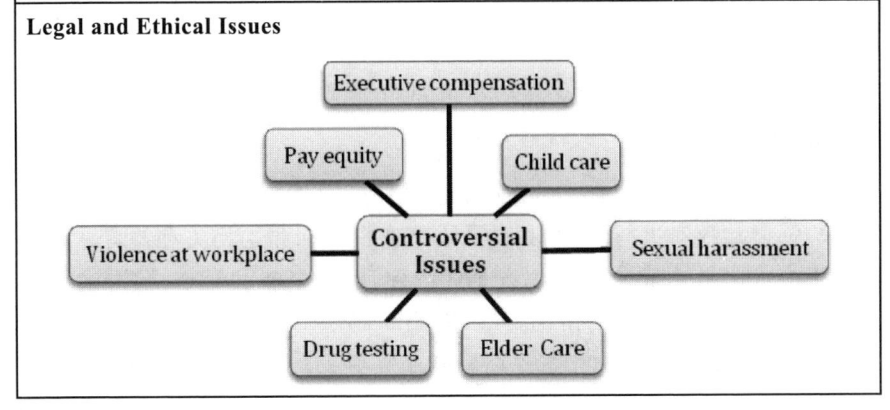

Union Tactics
- Strike — Employees temporarily walk off the job and refuse to work
- Picketing — Workers publicize their grievances at the entrance to an employer's facility
- Boycott — Workers refuse to buy the products of a targeted employer
- Slowdown — Workers perform jobs at a slower than normal pace

Management Tactics
- Lockouts — Workers are denied access to the employer's workplace
- Strikebreaker — Worker hired as permanent or temporary replacement for a striking employee

Mediation and Arbitration
- Mediation — Method of resolving a labor dispute in which a third party suggests, but does not impose, a settlement
- Arbitration —
  - In voluntary arbitration, both parties agree to submit to the judgement of a neutral third party (the arbitrator)
  - In compulsory arbitration, both parties are legally required to accept the judgement of a neutral party

Legal and Ethical Issues

Controversial Issues:
- Executive compensation
- Pay equity
- Child care
- Violence at workplace
- Sexual harassment
- Drug testing
- Elder Care

Equal Employment Opportunity
All people should be offered employment opportunities equally and treated the same, regardless of their race, color, religion, creed, age, sex, sex stereotype, gender, gender identity or expression, transgender, sexual orientation, national origin, citizenship, disability, marital and civil partnership/union status, pregnancy, veteran or military service status, genetic information, or any other characteristic protected by law.

Occupational Safety and Health
This is a multidisciplinary field concerned with the safety, health, and welfare of people at work. The goals of occupational safety and health programs include to foster a safe and healthy work environment.

Pay Equity
Equal pay for equal work is the concept of labor rights that individuals in the same workplace be given equal pay. It is most commonly used in the context of sexual discrimination, in relation to the gender pay gap. Equal pay relates to the full range of payments and benefits, including basic pay, non-salary payments, bonuses and allowances.

Sexual Harassment
Sexual harassment is bullying or coercion of a sexual nature, or the unwelcome or inappropriate promise of rewards in exchange for sexual favors. In most modern legal contexts, sexual harassment is illegal. Harassment can include "sexual harassment" or unwelcome sexual advances, requests for sexual favors, and other verbal or physical harassment of a sexual nature. The legal definition of sexual harassment varies by jurisdiction.

在中国

工会 (Labor Union)

在美国等大多数国家，Labor Union 是与资方相对立的组织，代表工人利益与资方和政府进行谈判，其会员不能有资方即雇主相关利益者。而中国的工会大多数由雇主或者用人企业组建，成为企业和党委、政府内部的一个职能部门，并由企业和党委、政府组织高层对工会进行人事任命，没有相对独立的组织和行动，主要起着联系党群关系的桥梁和纽带作用。

Key Terms	
Job analysis 工作分析	Disciplinary action 纪律处分
Job description 工作描述	Termination 解聘；解雇
Job specification 工作要求	Cutback/Downsizing 削减员工；裁员
Recruitment 招聘	Compensation 报酬

Part III Understanding People in Organizations

Selection 甄选	Base pay 基本工资
Contingency workers 临时员工	Commissions 提成，佣金
Application 应聘申请书	Bonus 奖金
Resume 简历	Stock option 股票期权
Aptitude test 资质测试	Gain sharing 利润分享
Reference check 背景调查；征信调查	Fringe benefits 福利待遇
Trial/probation period 试用期	Paid absence 带薪休假
Evaluation 评估	Labor union 工会
Scheduling 工作安排	Collective bargaining 集体谈判
Job offer 工作录用通知	Strike 罢工
Orientation 迎新培训	Picketing 抗议示威
Apprentice program 学徒训练计划	Boycott 联合抵制
Online training 在线培训	Slowdown 怠工
On-the-job training 在岗培训	Lockout 闭厂；封闭工厂；停工
Off-the-job training 脱岗培训	Strikebreaker 破坏罢工者
Job simulation 模拟培训	Mediation 调解；调停
Vestibule training 实战培训；仿真训练	Arbitration 仲裁
Demotion 降职	Equal Employment Opportunity 公平就业机会
Promotion 升职	Pay Equity 公平报酬
	Sexual harassment 性骚扰

Brainstorming

Find a job advertisement and analyze its job description and job specification.
Look around and you will find that Chinese enterprises are paying increasingly more attention to employee training. Think about why.
Search for more differences between Chinese labor unions and those in other countries and make comments.

Read More

Human Resource Management: Key Responsibilities

Human resource management is concerned with the development of both individuals and the organization in which they operate. HRM, then, is engaged not only in securing and developing the talents of individual workers, but also in implementing programs that enhance communication and cooperation between those individual workers in order to nurture organizational development.

The primary responsibilities associated with human resource management include: job analysis and staffing, organization and utilization of work force, measurement and appraisal of work force performance, implementation of reward systems for employees, professional development of workers, and maintenance of work force.

Job analysis consists of determining—often with the help of other company areas—the nature and responsibilities of various employment positions. This can encompass determination of the skills and experiences necessary to adequately perform in a position, identification of job and industry trends, and anticipation of future employment levels and skill requirements. "Job analysis is the cornerstone of HRM practice because it provides valid information about jobs that is used to hire and promote people, establish wages, determine training needs, and make other important HRM decisions," stated Thomas S. Bateman and Carl P. Zeithaml in *Management: Function and Strategy*. Staffing, meanwhile, is the actual process of managing the flow of personnel into, within (through transfers and promotions), and out of an organization. Once the recruiting part of the staffing process has been completed, selection is accomplished through job postings, interviews, reference checks, testing, and other tools.

Organization, utilization, and maintenance of a company's work force is another key function of HRM. This involves designing an organizational framework that makes maximum use of an enterprise's human resources and establishing systems of communication that help the organization operate in a unified manner. Other responsibilities in this area include safety and health and worker-management relations. Human resource maintenance activities related to safety and health usually entail compliance with federal laws that protect employees from hazards in the workplace. These regulations are handed down from several federal agencies, including the Occupational Safety and Health Administration (OSHA) and the Environmental Protection Agency (EPA), and various state agencies, which implement laws in the realms of worker's compensation, employee protection, and other areas. Maintenance tasks related to worker-management relations primarily entail: working with labor unions; handling grievances related to misconduct, such as theft or sexual harassment; and devising communication systems to foster cooperation and a shared sense of mission among employees.

Performance appraisal is the practice of assessing employee job performance and providing feedback to those employees about both positive and negative aspects of their performance. Performance measurements are very important both for the organization and the individual, for they are the primary data used in determining salary increases, promotions, and, in the case of workers who perform unsatisfactorily, dismissal.

Reward systems are typically managed by HR areas as well. This aspect of human resource management is very important, for it is the mechanism by which organizations provide their workers with rewards for past achievements and incentives for high performance in the future. It is also the mechanism by which organizations address problems within their work force, through institution of disciplinary measures. Aligning the work force with company goals, stated Gubman, "requires offering workers an employment relationship that motivates them to take ownership of the business plan."

Employee development and training is another vital responsibility of HR personnel. HR is responsible for researching an organization's training needs, and for initiating and evaluating employee development programs designed to address those needs. These training programs can range from orientation programs, which are designed to acclimate new hires to the company, to ambitious education programs intended to familiarize workers with a new software system.

"After getting the right talent into the organization," wrote Gubman, "the second traditional challenge to human resources is to align the workforce with the business—to constantly build the capacity of the workforce to execute the business plan." This is done through performance appraisals, training, and other activities. In the realm of performance appraisal, HRM professionals must devise uniform appraisal standards, develop review techniques, train managers to administer the appraisals, and then evaluate and follow up on the effectiveness of performance reviews. They must also tie the appraisal process into compensation and incentive strategies, and work to ensure that federal regulations are observed.

Responsibilities associated with training and development activities, meanwhile, include the determination, design, execution, and analysis of educational programs. The HRM professional should be aware of the fundamentals of learning and motivation, and must carefully design and monitor training and development programs that benefit the overall organization as well as the individual. The importance of this aspect of a business's operation can hardly be overstated. As Roberts, Seldon and Roberts indicated in Human Resources Management, "the quality of employees and their development through training and education are major factors in determining long-term profitability of a small business. Research has shown specific benefits that a small business receives from training and developing its workers, including: increased productivity; reduced employee turnover; increased efficiency resulting in financial gains; (and) decreased need for supervision."

Meaningful contributions to business processes are increasingly recognized as within the purview of active human resource management practices. Of course, human resource managers have always contributed to overall business processes in certain respects—by disseminating guidelines for and monitoring employee behavior, for instance, or ensuring that the organization is obeying worker-related regulatory guidelines. Now, increasing numbers of businesses are incorporating human resource managers into other business processes as well. In the past, human resource managers were cast in a support role in which their thoughts on cost/benefit justifications and other operational aspects of the business were rarely solicited. But as Johnston noted, the changing character of business structures and the marketplace are making it increasingly necessary for business owners and executives to pay greater attention to the human resource aspects of operation: "Tasks that were once neatly slotted into well-defined and narrow job descriptions have given way to broad job descriptions or role definitions. In some cases, completely new work relationships have developed; telecommuting, permanent part-time roles and outsourcing major non-strategic functions are becoming more frequent." All of these changes, which human resource managers are heavily involved in, are important factors in shaping business performance.

(1031)

https://www.inc.com/encyclopedia/human-resource-management.html

Part III Understanding People in Organizations

Chapter 6 Motivating People

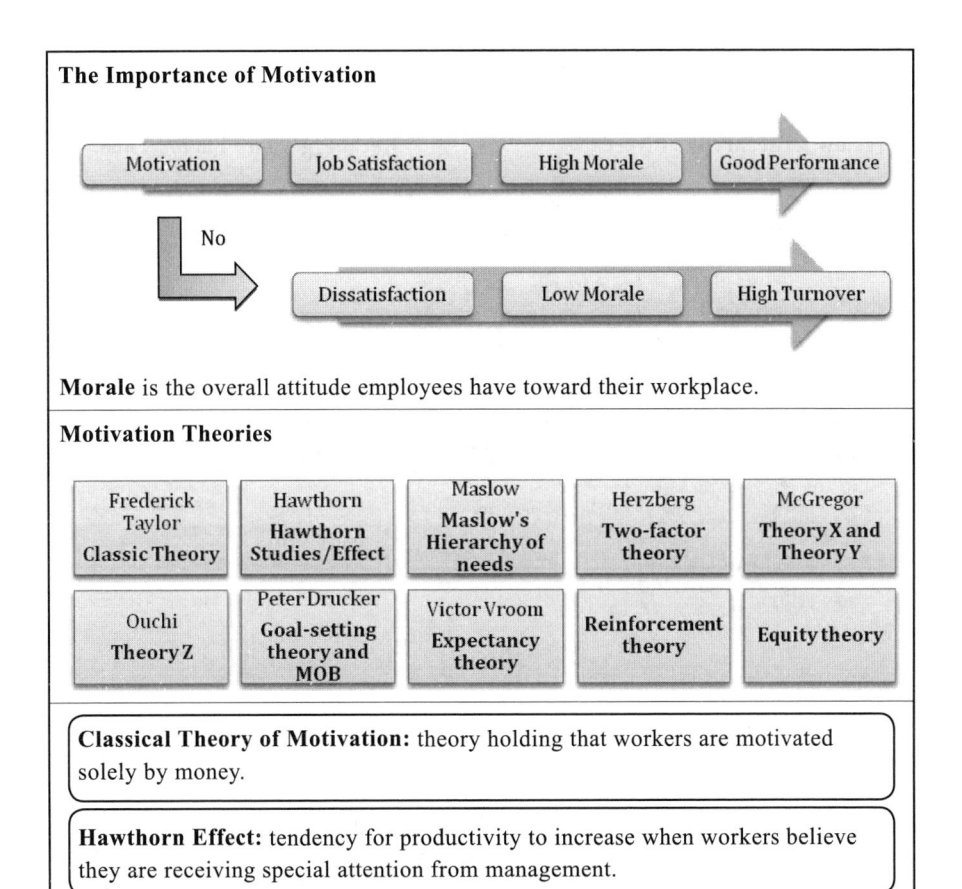

The Importance of Motivation

Motivation → Job Satisfaction → High Morale → Good Performance

No → Dissatisfaction → Low Morale → High Turnover

Morale is the overall attitude employees have toward their workplace.

Motivation Theories

Frederick Taylor Classic Theory	Hawthorn Hawthorn Studies/Effect	Maslow Maslow's Hierarchy of needs	Herzberg Two-factor theory	McGregor Theory X and Theory Y
Ouchi Theory Z	Peter Drucker Goal-setting theory and MOB	Victor Vroom Expectancy theory	Reinforcement theory	Equity theory

Classical Theory of Motivation: theory holding that workers are motivated solely by money.

Hawthorn Effect: tendency for productivity to increase when workers believe they are receiving special attention from management.

Maslow's Hierarchy of Needs: motivation comes from need. If a need is met, it's no longer a motivator, so a higher-level needs demand the support of lower-level needs.

Herzberg's Two Factor Theory: there are two groups of factors that influence job satisfaction and employee motivation. <u>Hygiene or hygienic factors</u> can cause dissatisfaction if missing but do not necessarily motivate employees if increased; <u>Motivation or motivating factors</u> can cause employees to be productive and that give them satisfaction, with the presence of hygiene factors.

· 51 ·

	Hygiene Factors Create dissatisfaction	**Motivational Factors** Create satisfaction
Absence	Dissatisfied	Not satisfied
Presence	Not dissatisfied	Satisfied

Maslow's Hierarchy of Needs vs. **Herzberg's Two Factor Theory**

Maslow	Herzberg	Category
Self-actualization needs	Work itself / Achievement / Possibility of growth	Motivational factors [Intrinsic rewards]
Esteem needs	Advancement / Recognition / Status	
Social needs	Interpersonal relations / Supervision	
Safety needs	Company policy and administration / Job security / Working conditions	Hygienic factors [Extrinsic rewards]
Physiological needs	Salary / Personal life	

McGregor found that managers' attitudes towards workers generally fall into two sets of assumptions, which he called Theory X and Theory Y.

	Theory X	Theory Y
Managers' Views	Employees dislike work and job responsibilities and will avoid work if possible	Employees are willing to work and prefer more responsibility
Implications	Supervisors cannot delegate responsibilities	Supervisors should delegate responsibilities, which will satisfy and motivate employees

Part III Understanding People in Organizations

Ouchi's Theory Z is a blend of American and Japanese management approaches.

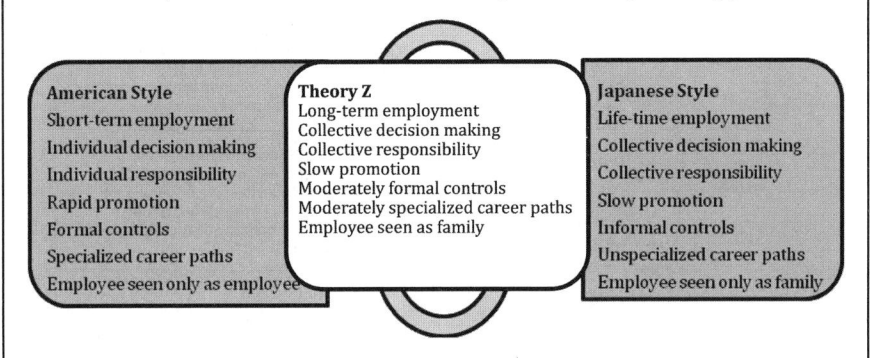

American Style	Theory Z	Japanese Style
Short-term employment	Long-term employment	Life-time employment
Individual decision making	Collective decision making	Collective decision making
Individual responsibility	Collective responsibility	Collective responsibility
Rapid promotion	Slow promotion	Slow promotion
Formal controls	Moderately formal controls	Informal controls
Specialized career paths	Moderately specialized career paths	Unspecialized career paths
Employee seen only as employee	Employee seen as family	Employee seen only as family

Other theories

Goal-setting theory sets that ambitious but attainable goals can motivate workers and improve performance if the goals are accepted, accompanied by feedback, and facilitated by organizational conditions.

MBO (Management by Objectives) is a system of goal setting and implementation; it involves a cycle of discussion, review, and evaluation of objectives among managers and employees.

Expectancy theory: the amount of effect employees exert on a task depends on their expectations of the outcome.

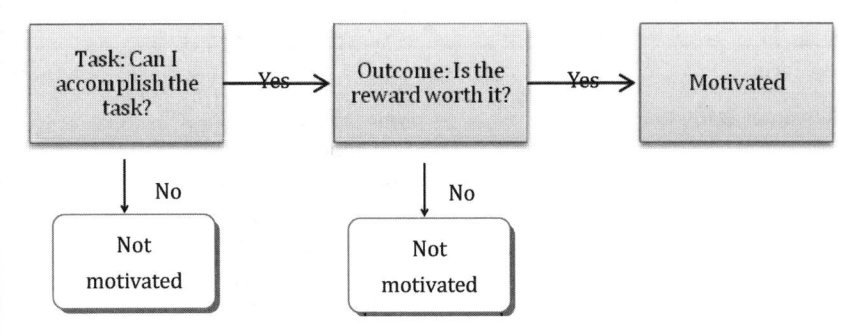

Task: Can I accomplish the task? —Yes→ Outcome: Is the reward worth it? —Yes→ Motivated

- Task → No → Not motivated
- Outcome → No → Not motivated

Reinforcement theory: behaviors can be encouraged or discouraged by means of rewards or punishments, respectively, also referred to as "behavior modification".

Equity theory: employees try to maintain equity between inputs and outputs compared to others in similar positions.

Putting Theories into Action

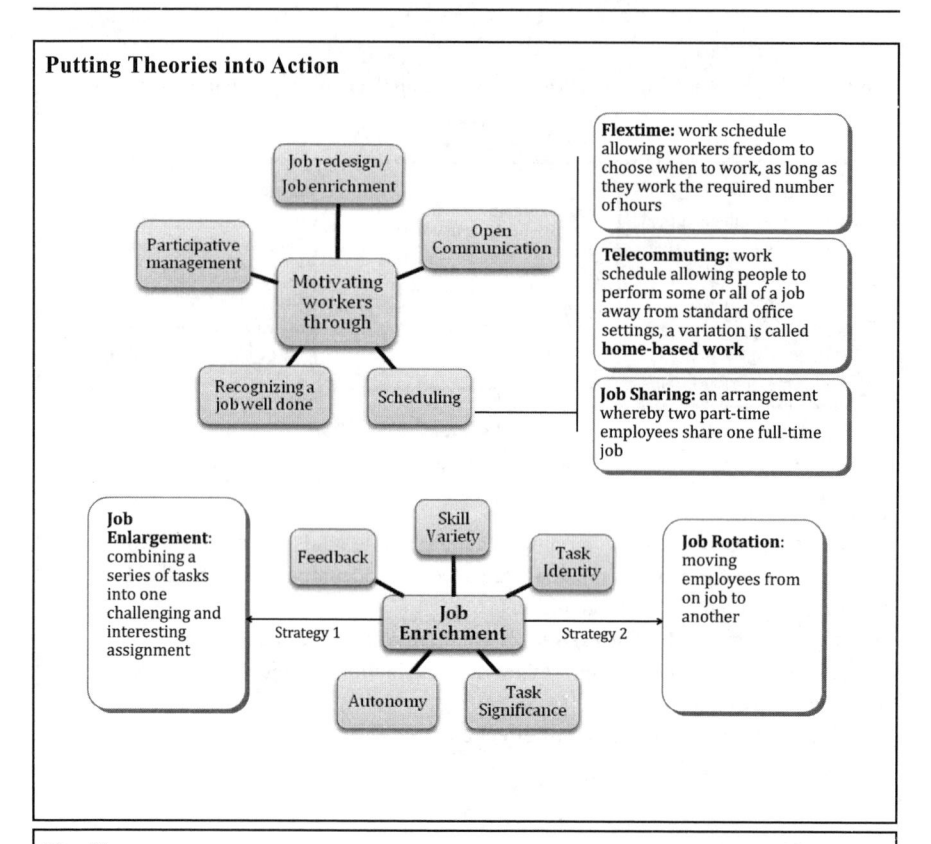

Motivating workers through:
- Job redesign/Job enrichment
- Open Communication
- Participative management
- Recognizing a job well done
- Scheduling

Flextime: work schedule allowing workers freedom to choose when to work, as long as they work the required number of hours

Telecommuting: work schedule allowing people to perform some or all of a job away from standard office settings, a variation is called **home-based work**

Job Sharing: an arrangement whereby two part-time employees share one full-time job

Job Enlargement: combining a series of tasks into one challenging and interesting assignment ← Strategy 1

Job Enrichment (Feedback, Skill Variety, Task Identity, Autonomy, Task Significance)

Strategy 2 → **Job Rotation:** moving employees from on job to another

Key Terms

Motivation 激励	Hygiene factor 卫生因素
Morale 士气	Motivation factor 激励因素
Turnover 人员流动	Intrinsic rewards 内在奖励
Classical theory 经典理论	Extrinsic rewards 外在奖励
Hawthorn effect 霍索恩效应	Flextime 灵活时间工作制
Maslow's hierarchy of needs 马斯洛需求层次	Telecommuting 远程办公
	Job sharing 工作分享
Two-factory theory 双因素理论	Job enrichment 工作丰富
MOB 目标管理	Job enlargement 工作扩大
Expectancy theory 期望理论	Job rotation 工作轮换
Reinforcement theory 强化理论	
Equity theory 公平理论	

Brainstorming

Discuss the effect of money in employee motivation.
Besides Google, find other examples excellent in motivating employees. Analyze their strategies.

Part III Understanding People in Organizations

Read More

What Can Managers Do to Motivate Employees

What can managers do to motivate employees? The reality, when you talk about how to motivate employees, is that employees are motivated. The manager's challenge is to figure out how to tap into that motivation to accomplish work goals. Fortunately, the manager controls the key environmental factors necessary to motivate employees.

The most significant factor, that the manager controls, is his or her relationship with each employee. The second most important factor in a manager's ability to motivate employees is creating a work environment and organizational culture that fosters employee motivation and engagement.

This work culture consists of an environment in which employees are trusted, treated like the adults they are, and not micromanaged. Employees are entrusted with the values, vision, mission, and strategic framework within which they are expected to accomplish their jobs.

They receive frequent communication, are treated with respect and civility, and have input to every facet of the work they are hired to produce. They are encouraged to speak up about what they believe when participating in solving a problem for their customer. They are further trusted by the organization with the most significant and critical financial information so they are not blindsided by business problems.

These are factors that help produce a work environment in which employees will choose motivation to accomplish the requirements of their work. Nothing is more powerful than a group of contributing, motivated employees. Trust this.

https://www.thebalancecareers.com/how-great-managers-motivate-their-employees-1918772

Additional Thoughts on How Managers Can Motivate Employees
Show your trust

The first sure way to motivate and inspire your employees is to demonstrate that you have faith in their abilities to get the job done. You can do this by assigning them more responsibilities and giving them the chance to rise to the challenge. Doing so shows that you trust them, which has a way of motivating people to keep doing their best.

Micromanaging your employees and hovering over their shoulders at every step is counterproductive because it makes them nervous. If your employees are too afraid to try new things, they won't be giving you their best. Give them greater autonomy and responsibility and they will rise to the occasion.

Incentivize with a prize

Reward people for a job well done, and they'll be more likely to repeat the performance and do what it takes to earn the coveted prize. Positive reinforcement, after all, is one of the oldest, tried and true psychological principals. You can incentivize your employees with prizes like a free lunch, an afternoon off, event tickets, or gift cards for people that reach certain targets. Not only will this tickle the reward centers of their brains, it will also inspire a little friendly, and healthy, competition in the workplace.

For example, years ago I worked at a call center and every time someone made a sale they got to spin a prize wheel that was mounted on the wall. The prizes where mostly candy bars and drinks, but every time I spun that wheel it was with a great sense of satisfaction and achievement. It gave me a reason to keep placing calls and striving for the next sale. This kind of activity also adds something to the culture of your company.

Invest in your employees

Similar to the first point about showing your trust, another way to inspire and motivate your employees is by investing in them. Offering things like tuition reimbursement, a mentoring program, one-on-one coaching, and job shadowing with people in higher positions sends a clear message: you care about their career and their future. Some companies, in fact, have periodic meetings with their employees to discuss their career paths and make sure they stay on track.

Aside from improving skills and increasing staff knowledge, this kind of investment in employee career pathing gives them a reason to stay with the company for the long haul rather than be on the lookout for a better offer.

Invest in your employees, and you'll give them a reason to stick around. When your employees grow and improve, so does the company.

Give them a purpose

No matter what your job is, whether it's packing orders at a distribution warehouse, or managing a Fortune 500 company at the executive level, we all want to know that our jobs matter. Show your employees why they matter to the company, and what the results of their work are, and they'll feel rewarded and motivated to keep at it. Emphasizing the importance of employee contributions (and giving people credit for good work) bolsters a sense of confidence and achievement, which can motivate people to keep working hard.

Include them in the big decisions

It can be discouraging to your employees when they see big company decisions being made without anything mentioned to them. It makes them feel isolated and unimportant. How do you get around this? By asking for your employees' opinions. Asking for their input creates a sense of belonging in the company, making them feel like they matter.

This goes hand-in-hand with employee investment, and giving them a purpose: by asking for their insight and opinion on how the company can improve, you will further engender their trust and loyalty to the company.

In today's highly competitive workplace, where people switch jobs every few years, employee turnover can be a big concern. You can stem the tide, though, by putting a focus on employee engagement and training. Doing so builds a solid foundation for employee management and growth, ensuring your staff is always motivated and inspired.

(673)

https://hiring.workopolis.com/article/5-ways-inspire-motivate-employees/

The Google Way of Motivating Employees

When it comes to motivating their employees, it can be said without question that Google stands out from the rest. Google was named the 2014 "Best Company to Work For" by the Great Place to Work Institute and Fortune Magazine. The organization topped the list for the fifth time. True, in its short lifespan, Google has acquired for itself a huge and bright workforce (over 50,000 employees spread throughout the world) that serves millions of people all over the globe. However, what is even more exemplary is how Google heavily pampers its employees while still being able to extract one-of-a-kind and outstanding ideas and products from them.

INTRODUCTION TO GOOGLE'S WORK CULTURE

Google's model of motivation and leadership topples traditional leadership theory which focuses more on results than on the people who deliver those results. The company's work culture is true to its philosophy:

"To create the happiest, most productive workplace in the world."

These words from the Vice President of people development at Google only serve to support that fact:

"It's less about the aspiration to be No. 1 in the world, and more that we want our employees and future employees to love it here, because that's what's going to make us successful."

While the company was in its early days, its co-founders Larry Page and Sergey Brin went looking out for organizations that were known to care for people, develop truly amazing brands and trigger extraordinary innovation. The objective of this search was to be able to draw and keep great talent. In their search, they found the SAS institute (which was then ranked No. 1 on the Great Place to Work Institute's list of best multinational companies to work for) as one company that was worth modeling. Interactions with SAS executives led the Google founders to understand that people were really successful in their jobs and loyal too when they felt truly valued and thoroughly supported. The result was the Google work culture as we know it now with huge and plentiful perks, unconventional (or weird) office designs, and amazing freedom, flexibility and transparency, among other things.

EMPLOYEE MOTIVATION THE GOOGLE WAY
Uncommon Yet Affordable, Amazing Perks and Benefits

Just like other companies, Google offers the usual extrinsic benefits such as flex spending accounts, no-cost health and dental benefits, insurance, 401K plans, vacation packages and tuition reimbursements. However, Google is better known for some really distinctive and "more than just attractive" perks and benefits which just serve to show the very extreme lengths the company goes to make its employees consistently happy. What follows are some examples of these remarkable perks and benefits.

Reimbursement of up to $5,000 to employees for legal expenses.

Maternity benefits of a maximum of 18 weeks off at about 100 percent pay. The father and mother of the newborn are given expenses of a maximum of $500 for take-out meals in the initial 3 months they spend at home with the baby (Take-Out Benefits).

Financial support for adopting a child (Google's Adoption Assistance).

On-site car wash, oil change, bike repair, dry cleaning, gym, massage therapy and hair stylist are available at the company's headquarters in Mountain View.

At the Googleplex, there's an onsite doctor and free fitness center and trainer and facility to wash clothes among other benefits.

Lunch and dinner is available free of charge. In addition, an assortment of delicious but healthy meals are available every day, prepared by gourmet chefs.

Voice and Value

At Google, democracy prevails with employees given a considerable voice. Here are some ways how.

The company hosts employee forums on all Fridays where there is an examination of the 20 most asked questions.

Employees can make use of any of a number of channels of expression to communicate their ideas and thoughts. Channels include Google+ conversations, a wide variety of surveys, Fixits (24-hour sprints wholly dedicated to fixing a specific problem), TGIF and even direct emails to any of the Google leaders.

Googlegeist, the company's biggest survey seeks feedback on hundreds of issues and then employs volunteer employee teams all over the company to resolve the major problems.

Employees are regularly surveyed about their managers. The results of the survey are used to publicly acknowledge the best managers and make them role models or teachers for the next year. The worst managers are provided with vigorous support and coaching, with the help of which 75 percent improve within a quarter.

Transparency

As Google is a company that considers its people to be its biggest asset, everything that can be shared, is shared. In this way, they are able to show their employees that they trust them with confidentiality and trust their judgment.

After the first few weeks of every quarter, Google's Executive Chairman shares with all Googlers, practically the same material that Google shared with their Board of Directors at their most recent meeting. The material includes launch plans and product roadmaps in addition to team and employee OKRs (quarterly goals) so that all Googlers are aware of what fellow Googlers are working on.

Following annual surveys of employees in which 90 percent of them participate, not only do the employees see the results of their own group, they also see those of all the other groups (privacy is protected). In addition, when the company takes action on the collective feedback from their employees, the action(s) taken is also shared with everyone.

30 minutes of a weekly all-hands meeting hosted by Google's co-founders and called TGIF are devoted to a Q and A session where almost anything can be debated or questioned from the founder's attire to whether the company is proceeding along the right direction.

Freedom over How and When Work is Completed

One of Google's strongly held beliefs is that they can get amazing output from people by giving them freedom. Indeed, research by Sir Michael Marmot, Professor of Epidemiology and Public Health at the University College, London is proof of that fact. From research that he carried out over a period of 4 decades into the health of government workers in Great Britain, he found out the highest mortality and poorest well-being were consistently associated with employees who had the smallest degree of control over their work lives.

Google's employees are allowed greater discretion on their hours of work and also on when they can go and have some fun whether it involves getting a massage, heading to the gym or just indulging in volleyball. In addition, the firm allows each of its employees to give 20 percent of his time (1 day every week) to doing anything they like. This can range from assisting with another project to even just sleeping. Anything that is ethical and lawful is okay with Google.

Flexibility

In this flat hierarchy organization, engineers have plenty of flexibility when it comes to selecting the projects they work on. The organization also encourages its staff to pursue company-associated interests. In addition, instead of being trained by top management on the protocol for tasks, employees can approach tasks in their own unique ways. For example, employees are allowed to express themselves by scrawling on the walls. They can also arrive for work at any time they like, wear pajamas if they want or even bring their dog along. The relaxed, creative and fun environment psychologically benefits Google's employees while giving Google the benefit of a more motivated, dedicated and productive workforce.

Inspiring Work

One of the reasons why people don't feel motivated at their jobs is that the work assigned to them is frequently deficient in variety or challenge. The monotonous nature of the work with no growth in sight dulls employee enthusiasm.

At Google, things are different with the organization putting in effort to make sure its employees have inspiring work. The 20 percent allowance for projects of their own interest is one step in this direction. One Google engineer by the name of Chade-Ment Tan appears to have really benefited from this 80-20 rule. He had a desire to make world peace a reality in his lifetime. Though this may have seemed an impossible and strange dream to many, Google didn't discourage him. Eventually Tan designed a very successful course on mindfulness with the assistance of a Stanford University professor, Daniel Goleman (author of *Emotional Intelligence*) and other leading lights in the business industry. Tan's course is a great hit in his company. Tan is additionally credited with authorship of the New York Times best seller entitled "Inside Yourself".

Fun is a Regular Aspect of Work

In keeping with Google's philosophy, life at Google is not all work. There are plenty of opportunities for fun which help Googlers get out of their office and even interact more with each other. The opportunities include frequent breaks, facilities for wall climbing, beach volleyball or bowling; and personal creative sessions. In addition, there are pajama days, dress up days and a Halloween costume party. Every April Fool's Day, Googlers are permitted to plan and implement some major gags and tricks to the world. Google's office design too incorporates some fun with one example being that employees can literally slide down to the next floor with the help of a slide-type construction. Similar to that is a ladder in the Mountain View California office which employees must scurry up to get between floors.

Food is Pretty Easy to Get—150 Feet from Food Rule

Wherever they are, Googlers don't have to go far to get access to food. With respect to Google's East Coast headquarters, not even a single area of the office is situated at a distance exceeding 150 feet, from sources of food, whether it is a restaurant, a micro-kitchen or a huge cafeteria. The convenience obviously makes it possible for Google's employees to snack frequently and possibly even find their co-workers from other teams there.

Googlers benefit from free food and a great variety of food types to choose from. Food stocked in open kitchen areas includes waters, beverages, snacks and candy. The healthier options are more easily visible than their non-healthy counterparts showing how much Google cares about their employees' health. For example, while sodas are somewhat hidden behind translucent glass, various kinds of waters and juices are visible straight away. Healthier snacks (such as almonds and dried banana chips) occupy transparent glass jars while the non-healthier kinds (such as Life Savers and M&Ms) occupy opaque ceramic jars with conspicuous nutritional labels.

Unconventional Office Designs

Google is known for its unusual and often wild office designs. The designs are done to serve several purposes including casual collisions for creative people and engineers to come together, idea generation and the triggering of maximum creativity while also ensuring employee happiness. Thus, rooms for Googlers include a meeting room that resembles a pub, in Dublin; ski gondolas in the Zurich office, and a sidewalk café in Istanbul.

If one were to take the organization's Mountain View, California campus as an example, conversation areas resemble vintage subway cars. In addition, there are conference rooms which are Broadway-themed with velvet drapes, and a labyrinth of play areas.

Google permits its software engineers to design their own work stations or desks out of what look like huge Tinker toys. While some of the engineers have standing desks, a few others additionally have attached treadmills that enable them to walk while working.

To create the perfect workspaces, everything from ceilings and floors to the impact of different colors of paint are analyzed.

Part IV Understanding Marketing

Chapter 7 Marketing and Product Developing

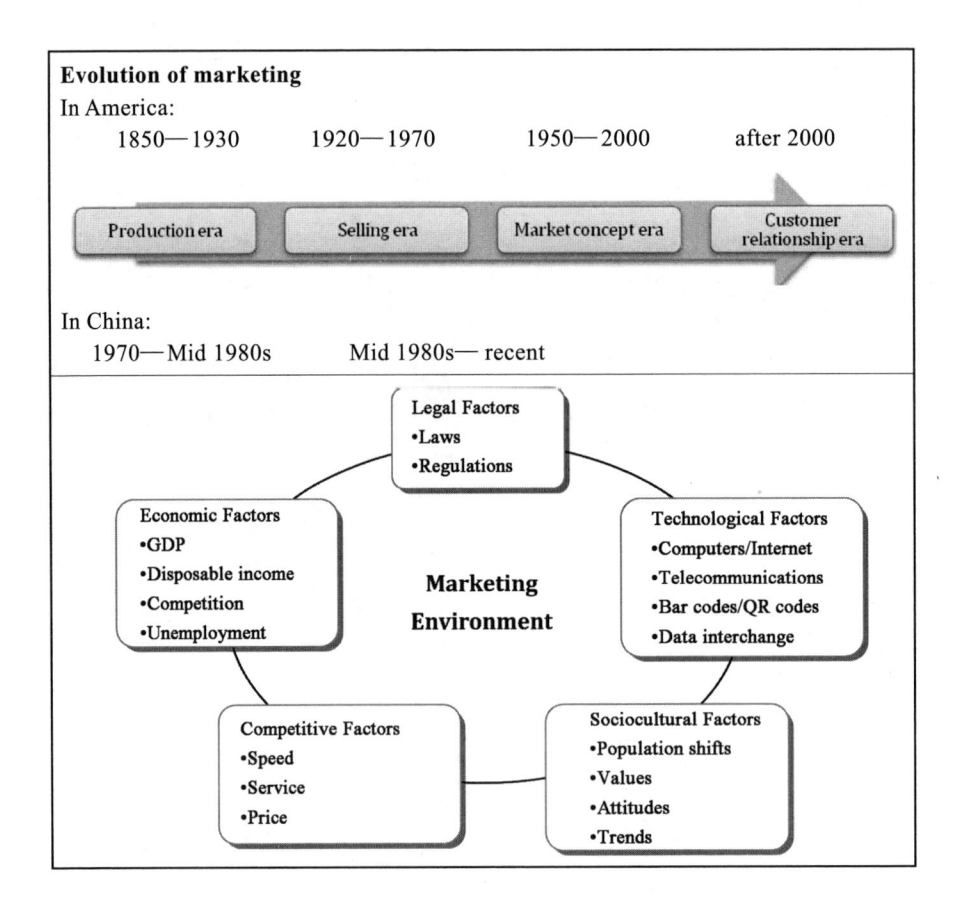

Evolution of marketing

In America:
  1850—1930   1920—1970   1950—2000   after 2000

| Production era | Selling era | Market concept era | Customer relationship era |

In China:
  1970—Mid 1980s   Mid 1980s—recent

Legal Factors
- Laws
- Regulations

Economic Factors
- GDP
- Disposable income
- Competition
- Unemployment

Technological Factors
- Computers/Internet
- Telecommunications
- Bar codes/QR codes
- Data interchange

Marketing Environment

Competitive Factors
- Speed
- Service
- Price

Sociocultural Factors
- Population shifts
- Values
- Attitudes
- Trends

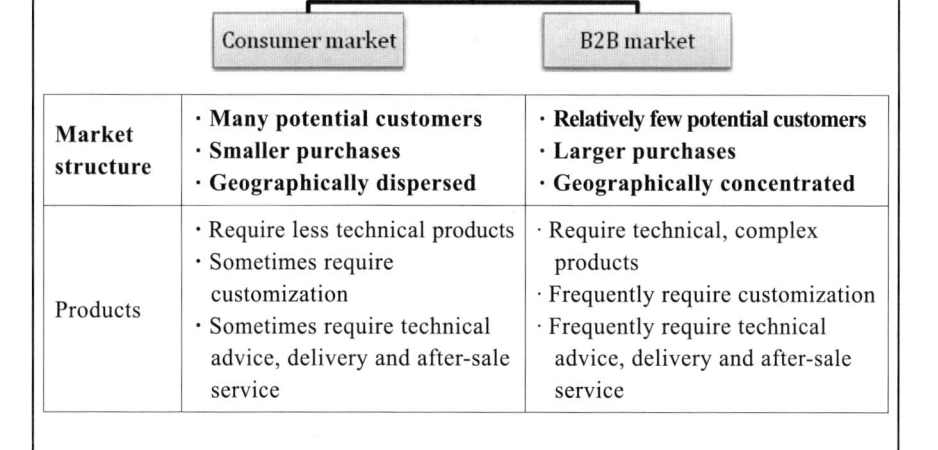

Part IV Understanding Marketing

Marketing research
The analysis of markets to determine opportunities and challenges, and to find the information needed to make good decisions.

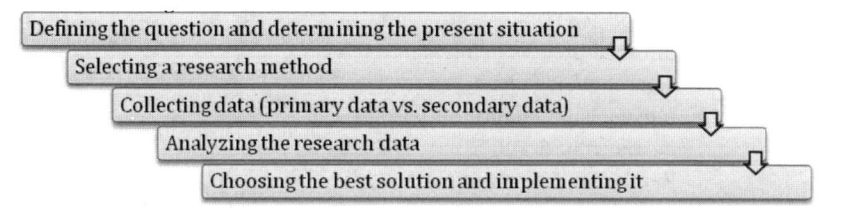

- Defining the question and determining the present situation
- Selecting a research method
- Collecting data (primary data vs. secondary data)
- Analyzing the research data
- Choosing the best solution and implementing it

Research methods

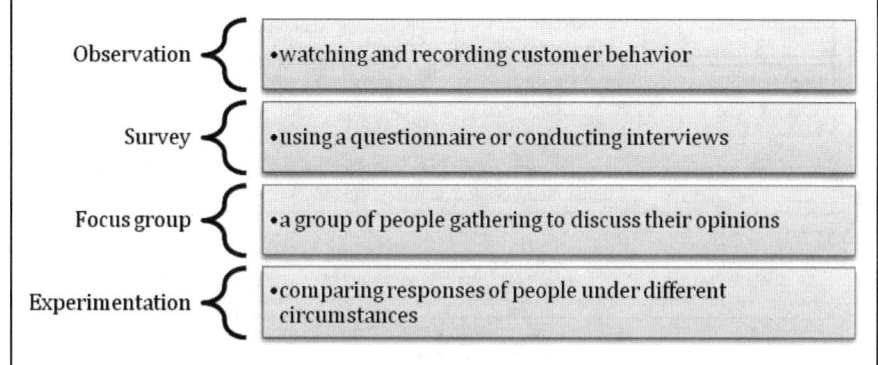

- Observation — watching and recording customer behavior
- Survey — using a questionnaire or conducting interviews
- Focus group — a group of people gathering to discuss their opinions
- Experimentation — comparing responses of people under different circumstances

Secondary data are information that has already been compiled by others and published in journals and books or made available online. **Primary data** are collected by yourself rather than from the above mentioned sources.

Two Markets
- Consumer market
- B2B market

	Consumer market	B2B market
Market structure	· **Many potential customers** · **Smaller purchases** · **Geographically dispersed**	· **Relatively few potential customers** · **Larger purchases** · **Geographically concentrated**
Products	· Require less technical products · Sometimes require customization · Sometimes require technical advice, delivery and after-sale service	· Require technical, complex products · Frequently require customization · Frequently require technical advice, delivery and after-sale service

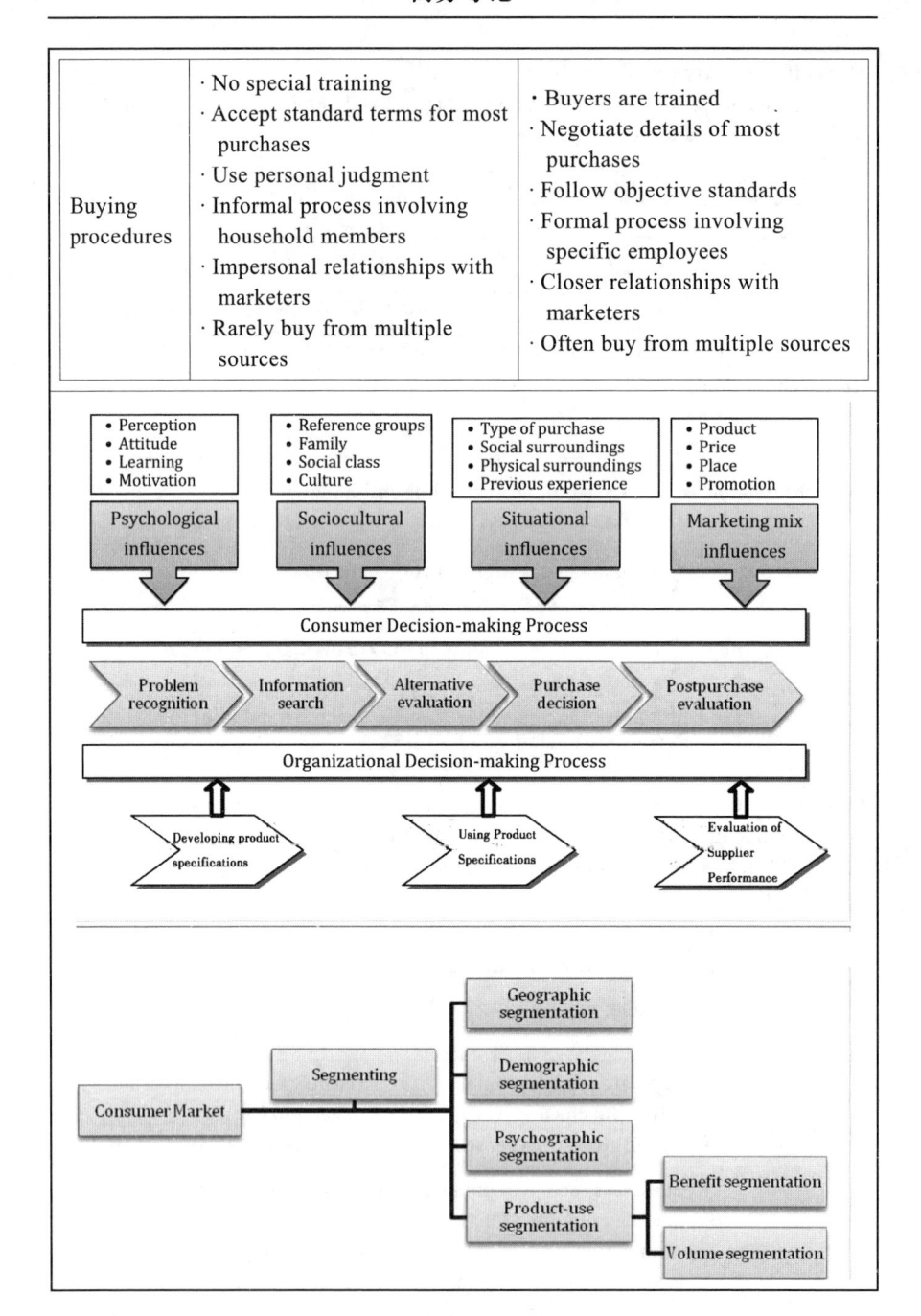

Buying procedures	· No special training · Accept standard terms for most purchases · Use personal judgment · Informal process involving household members · Impersonal relationships with marketers · Rarely buy from multiple sources	· Buyers are trained · Negotiate details of most purchases · Follow objective standards · Formal process involving specific employees · Closer relationships with marketers · Often buy from multiple sources

- Perception
- Attitude
- Learning
- Motivation

Psychological influences

- Reference groups
- Family
- Social class
- Culture

Sociocultural influences

- Type of purchase
- Social surroundings
- Physical surroundings
- Previous experience

Situational influences

- Product
- Price
- Place
- Promotion

Marketing mix influences

Consumer Decision-making Process

Problem recognition → Information search → Alternative evaluation → Purchase decision → Postpurchase evaluation

Organizational Decision-making Process

Developing product specifications → Using Product Specifications → Evaluation of Supplier Performance

Consumer Market → Segmenting →
- Geographic segmentation
- Demographic segmentation
- Psychographic segmentation
- Product-use segmentation → Benefit segmentation / Volume segmentation

Main Dimension	Sample Variables	Typical Segments
Geographic	Region	Northeast, Midwest, Southeast
	City or county size	Under 1 million; 1million ~ 5million; 5million ~ 10 million; over 10 million
	Density	Urban; suburban; rural
	Climate	Dry or damp; hot or cold
	Terrain	Mountain area; plain; plateau
Demographic	Gender	Male; female
	Age	Under 10; teens; 20 ~ 34; 35 ~ 49; 50 ~ 64; over 65
	Education	Some high school or less; high school graduate; college graduate; postgraduate
	Race/Nationality	Chinese; American; African; American-Chinese
	Life stage	Infant; preschool; child; teenager; collegiate; adult; senior; single or married; with or without child
	Income	Under 3,000; 3,000 ~ 6,000; 6,000 ~ 10,000; 10,000 ~ 20,000; over 20,000
	Household size	1, 2, 3 ~ 4, 5 or more
	Occupation	Professional, technical, clerical, salespersons, farmers, students, business owners, managers, retired, unemployed
Psychographic	Personality	Gregarious or solitude; passive or active; extroverted or introverted; aggressive or gentle
	Values	Achievers; experiencers; believers; strivers; makers; strugglers
	Lifestyle	Upscale; moderate
Product-use	Benefit	Convenience; comfort; durability; economy; health; luxury; safety; status
	Usage volume	Heavy users; light users; nonusers
	Loyalty status	None; medium; strong

Note: benefit segmentation divides an already established market into smaller, more homogeneous segments.

Approaches to market segmentation
- No market segmentation → A product is targeted at average consumer
- High market segmentation → A different product is offered to each market segment
- Focused market segmentation → A product is offered to one or a few market segments

Marketing Stratiges

Niche marketing	Mass marketing
The process of finding small but profitable market segments and designing or finding products for them	Developing products and promotions to please large groups of people, with mass media like TV, for example
One-to-one marketing	Relationship marketing
Developing a unique mix of goods and services for each individual customer, e.g. travel packages; Dell computers	Marketing strategy with the goal of keeping individual customers over time by offering them products that exactly meet their requirements

Product differentiating is the process of setting a product apart from its competitors by designing and marketing it to better satisfy customers' needs.

↓ achieved through →

Marketing Mix

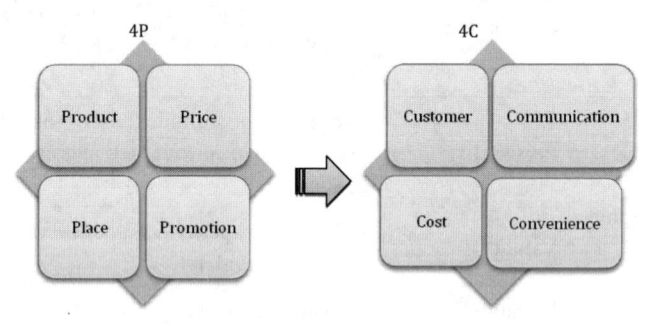

4P: Product, Price, Place, Promotion ⇨ 4C: Customer, Communication, Cost, Convenience

Note: 4C theory shows the tendency of shifting focus to customer relationship; however, the following chapter will adopt the classical 4P theory as the framework.

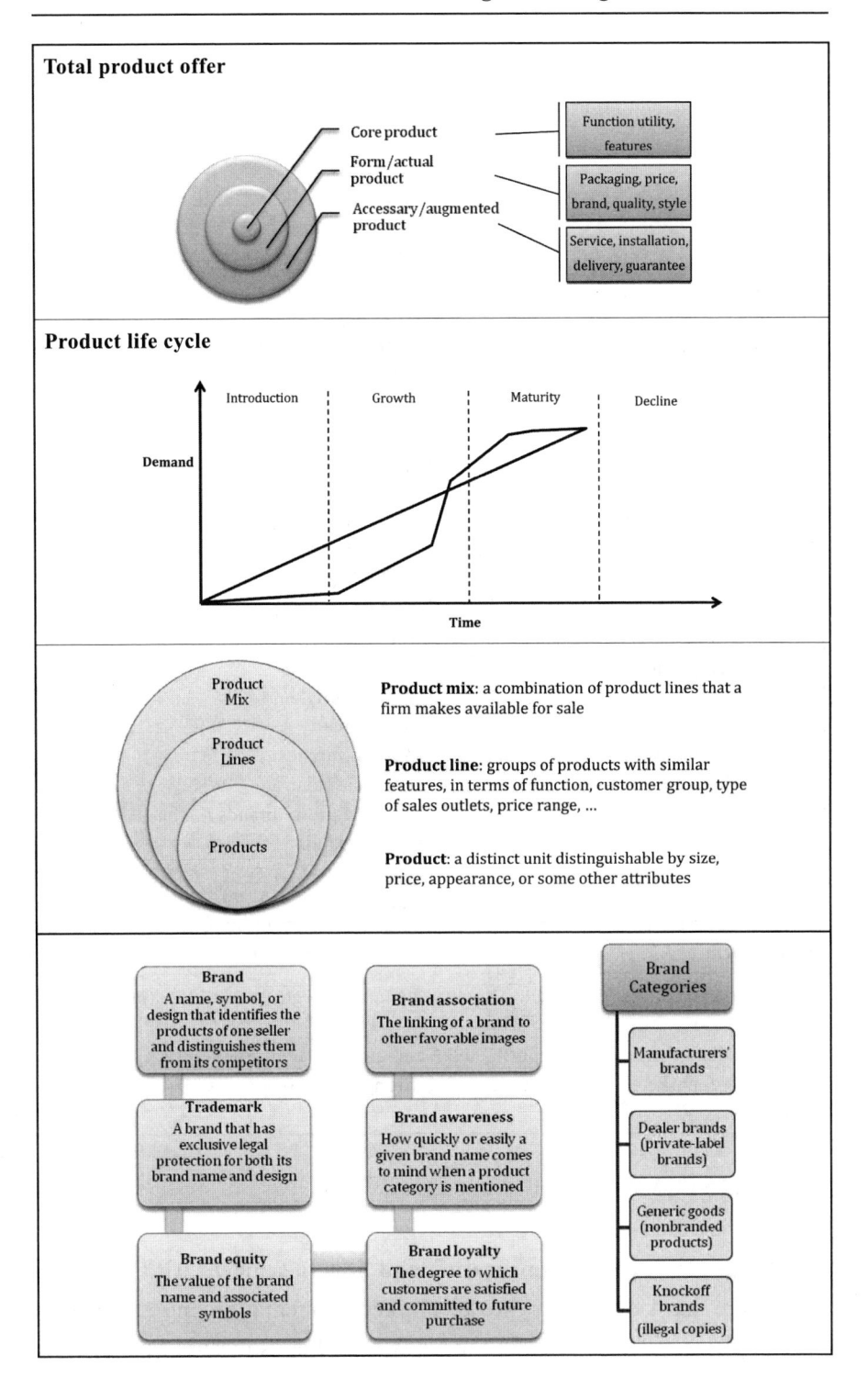

Part IV Understanding Marketing

Total product offer

- Core product → Function utility, features
- Form/actual product → Packaging, price, brand, quality, style
- Accessary/augmented product → Service, installation, delivery, guarantee

Product life cycle

Stages: Introduction | Growth | Maturity | Decline

Axes: Demand (vertical), Time (horizontal)

Product Mix / Product Lines / Products

Product mix: a combination of product lines that a firm makes available for sale

Product line: groups of products with similar features, in terms of function, customer group, type of sales outlets, price range, …

Product: a distinct unit distinguishable by size, price, appearance, or some other attributes

Brand

Brand: A name, symbol, or design that identifies the products of one seller and distinguishes them from its competitors

Trademark: A brand that has exclusive legal protection for both its brand name and design

Brand equity: The value of the brand name and associated symbols

Brand association: The linking of a brand to other favorable images

Brand awareness: How quickly or easily a given brand name comes to mind when a product category is mentioned

Brand loyalty: The degree to which customers are satisfied and committed to future purchase

Brand Categories

- Manufacturers' brands
- Dealer brands (private-label brands)
- Generic goods (nonbranded products)
- Knockoff brands (illegal copies)

Key Terms

Marketing research 市场调研	Core product 核心产品
Observation 观察法	Form/actual product 形式产品
Survey 调查法	Accessary/augmented product 外延产品
Focus group 焦点小组；小组座谈会	Product life cycle 产品生命周期
Experiment 实验法	Introduction 引入期
Primary data 一手数据	Growth 成长期
Secondary data 二手数据	Maturity 成熟期
Consumer market 消费者市场	Decline 衰退期
B2B market 企业对企业市场	Consumer goods/services 消费商品
Market segmentation 市场划分	Industrial goods/services 工业商品
Market segment 市场细分	Convenience goods/services 方便商品
Target market 目标市场	Shopping goods/services 选购商品
Geographic segmentation 地理划分	Specialty goods/services 特殊商品
Demographic segmentation 人口学划分	Unsought goods/services 意外商品
Psychographic segmentation 心理学划分	Capital items 资本项目
Product-use segmentation 产品使用划分	Expense items 费用项目
Benefit segmentation 用途划分	Product line 产品系列
Volume segmentation 使用量划分	Product mix 产品组合
No market segmentation 无市场划分	Brand 品牌
High market segmentation 高市场划分	Trademark 商标
Focused-market segmentation 焦点市场划分	Brand equity 品牌价值；品牌权益
Niche marketing 利基营销	Brand loyalty 品牌忠实度
One-to-one marketing 一对一营销	Brand awareness 品牌意识
Mass marketing 大众营销	Brand association 品牌联想
Relationship marketing 关系营销	Manufacturers' brands 生产商品牌
Product differentiation 产品差异化	Dealer brands 经销商品牌
Marketing mix 营销组合	Generic goods 杂牌货；无品牌产品
Total product offer 完整产品内容	Knockoff brands 山寨品牌；冒牌货

Brainstorming

Choose a representative product to analyze its market segments and total product offer.

Pick a basket of products, categorize them and analyze their product life cycle.

Do Chinese marketers and consumers have strong brand awareness? Discuss with examples.

Read More

4 types of Market segmentation and how to segment with them

There are 4 different types of market segmentation and all of them vary in their implementation in the real world. Let us discuss each of them in detail.

Types of Market Segmentation
1. Demographic segmentation

Demographic segmentation is one of the simplest and widest type of market segmentation used. Most companies use it to get the right population in using their products. Segmentation generally divides a population based on variables. Thus demographic segmentation too has its own variables such as age, gender, family size, income, occupation, religion, race and nationality.

Demographic segmentation can be seen applied in the automobile market. The automobile market has different price brackets in which automobiles are manufactured. For example, Maruti has the low price bracket and therefore manufactures human-powered cars. Audi and BMW have the high price bracket so it targets high end buyers. Thus in this case, the segmentation is being done on the basis of earnings which is a part of demography. Similarly, age, life cycle stages, gender, income etc can be used for demographic segmentation.

2. Behavioral segmentation

This type of market segmentation divides the population on the basis of their behavior, usage and decision making pattern. For example, young people will always prefer Dove as a soap, whereas sports enthusiast will use Lifebuoy. This is an example of behavior based segmentation. Based on the behavior of an individual, the product is marketed.

This type of market segmentation is in boom especially in the smart phone market. For example, Blackberry was launched for users who were business people, Samsung was launched for users who like android and like various applications for a free price, and Apple was launched for the premium customers who want to be a part of a unique and popular niche.

Another example of behavioral segmentation is marketing during festivals. Say on Christmas, the buying patterns will be completely different as compared to buying patterns on normal days. Thus, the usage segmentation is also a type of behavioral segmentation. To read more in depth about behavioral segmentation, do read this article.

3. Psychographic segmentation

Psychographic segmentation is one which uses lifestyle of people, their activities, interests as well as opinions to define a market segment. Psychographic segmentation is quite similar to behavioral segmentation. But psychographic segmentation also takes the psychological aspects of consumer buying behavior into accounts. These psychological aspects may be consumers lifestyle, his social standing as well as his AIO (activities, interests and opinions).

Application of psychographic segmentation can be seen all across nowadays. For example, Zara markets itself on the basis of lifestyle, where customers who want the latest and differential clothing can visit the Zara stores. Similarly Arrow markets itself to the premium office lifestyle where probably your bosses and super bosses shop for the sharp clothing. Thus, this type of segmentation is mainly based on lifestyle or AIO.

4. Geographic segmentation

This type of market segmentation divides people on the basis of geography. Your potential customers will have different needs based on the geography they are located in. In the article on geographic segmentation, I have explained how people who are located in non municipal areas might require a RO water purifier whereas those located in municipal areas might need UV based purifiers. Thus, the need can vary on the basis of geography.

Similarly in cold countries, the same company might be marketing for heaters whereas in hot countries, the same company might be targeting air conditioners. Thus, many companies use geographic segmentation as a basis for market segmentation.

This type of segmentation is the easiest but it was actually used in the last decade where the industries were new and the reach was less. Today, the reach is high but still geographic segmentation principles are used when you are expanding the business in more local areas as well as international territories.

Thus, the above are the 4 main types of market segmentation. Usage based market segmentation, benefit segmentation, price based market segmentation, all these different types of segmentation are a derivative of the above 4 types only.

So what type of market segmentation can you use for business and how would you like to implement segmentation?

(723)

https://www.marketing91.com/4-types-market-segmentation-segment/

Niche Marketing

Creating a good niche involves following this seven-step process:

1. Make a wish list

With whom do you want to do business? Be as specific as you can: Identify the geographical range and the types of businesses or customers you want your business to target. If you don't know whom you want to do business with, you can't make contact.

These days, the trend is toward smaller niches. Targeting teenagers isn't specific enough; targeting male, African-American teenagers with family incomes of $40,000 and up is. Aiming at companies that sell software is too broad; aiming at Northern California-based companies that provide internet software sales and training and have sales of $15 million or more is a better goal.

2. Focus

Clarify what you want to sell, remembering this: a) You can't be all things to all people and b) "smaller is bigger". Your niche is not the same as the field in which you work. For example, a retail clothing business is not a niche but a field. A more specific niche may be "maternity clothes for executive women".

To begin this focusing process, use these techniques to help you:

Make a list of things you do best and the skills implicit in each of them.

List your achievements.

Identify the most important lessons you have learned in life.

Look for patterns that reveal your style or approach to resolving problems.

Your niche should arise naturally from your interests and experience. For example, if you spent 10 years working in a consulting firm, but also spent 10 years working for a small, family-owned business, you may decide to start a consulting business that specializes in small, family-owned companies.

3. Describe the customer's worldview

When you look at the world from your prospective customers' perspective, you can identify their needs or wants. The best way to do this is to talk to prospective customers and identify their main concerns.

4. Synthesize

At this stage, your niche should begin to take shape as your ideas and the client's needs and wants coalesce to create something new. A good niche has five qualities:

It takes you where you want to go—in other words, it conforms to your long-term vision.

Somebody else wants it—namely, customers.

It's carefully planned.

It's one-of-a-kind, the "only game in town."

It evolves, allowing you to develop different profit centers and still retain the core business, thus ensuring long-term success.

5. Evaluate

Now it's time to evaluate your proposed product or service against the five criteria in Step 4. Perhaps you'll find that the niche you had in mind requires more business travel than you're ready for. That means it doesn't fulfill one of the above criteria—it won't take you where you want to go. So scrap it, and move on to the next idea.

6. Test

Once you have a match between niche and product, test-market it. This can be done by offering samples, such as a free mini-seminar or a sample copy of your newsletter.

7. Go for it

It's time to implement your idea. For many entrepreneurs, this is the most difficult stage. But fear not: If you did your homework, entering the market will be a calculated risk, not just a gamble.

Once your niche is established and well received by your market, you may be tempted to rest on your laurels. Not a good idea. Ask yourself the following questions when you think you have found your niche, and ask them again every six months or so to make sure your niche is still on target:

Who are your target clients?

Who aren't your target clients?

Do you refuse certain kinds of business if it falls outside your niche?

What do clients think you stand for?

Is your niche in a constant state of evolution?

Does your niche offer what prospective customers want?

Do you have a plan and delivery system that effectively conveys the need for your niche to the right market?

Can you confidently predict the life cycle of your niche?

How can your niche be expanded into a variety of products or services that act as profit centers?

Do you have a sense of passion and focused energy with respect to your niche?

Does your niche feel comfortable and natural?

How will pursuing your niche contribute to achieving the goals you have set for your business?

(729)

https://www.entrepreneur.com/encyclopedia/niche-marketing

Apple's Product Strategy
Quality Product with Premium Offerings

The entrance of other players in the consumer electronics market meant that Apple is getting stiffer competition, especially since these competitors are churning out smartphones and tablets that are significantly lower in price. Apple CEO Tim Cook, however, is unfazed by this non-threat, calling these lower-cost counterparts as the "junk market". According to Cook, Apple is not catering to this junk market, which is why it opts to stick to offering more expensive products that have a lot more, and better, things to offer, than what these "junk markets" are currently fielding to buying customers.

There is no denying, however, that the best product strategy that Apple employs is coming up with very good products. They call it the "great product" strategy. By continuing to hold on to high standards of quality, Apple refuses to get on the bandwagon that most other device makers are using, where they pack their products chock-full of features that, while they may be impressively advanced, actually end up making operating the device actually more complicated and not at all user-friendly.

Packaging is certainly not an area where Apple is lacking. It is known for being a company that provides clean and simple, yet functional packaging to its products. More than being flashy, it tends to boast more of a utilitarian aesthetic, but without coming across as boring or plain.

The "great product" strategy also focuses on quality over quantity. While other manufacturers' strategy entail churning out products one after another in a short span of time and having such a diversified product mix, Apple preferred to stick to what it does best. This means that it focuses on selected products and continues enhancing them, instead of branching out to create other products within the same category.

If you look at the numbers, it is true that other companies, such as Samsung, are showing higher figures when it comes to unit sales. They are starting to occupy a larger share of the market. But this does not worry Apple. Instead, it continues to focus on its loyal customers and, despite occupying a smaller percentage of the market, is able to position itself as a premium brand and a maker and provider of top quality products.

As such, Samsung was able to eat up a huge chunk of the market because of its production of cheap and low-end gadgets. That market is not really what Apple is aiming for, and it is comfortable with the market it has right now.

New Updates, Not Necessarily New Products

Market trends are constantly changing, and demands are certainly increasing. Other companies' response to these changes may be "give them new products". What Apple does is to "improve the products that it has". This explains the product refreshes and updates that are released on a schedule set by Apple. Thus, the tweaked or updated versions retain the best parts of the old versions, with the "problematic" features corrected or improved. Clearly, this means that the latest iPhone, the iPhone 6 Plus, is a much improved version of the first generation iPhone, or even the previously released iPhone 6.

These changes put the Apple product development team in a good light, particularly in the eyes of Apple users, since it implies a commitment on their part of seeking continuous improvement for their product offerings. It also effectively attracts new users, thereby increasing the market share of Apple.

Control of Both Software and Hardware

Aside from producing the hardware—the smartphones and the tablets—Apple maintains total control of its platform, which is not something that can be completely said of Apple's main rival platform, Android, which can be modified and tweaked by device manufacturers. Having total control means that Apple users are guaranteed to have the latest version of the operating system, with updates readily and immediately made available to Apple users.

Giving Meticulous Attention to Detail

The strategy employed by Apple in its product development largely depends on what the product is. If we look into the key points in the strategy used by Apple for its flagship product, the iPhone, we will find that there are four major factors involved: the competitors, a SWOT analysis of your competitors' product, the target market, and market survey pertaining to the product.

1. Competitors

Compared to when Apple was founded and started its operations, there are now a lot more consumer electronics companies and mobile phone manufacturers that are attempting to compete with Apple. However, out of this sea of competitors, there are only a few companies that are considered to be major threats or those that provide serious competition. These companies include Samsung, Google, Blackberry, Nokia, HTC, and Sony, to name a few. Granted, some of these companies do not really pose a serious threat to Apple, not like Samsung and Google.

Case in point: Google is seen as the biggest competitor of Apple when it comes to operating systems and software development. Google has singlehandedly brought about the boom of the Android market, and its app store, Google Play, is currently competing with Apple's App Store for the top spot.

2. Product SWOT

Other companies focus on conducting SWOT (Strengths, Weaknesses, Opportunities, Threats) analysis of their products. Apple does, too, but it does not stop there. It also conducts SWOT analysis of the products of its competitors.

Why is that?

Doing a product SWOT on your own products will not really give you the whole picture. It only gives you one angle: yours. By checking out the competitor's product, you will know exactly what you are up against. What makes their product better? What makes yours the best? What are the possible opportunities and threats that the competitor's products are faced with, and how can you take advantage of that?

This practice has certainly paid off for Apple, particularly when it was starting to release new products into the market. They were able to come out with products that are unique and innovative. For example, in the past, phones were bulky and on the heavy side. This was seen by Apple as a weakness, so it zeroed in on that and developed sleeker, thinner, and lighter mobile phone units.

3. Target Market

Usually, a business would study the market and identify the segments that it will specifically target, and that will figure greatly in its overall product development and strategy. However, Apple does things differently.

Apple is primarily product-driven in its approach, in that it develops the product first, and then seeking out the market for it. This worked thanks, in large part, to the high quality and unique products that Apple has churned out. It did not take long for Apple to become established as a global market. That meant market segmentation is no longer a priority, because Apple's target market is now the global market.

Apple markets its products to cater to anyone and everyone who is looking for great value and high quality all over the world. You will find Apple stores and outlets in major areas of the world, a sure sign that Apple is targeting customers globally.

4. Product Related Market Survey

As mentioned earlier, Apple adapts a product-driven attitude. When it creates products, it automatically assumes that there is a market for it; it's just that the customers are still unaware that they need the product Apple is developing. It will now be up to Apple, once the product has finished development, to make the market realize that it wants and needs the product that it has to offer. After all, according to Steve Jobs, the customer does not know what he wants.

The updates and upgraded versions of products that Apple has been doing in recent years is the result of market surveys that it conducted, asking customers what products they liked, or what specific features they thought were excellent or outstanding.

Using the Music Business

The computing branch of Apple makes heavy use of the music industry to boost its presence and, consequently, its sales. This has been described as the Halo Effect of the Apple brand, and a good example would be with regards to iTunes.

It all started with the iPod, which started out as a simple music player. When the iPod hit the ground running, along with iTunes, Apple made sure to capitalize on the tandem's popularity to lure other customers to make use of other Apple computing products. The features that users loved using on iPod and iTunes were craftily integrated in other Apple products, so that others who liked them would not hesitate to try other Apple products with similar offerings. The result is a customer experience that has become common across different Apple products.

Use of Product Experience in Branding

We cannot discuss Apple's product strategy without focusing on its branding. "Apple" has become such a household name globally, and this is attributed to the company's branding strategy, which was primarily focused on human's emotions.

Anything that strikes a chord in one's consciousness tends to make a lasting impression, and that's what Apple capitalized on when it put its brand out there. Customers these days are smarter, looking at the overall experience a product gives them, instead of isolated moments and fleeting flashes. Apple made its brand synonymous with technology playing a major role in one's lifestyle, innovation, passion, imagination, and human nature's innate desire to have power or even a small measure of control. Their products offer that sense of control, by integrating concepts of simplicity and convenience.

Apple has successfully established a relationship with its customers that can best be described as "intimate". Take note of the long queues or lines of prospective Apple product buyers that reach all the way down across the street, or the long lists of preorders, whenever a new Apple product is due for release. It takes a lot of dedications and commitments to be one of those people lining up, which is pretty much like being in an intimate relationship.

In the same way, the Apple brand also puts emphasis on customer experience by enhancing that sense of community among Apple users. Apple users are inclined to be drawn towards other Apple users, because they somehow get a sense of kinship just by becoming users of the same product, or of different products but belonging within the same product line of the Apple brand.

Apple was smart enough to play on the strong brand preference that customers tend to develop when they have tried and tested a specific product. Users will not mind developing an attachment or loyalty to a brand or a product as long as it provides what they are looking for, and by ensuring that this is the case, Apple is able to keep its customers, and keep them coming back.

This halo strategy is also seen in how Apple targets its markets. Apple started its computing segment, focusing largely on corporate markets. It used to have a strong presence in business environments. It wasn't until the 1990s that it withdrew from corporate settings and focused on the individual instead. But that did not last long, as Apple started to go back to the corporate market and prove to be useful to business users. Apple is banking on the popularity of the iPhone, as well as the iPad, to become business tools. Today, what used to be a personal tablet can now be used in an office or workplace setting.

Getting Close to the Apple User

Apple is confident about having a very good—extraordinary, even—product that it can only introduce once. Therefore, it is important to make the introduction have such an impact. Apple is quite good at that, increasing customer anticipation before the release of a product. But what about when the product has already been launched and introduced?

This is where Apple's product strategy becomes more personal, in that it surrounds the product with excellent service and support—before, during and after sale—as well as applications software. Part of the product strategy of Apple is to ensure that the customer experience is always highly positive. Its efforts to improve the Apple customer experience is apparent in how its distribution channels are continuously expanding. Currently, the major and key cities all over the world are not without an Apple retail store. It has even struck up partnerships with leading telecommunication companies in different countries all over the world, so that the latter would become retail outlets of Apple products. Resellers are also tapped into, both online and brick-and-mortar stores.

(2098)

https://www.cleverism.com/apple-product-strategy/

Chapter 8 Pricing, Distributing and Promoting

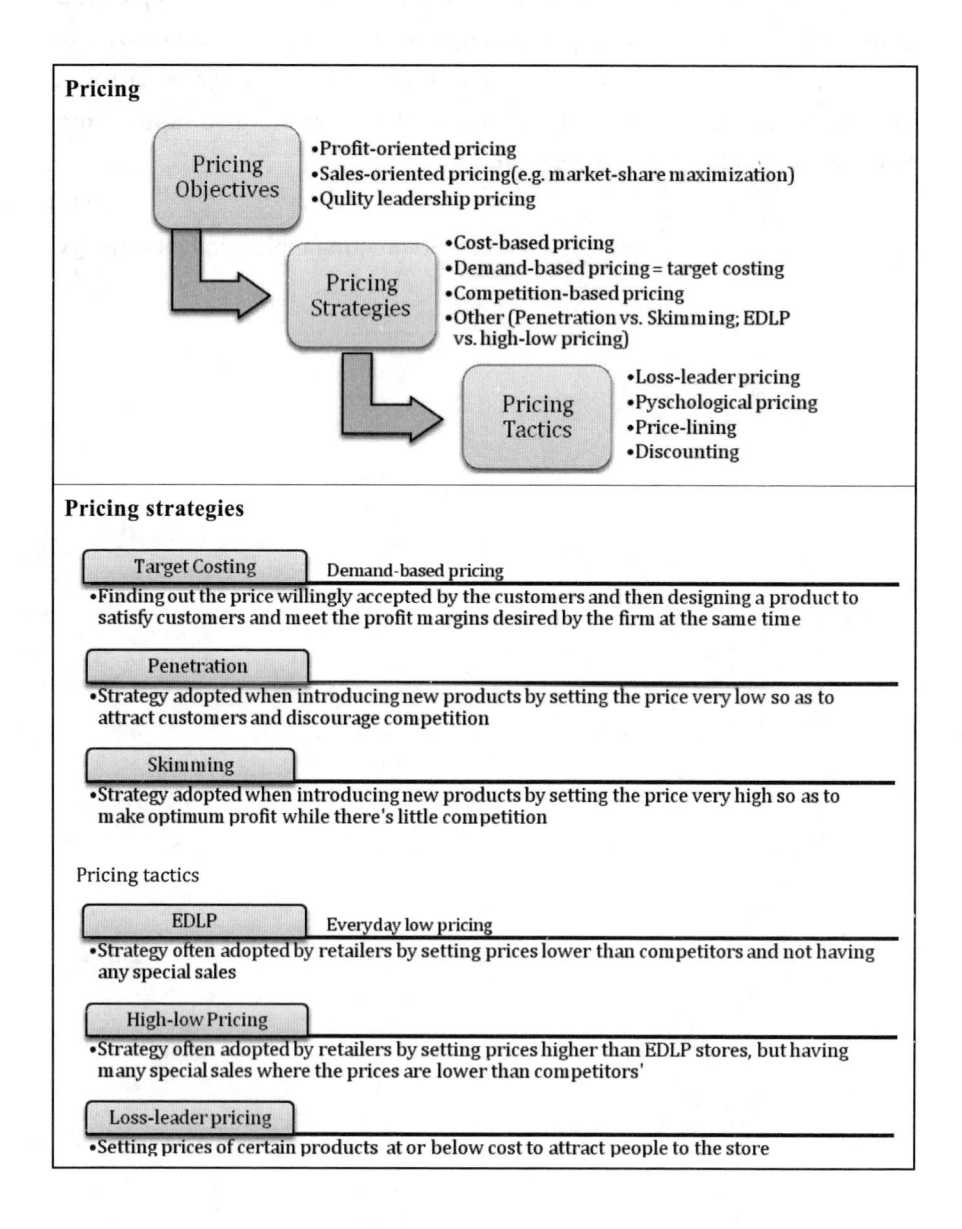

Pricing

Pricing Objectives
- Profit-oriented pricing
- Sales-oriented pricing (e.g. market-share maximization)
- Qulity leadership pricing

Pricing Strategies
- Cost-based pricing
- Demand-based pricing = target costing
- Competition-based pricing
- Other (Penetration vs. Skimming; EDLP vs. high-low pricing)

Pricing Tactics
- Loss-leader pricing
- Pyschological pricing
- Price-lining
- Discounting

Pricing strategies

Target Costing — Demand-based pricing
- Finding out the price willingly accepted by the customers and then designing a product to satisfy customers and meet the profit margins desired by the firm at the same time

Penetration
- Strategy adopted when introducing new products by setting the price very low so as to attract customers and discourage competition

Skimming
- Strategy adopted when introducing new products by setting the price very high so as to make optimum profit while there's little competition

Pricing tactics

EDLP — Everyday low pricing
- Strategy often adopted by retailers by setting prices lower than competitors and not having any special sales

High-low Pricing
- Strategy often adopted by retailers by setting prices higher than EDLP stores, but having many special sales where the prices are lower than competitors'

Loss-leader pricing
- Setting prices of certain products at or below cost to attract people to the store

Part IV Understanding Marketing

Pricing tactics

Psychological pricing | Odd pricing
- Setting the price at the point that seems less expensive than it is, e.g. 0.99, 99, 298; or using lucky numbers in prices, such as 6, 8, 9 in China or odd numbers in the US

Price lining
- Setting a group of products at the same price so as to simplify the choice of customers

Discounting
- Setting prices higher than the desired level and giving discounts for certain reasons, like seasonal discount, promotional dicount

Price Setting Tool

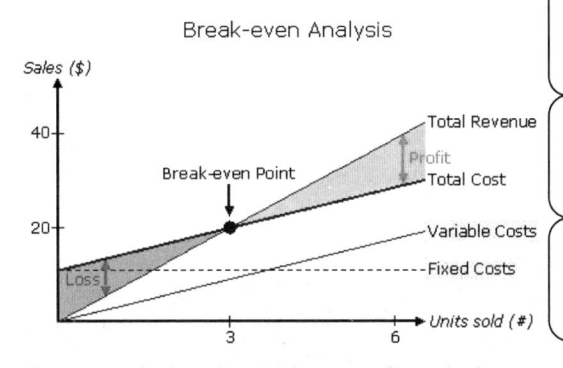

Break-even analysis
The process used to determine profitability at various levels of sales

Variable costs
Costs that change with the quantity of sales or production

Fixed costs
Costs unaffected by the quantity of sales or production

Break-even analysis = Cost-Volume-profit analysis
Breakeven point = zero profitability
Total revenue = total fixed costs + total variable costs
Unit price × units sold = total fixed costs + unit variable cost × units sold
→ Break-even point : units sold = total fixed costs/ (unit price −unit variable cost)

Price War and Nonprice Competition

If all companies focus competition on price, the price war would break out, a situation in which several companies reduce the prices of what they sell, because they are all trying to get the most customers.

Therefore, marketers often compete on product attributes other than price, including but not limited to:
- adding value to products
- providing quality service
- establishing good relationship with customers
- stressing brand image or consumer benefits

Channels of distribution

Channel	Producer	Agent or Broker	Wholesaler	Retailer	End Users (consumers and industrial buyers)
Channel 1 – Direct Distribution	✓				✓
Channel 2 – Retail Distribution	✓			✓	✓
Channel 3 – Wholesale Distribution	✓		✓	✓	✓
Channel 4 – Distribution by Agents or Brokers	✓	✓	✓	✓	✓

Agents and brokers

Commonalities
- Take no title to goods
- Make profits by earning commissions based on sales

Differences
- Agents work on permanent basis
- Brokers work on deal-by-deal basis

Wholesalers and retailers

Commonalities
- Take title to goods for resale
- Make profits by adding markups to products

Differences
- Wholesalers sell to ogranizations for use in the business, or to wholesalers or retailers for resale; they make B2B sales.
- Retailers sell to consumers for their own use; they make B2C sales.

Values and cost of intermediaries

Intermediaries add lots of cost to products, but they provide lots of activities that cannot be eliminated, adding great value in marketing.

Utilities: Time Utility, Possession Utility, Place Utility, Information Utility, Form Utility.

Utility: adding value to products, by making them available when they are needed, where people want them, by providing services before, during or after the sales, by giving sufficient communication and information, or by facilitating the transfer of ownership, like extending credit.

Promotion Mix
| Advertising | Personal selling |
| Public relations | Sales promotion |

Part IV Understanding Marketing

Advertising is paid, non-personal communication through various media by organizations and individuals who are in some way identified in the advertising message.

- Advertising purposes
  - Informating
  - Persuading
  - Reminding
- Advertising principle
  - Meaningful
  - Distinctive
  - Believable

New media: New media is a broad term in media studies that emerged in the later part of the 20th century. For example, new media holds out a possibility of on-demand access to content anytime, anywhere, on any digital device, as well as interactive user feedback, creative participation and community formation around the media content. Another important promise of New Media is the "democratization" of the creation, publishing, distribution and consumption of media content. What distinguishes new media from traditional media is the digitizing of content into bits.

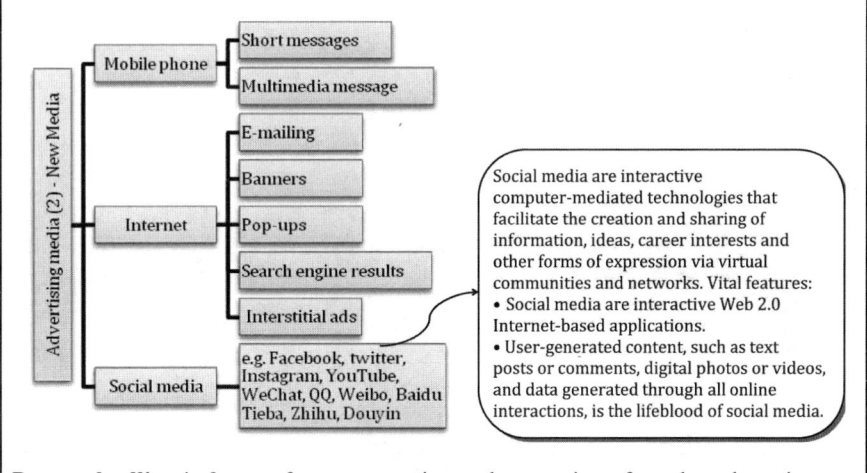

Advertising media (2) - New Media
- Mobile phone
  - Short messages
  - Multimedia message
- Internet
  - E-mailing
  - Banners
  - Pop-ups
  - Search engine results
  - Interstitial ads
- Social media
  - e.g. Facebook, twitter, Instagram, YouTube, WeChat, QQ, Weibo, Baidu Tieba, Zhihu, Douyin

Social media are interactive computer-mediated technologies that facilitate the creation and sharing of information, ideas, career interests and other forms of expression via virtual communities and networks. Vital features:
- Social media are interactive Web 2.0 Internet-based applications.
- User-generated content, such as text posts or comments, digital photos or videos, and data generated through all online interactions, is the lifeblood of social media.

Personal selling is face-to-face presentation and promotion of goods and services.

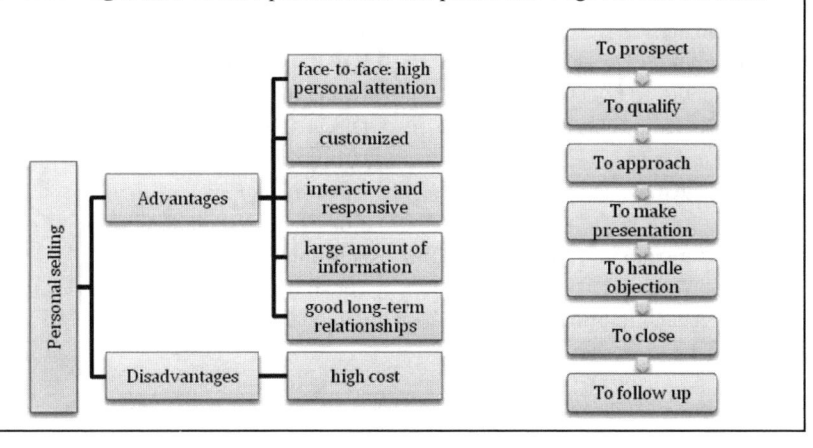

Personal selling
- Advantages
  - face-to-face: high personal attention
  - customized
  - interactive and responsive
  - large amount of information
  - good long-term relationships
- Disadvantages
  - high cost

- To prospect
- To qualify
- To approach
- To make presentation
- To handle objection
- To close
- To follow up

Public Relations (PR) is the planned and sustained effort to establish and maintain goodwill and mutual understanding between an organization and its publics.
Publicity is an important tool of public relations. It is a news report about an organization or its products and it's not paid for or controlled by the seller.

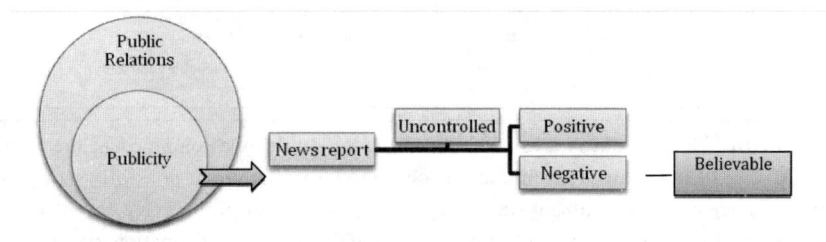

Sales promotion: giving buyers incentives by means of short-term promotional activities.

Sales promotion tools:
- Point-of-sale display/Demonstration
- Specialty advertising
- Trade shows
- Sponsorship/Special Events
- Contests
- Sweepstakes/lotteries
- Coupons/Trade stamps
- Bonuses/Premiums/Gifts
- Sampling
- Catalogs
- Deals/Price discounts

Other

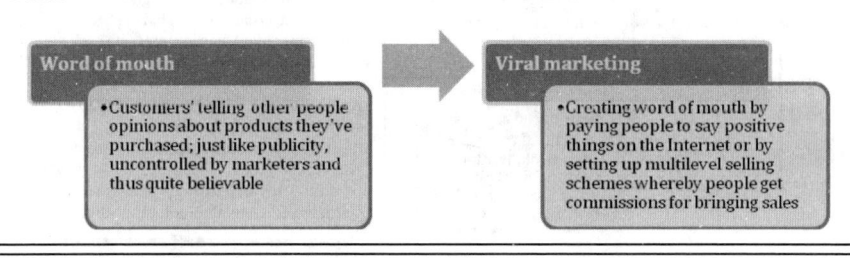

Word of mouth
- Customers' telling other people opinions about products they've purchased; just like publicity, uncontrolled by marketers and thus quite believable

Viral marketing
- Creating word of mouth by paying people to say positive things on the Internet or by setting up multilevel selling schemes whereby people get commissions for bringing sales

Key Terms	
Pricing objectives 定价目标	Wholesalers 批发商
Pricing strategies 定价策略	Retailers 零售商
Pricing tactics 定价技巧	Direct marketing 直接营销
Profit-oriented pricing 利润导向的定价策略	Direct selling 直接销售；直销
Sales-oriented pricing 销售量导向的定价策略	Utility 便利；效用
	Advertising 广告
Market-share maximization 市场份额最大化	Advertising media 广告媒体
	New media 新媒体
	Social media 社交媒体
Quality leadership pricing 质量领先定价	Personal selling 人员推销

Cost-based pricing 基本成本定价策略 Demand-based pricing 基于需求定价策略 Target costing 目标成本法 Competition-based pricing 基于竞争定价策略 Penetration 渗透策略 Skimming 撇脂策略 EDLP 天天低价策略 High-low pricing 高低价策略 Loss-leader pricing 低价引诱定价法 Psychological pricing 心理定价法 Odd pricing 奇数定价法 Price-lining 统一定价法 Discounting 打折法 Break-even analysis 盈亏平衡点分析 Variable costs 可变成本 Fixed costs 固定成本 Price war 价格战 Non-price competition 非价格竞争 Channels of distribution 分销渠道 Agents and brokers 经纪；代理	Public relations 公共关系 Publicity 媒体推介 Sales promotion 销售促进 Point-of-sale display/ Demonstration 销售点的摆设、展示/演示 Specialty advertising 专业广告 Trade show 展销会 Sponsorship 赞助 Contests 销售竞赛 Sweepstakes/lotteries 抽奖 Coupons/Trade stamps 优惠券；折扣券 Bonuses/Premiums/Gifts 礼品；奖品；赠品 Sampling 免费试用 Catalogs 宣传册；产品目录 Deals/Price discounts 特价；折价销售 Word of mouth 口碑 Viral marketing 病毒式营销

Brainstorming

What are the trends and characteristics of social media in China?
Discuss new methods of promotion in the new media era.

在中国

直销

　　中国的直销经营及立法经历了多次变革。从1990年雅芳公司进入中国，直销这种经营模式正式进入中国内地市场，随后非法传销活动猖獗，国家严厉查处多层次传销活动并一度全面禁止多层次传销，并规定外商直销经营必须与实体店铺经营相结合。2001年我国加入WTO，承诺在3年内逐步取消对直销经营的限制，随后出台了多部法规管理并规范直销经营，在中国从事直销经营须经过严格审核并获取牌照。目前，中国政府一方面严厉打击非法传销，另一方面完善对直销的立法和监管并积极推动对公众的直销知识普及。

Read More

In pricing, managers decide what the company will get in exchange for products. Pricing objectives refer to the goals that producers hope to attain as a result of pricing decisions. These objectives can be divided into two major categories. (1) pricing to maximize profits: if prices are too low, the company will probably sell many product units but miss the chance to make additional profits on each one. If prices are set too high, it will make a large profit on each unit but will sell fewer units. (2) market share objectives: many companies are willing to accept minimal profits, even losses, to get buyers to try products. They may use pricing to establish market share—a company's percentage of the total market sales for specific product type.

Managers must measure the potential impact before deciding on final prices. For this purpose, they use two basic tools (which are often combined): (1) cost oriented pricing: managers price products by calculating the cost of making them available to shoppers; when they total these costs and add a figure for profit, they arrive at a markup. (2) breakeven analysis: breakeven analysis assesses total costs vs. revenues for various sales volumes. It shows, any particular sale price, the financial results—the amount of profit or loss—for each possible sales volume. The number of units that must be sold for total revenue to equal total cost is the breakeven point.

The distribution mix

The success of any product depends on its distribution mix: the combination of distribution channels of the firm uses to get products to end-users. Intermediaries help to distribute a producer's goods: wholesalers sell products to other businesses, which resell them the final consumers. Retailers sell products directly to consumers.

Among the eight distribution channels, the first four are aimed at getting products to consumers, the fifth is for consumers or business customers, and the last three are aimed at getting products to business customers.

Channel 1 involves direct sales to consumers
Channel 2 includes a retailer
Channel 3 involves both a retailer and a wholesaler
Channel 4 includes an agent or broker
Channel 5 includes only an aged man between the producer and consumer
Channel 6 which is used extensively for e-commerce, involves a direct sale to an industrial user
Channel 7 entails selling to business users through wholesalers
Channel 8 includes retail superstores they get products from producers or wholesalers (or both) for reselling to business customers

Retailing

U.S. retail operations fall under two classifications.

Product line retailers featuring broad product lines include department stores in supermarkets. Small specialty stores are clearly defined market segments by offering full product lines in their rope product fields.

Nonstore retailing includes direct response retailing, in which firms make direct contact with customers to inform them about products and take sales orders. Mail order (or catalog marketing) is a form of direct response retailing, as is telemarketing. Electronic retailing uses communications networks that allow sellers to connect to consumers' computers. Internet retail shopping includes electronic storefronts where customers can examine the stores products, place orders, and make payments electronically. Customers can also visit cyber malls—a collection of virtual storefronts representing a variety of product lines on the Internet.

Physical Distribution

Physical distribution refers to all the activities needed to move products from producers to consumers, so that products are available when and where customers want them at reasonable cost. Physical distribution activities include providing customer services, warehousing, and transportation of products. Warehouses provide storage for products and may be either public or private. Transportation operations physically move products from suppliers to customers. Trains, railroads, planes, water carriers (boats and barges), and pipelines are major transportation modes used in the distribution process.

Promotions

Although the ultimate goal of promotion is to increase sales, other roles include communicating information, positioning a product, adding value, and controlling sales volume. In deciding on the appropriate promotional mix—the best combination of promotional tools (for example, advertising, personal selling, public relations)—marketers must consider the good or service being offered, characteristics of the target audience and the buyer's decision process, and of course the promotional mix budget.

Advertising media includes television, newspapers, direct mail, radio, magazines, outdoor advertising, and the Internet, as well as other channels such as Yellow Pages, movies, special events, and door-to-door selling. The combination of media that a company chooses is called its media mix.

Personal Selling

Personal selling tasks include order processing, creative selling (activities that helped persuade buyers), and missionary selling (activity that promoted firms and products). Point-of-purchase (POP) displays are intended to grab attention and help customers find products in stores. Purchasing incentives include samples (which let customers try products without having to buy them) and premiums (rewards for buying products). At trade shows, sellers rent booths to display products to customers who have an interest in buying. Contests are intended to increase sales by stimulating buyers interest in a product.

(853)

http://destinydawnmarie.blogspot.com/2005/08/pricing-distributing-and-promoting.html

Google's Marketing Mix (4Ps)

UPDATED ONUPDATED ON JANUARY 28, 2017 BY ROBERTA GREENSPAN

Google's marketing mix is a major contributor to the global success of the business. Founded in 1998, the company's business has expanded to include Google Search, as well as a host of other products, such as Google Fiber and Google Glass. With this level of success, the firm's marketing mix is an example of how carefully designed strategies can support the growth of an originally purely online business. Google's marketing mix

Part IV Understanding Marketing

has different approaches because of the company's diversification. The company has already expanded from being a purely web-based business and now provides goods like Nexus smartphones and Chromecast media players.

Google's marketing mix is an effective combination of a wide array of product lines, a suitable pricing strategy and ubiquitous product distribution, along with cost-effective promotions.

Google's Products

Google's marketing mix involves a diverse array of products. The company has grown and diversified. These products are generally grouped into the following product lines:

- Web-based products
- Operating systems
- Desktop apps
- Mobile apps
- Hardware products
- Services

The diversity of Google's products is a reflection of the firm's strategy of growth and expansion. The company uses product development as a major intensive growth strategy. Because of this strategy, the firm keeps developing new products to expand its business, while growing its market share for existing products like Google AdWords, Nexus, and others.

Place/Distribution in Google's Marketing Mix

The place or distribution component of Google's marketing mix is typical of mostly-online businesses. Mostly-online firms use the Internet to distribute their products. Most of the company's products are available around the world via the Internet. For example, Google apps can be downloaded anywhere where there is Internet connectivity. Thus, the company uses the Internet as its distribution mechanism to reach target users/customers. For goods like Nexus smartphones, Google uses retailers as the main outlets. Large retailers usually include Nexus models as part of their consumer electronics offerings.

Google's place/distribution strategy contributes to the success of the company's marketing mix. The ubiquity of the Internet maximizes the firm's efficiency of distributing its digital products. The choice of major retailers as outlets for goods like Nexus also increases Google's ability to reach large populations of target consumers.

Google's Promotions (Promotional Mix)

Google's marketing mix involves only minimal promotion. The company's global popularity and market dominance means that it does not need to engage in extensive promotion campaigns. Still, Google occasionally promotes it products. For example, online advertisements for Gmail for Work are sometimes used.

The minimal promotion in Google's marketing mix has beneficial effects on the business. The company spends little for promotion. As a result, more funds are available for other areas of the business. Google can have more funds for research and development or product development.

Google's Prices and Pricing Strategies

Google's marketing mix involves different pricing strategies. Different pricing strategies satisfy the different kinds of products available from the company. The most notable pricing strategies in Google's business are:

- Freemium pricing
- Market-oriented pricing
- Penetration pricing
- Value-based pricing

The freemium pricing strategy involves offering free products, but selling premium or add-on features of the product. In Google's marketing mix, this pricing strategy is used for products like Gmail, which has a premium version for businesses. The market-oriented pricing strategy determines prices based on market conditions. Google's marketing mix uses this strategy for pricing its products like Chromecast. On the other hand, the penetration pricing strategy involves low prices that allow the company to gain market share despite the presence of large competitors. In Google's marketing mix, penetration pricing is used for the Google Fiber Internet and cable television service, which directly competes against Comcast. The value-based pricing strategy determines prices based on customers' perceived value of the product. In Google's marketing mix, the value-based pricing strategy is used for its AdWords online advertising service, where advertisers could place bids based on their perceptions of the importance of these advertisements.

(654)

Chapter 9 International E-commerce and Logistics

E-commerce is the use of the Internet, the Web, and apps to transact business. More formally, digitally enabled commercial transactions between and among organizations and individuals.

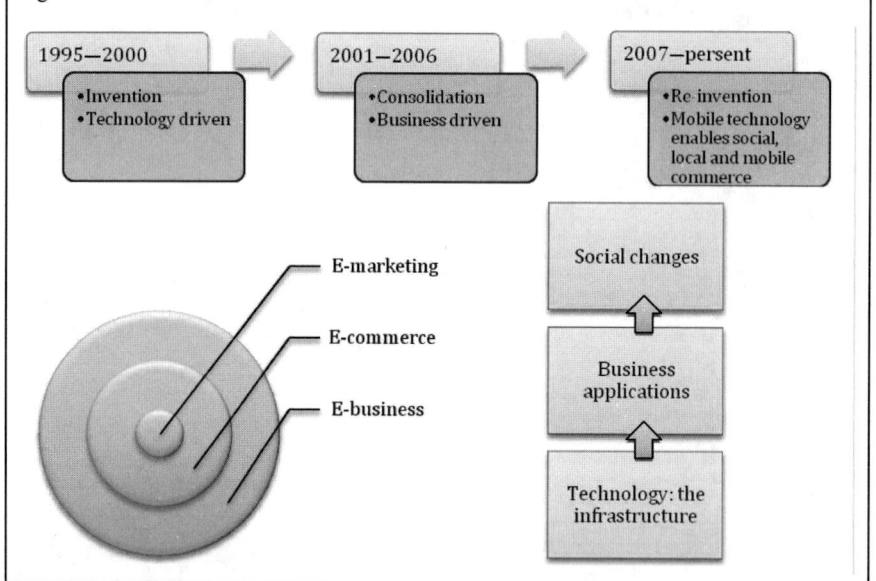

1995—2000	2001—2006	2007—persent
• Invention • Technology driven	• Consolidation • Business driven	• Re-invention • Mobile technology enables social, local and mobile commerce

- E-marketing
- E-commerce
- E-business

Social changes ← Business applications ← Technology: the infrastructure

Types of e-commerce	
B2C — business-to-consumer	online businesses selling to individual consumers, e.g. Amazon, JD, Dangdang
B2B — business-to-business	online businesses selling to other businesses, e.g. Alibaba
C2C — consumer-to-consumer	consumer selling to other consumers, e.g. Taobao
Social e-commerce	e-commerce enabled by social networks and online social relationships, e.g. Facebook, Weibo, Douyin
M-commerce — mobile e-commerce	use of mobile devices to enable online transactions, e.g. WeChat Moments
Local e-commerce	e-commerce that is focused on engaging the consumers based on the current geographic location

Revenue models

Advertising revenue model	a company provides a forum for advertisements and receives fees from advertisers	Most free websites and apps, e.g. Baidu, Taobao
Subscription revenue model	a company offers its users content or services and charges a subscription fee for access to some or all of its offerings	Most video and audio content providers, e.g. Aiqiyi, Tencent Video, Ximalaya, Dragonfly FM
Transaction fee revenue model	a company receives a fee (commission) for enabling or executing a transaction	Some platforms for transactions, e.g., E-bay
Sales revenue model	a company derives revenue by selling goods, information, or services	On-line retailers, e.g. Amazon, JD, Gap
Affiliate revenue model	a company steers business to an affiliate and receives a referral fee or percentage of the revenue from any resulting sales	Website providing coupons, rebounds, e.g. Fanliwang, MyPoints

Logistics

In broad sense, logistics is the detailed coordination of a complex operation involving many people, facilities, or supplies.

In general business sense, logistics is the managemnent of the flow of things between the point of origion and the point of consumption in order to meet requirements of cutomers or corporations.

Components of logistics

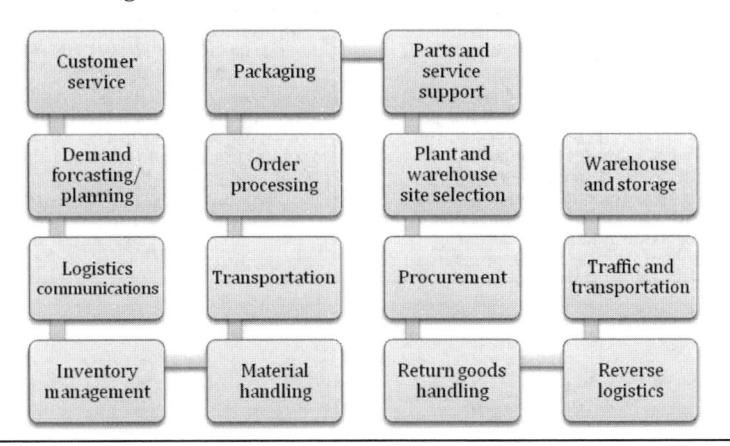

- Customer service
- Packaging
- Parts and service support
- Demand forcasting/planning
- Order processing
- Plant and warehouse site selection
- Warehouse and storage
- Logistics communications
- Transportation
- Procurement
- Traffic and transportation
- Inventory management
- Material handling
- Return goods handling
- Reverse logistics

Material management

Aims:
- Anticipating materials requirements
- Sourcing and obtaining materials
- Introducing materials into organization
- Monitoring the status of materials as a current asset

- Low cost
- High level of service
- Quality assurance
- Low-level of tied-up capital
- Support of other functions

Inventory management

Inventory (American English) or stock (British English) is the goods and materials that a business holds for the ultimate goal of resale (or repair).

Inventory management is a discipline primarily about specifying the shape and placement of stocked goods. It is required at different locations within a facility or within many locations of a supply network to precede the regular and planned course of production and stock of materials.

Purposes of Inventory

- To take advantage of economic purchase order size
- To allow flexibility in production scheduling
- To meet variation in product demand
- To maintain independence of operations
- To provide a safeguard for variation in raw material delivery time.

Just-in-Time Inventory Management

Just in Case	Just in Time
• Just in case (JIC) is an inventory strategy in which companies keep large inventories on hand. This type of inventory management strategy aims to minimize the probability that a product will sell out of stock. The company that utilizes this strategy likely has a hard time predicting consumer demand, or experiences large surges in demand at unpredictable times. A company practicing this strategy essentially incurs higher inventory holding costs in return for a reduction in the number of sales lost due to sold out inventory.	• The just-in-time inventory system is a management strategy that aligns raw-material orders from suppliers directly with production schedules. Companies use this inventory strategy to increase efficiency and decrease waste by receiving goods only as they need them for the production process, which reduces inventory costs. This method requires producers to forecast demand accurately.

Requirements:
steady demand, high-quality workmanship, no machine breakdowns at the plant, reliable suppliers and quick production, etc.

Alternatives:
Short-cycle manufacturing (SCM) (Motorola)
Continuous-flow manufacturing (CFM) (IBM)
Demand-flow manufacturing (DFM)

Warehousing

Private warehousing	Public warehousing	Contract warehousing
• Owned and operated by the company who uses this warehouse	• Operated by a third party that stores goods for multiple shippers/owners	• Operated by a third party, who handles the shipping, receiving and storage of goods on a contract basis.

Warehousing operations

Receiving → Inventory movement → Shipping

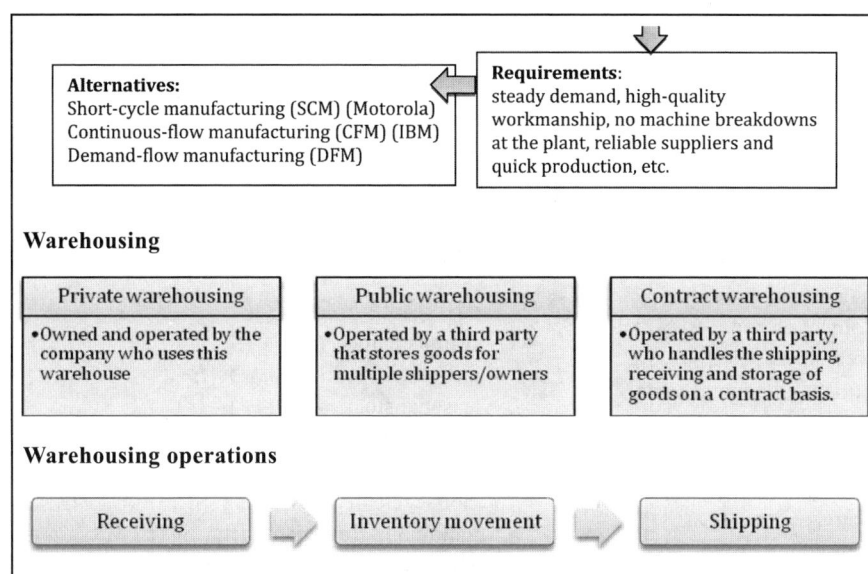

A bonded warehouse, or bond, is a building or other secured area in which dutiable goods may be stored, manipulated, or undergo manufacturing operations without payment of duty. Upon entry of goods into the warehouse, the importer and warehouse proprietor incur liability under a bond. This liability is generally cancelled when the goods are:
· exported; or deemed exported;
· withdrawn for supplies to a vessel or aircraft in international traffic;
· destroyed under Customs supervision; or
· withdrawn for consumption domestically after payment of duty.

While the goods are in the bonded warehouse, they may, under supervision by the customs authority, be manipulated by cleaning, sorting, repacking, or otherwise changing their condition by processes that do not amount to manufacturing. After manipulation, and within the warehousing period, the goods may be exported without the payment of duty, or they may be withdrawn for consumption upon payment of duty at the rate applicable to the goods in their manipulated condition at the time of withdrawal.

Key Terms

e-commerce 电子商务	logistics 后勤；物流
e-marketing 电子营销	logistics communications 物流信息
e-business 电子商业	inventory management 库存管理
ubiquity 普遍性	packaging 包装
global reach 全球覆盖	order processing 订单处理
universal standards 统一标准	transportation 运输
richness 丰富性	material handling 物料处理
interactivity 互动性	procurement 采购
information density 信息密度	warehouse 仓库

personalization 个性化	reverse logistics 逆向物流
B2C 商业对个人	third party logistics (TPL) 第三方物流
B2B 商业对商业	fourth party logistics (FPL) 第四方物流
C2C 个人对个人	materials management 物料管理
m-commerce 手机商务	tied-up capital 占用资金
local e-commerce 本地电子商务	inventory 库存
e-tailer 电子零售商	inventory management 库存管理
bricks and clicks 线上线下	cycle stock 经常库存；周转库存
community provider 社区提供商	safety stock 安全库存
content provider 内容提供商	in-transit stock 在途库存
web portal 网络门户	speculative stock 投机性库存
horizontal/general portal 横向/综合性网站	seasonal stock 季节性库存
vertical/specialized portal (vortal) 垂直/专业网站	just-in-case (JIC) "以防万一"生产模式
	just-in-time (JIT) 适时生产；准时化生产模式
search engine 搜索引擎	short-cycle manufacturing (SCM) 短周期制造
transaction broker 交易经纪	continuous-flow manufacturing (CFM) 连续流水线制造
service provider 服务提供商	
revenue model 收益模式	demand-flow manufacturing (DFM) 需求流水线制造
advertising revenue model 广告收益模式	warehousing 仓储
subscription revenue model 订阅收益模式	private warehousing 私人仓储
	public warehousing 公共仓储
transaction fee revenue 交易费收益模式	contract warehousing 合同仓储
	inventory movement 库存管理
sales revenue model 销售收入模式	shipping 装运
affiliate revenue model 合作收益模式	bonded warehouse 保税仓

在中国

电子商务在中国的发展

中国电商刚起步时，在全球的影响几乎可忽略不计。到 2003 年，中国电子商务交易额还不到 100 亿美元。到 2007 年时，中国电子商务在全球的市场份额达到了 1%，在我国 GDP 中的比重约为 0.2%。2013 年中国成为全球第一大网络零售市场。2014 年，我国快递业务量接近 140 亿件，跃居世界第一。2017 年，中国网络零售额在全球的比重超过 40%。

到 2018 年，中国成为全球电子商务最为发达的国家，网络零售额占社会消费品零售总额的比重达到 17.5%，居全球第一位。

（引自网络：https://baijiahao.baidu.com/s?id=1616842934308119131&wfr=spider&for=pc）

中国电商的特点及趋势：

（1）中国消费者对海外产品的巨大需求，催生了"跨境电商"的发展，以及"代购"这一非正式卖家的职业。2016年，中国跨境零售电商市场规模为785亿美元（约5400亿人民币）；到2021年，这一规模有望超过1400亿美元（约9600亿人民币）。

（2）中国消费者开始通过关键意见领袖（即数字媒体上的影响者）来了解最新产品及最新趋势。意见领袖传播相关内容的途径既包括在微信（即中国版的Facebook）公众号上发表文章，也包括在社交媒体上进行直播。意见领袖在中国市场上的产品推销能力十分惊人。（引自网络：https://www.sohu.com/a/257257443_396568）

（3）其他：自媒体蓬勃发展，主要聚集地为微信、微博，成为电商的一种独特形式；移动支付普及，在中国几乎实现了无货币交易的全覆盖，包括小商小贩都能接受电子支付；电商开始和线下实体店结合，开启了新一代的数字化零售方式；中国电商在未来将越来越深入农村和内陆地区，这些地区仍存在巨大的发展空间。

Brainstorming

How is e-commerce different from traditional commerce?
What are the pros and cons of e-commerce compared with traditional commerce?
Choose an industry and discuss the impact of e-commerce on it.
Select an e-commerce company. Visit its website and search for information about the company and analyze its business model.

Read More

What Is Facebook's Future As An E-commerce Platform?

Facebook is a powerhouse for advertising and virtual goods with 500 million people using the service to communicate and share information with their friends. But are people as eager to click "buy" as they are to click "share" on Facebook?

While Facebook has become a standard advertising and marketing channel for retailers, its development as an e-commerce platform is still in its early stages. But companies are testing out new ways to get people to buy on Facebook.

The biggest e-commerce use of Facebook thus far has been to drive traffic back to their websites through ads, or by posting deals or new products on Facebook. Retailers have also placed Facebook's "Like" button on their own sites as a quick way for users to automatically create links on Facebook. Or they have placed product reviews on Facebook using services like PowerReviews. They are also integrating Facebook's Open Graph technology into their sites to show customers, for example, friends who have a birthday so that they can buy a gift for them.

Going further, start-up such as 8th Bridge and Payvment are enabling companies to sell products directly on Facebook, so consumers don't have to click off to a third-party site. More companies are becoming comfortable with selling products direct on Facebook, these companies say.

But a new report by Forrester Research says that Facebook is more suitable for small retailers, niche products, or steeply discounted items, while most ecommerce retailers find little benefit from Facebook. Forrester analyst Sucharita Mulpuru says most of the benefit that big retailers get from Facebook is still what marketers call "top of the funnel" —branding of their company but not actual purchases.

A Facebook spokeswoman points out Facebook is a key and growing driver of online traffic to retailers. Facebook's referral traffic to Amazon grew 328% year over year in Oct. 2010, while Google's traffic dropped 2%. Facebook traffic to eBay grew 81% while Google traffic dropped 3%.

Facebook also pointed to social advertising tools the company offers to drive sales, including Sponsored Stories, which are ads that show that a friend has liked a company or product. In one example, a Valentine's Day promotion from 1-800-Flowers.com on Facebook generated 4,000 transactions from a promotion that offered 50 Facebook Credits (Facebook's virtual currency) and a 15% discount on flowers.

Buying Direct on Facebook

While recommendations from friends drive people to buy on third-party websites, another growing trend is buying direct on Facebook.

Start-up 8thBridge has been helping companies like Delta Airlines, 1-800-Flowers, HauteLook and Brooks Brothers sell on Facebook. The company has had particular traction with its Facebook stores that enable people to buy products directly in their Facebook News Feed.

With this service, people see what looks like a video on their News Feed, and when they click the "play" arrow, they can immediately scroll through products and purchase. People are 18 times more likely to buy directly in their News Feed than when clicking off to a separate website, said Wade Gerten, chief executive of 8thBridge. In addition, placing a store on the News Feed has made it much more likely that people will share the product with a friend.

"What's happening is that more and more of us are now hearing about things from friends on Facebook and less and less are hearing from brands on Facebook." Gerten said.

Flash sales have been especially popular on Facebook. A special deal 8thBridge ran for designer goods retailer HauteLook on Dec. 7 with designer Diane von Furstenberg generated more than $100,000 in sales in one day, and 40% of those sales were from new HauteLook members. Users were incentivized with a $10 coupon for every new member they brought in. The conversion rates—the number of people who purchased an offer—were above 6%, much higher than the typical rates. (HauteLook recently agreed to be acquired by Nordstrom for $180 million.)

The sale was a way to provide a new way for a brand to reach Facebook users, said Greg Bettinelli, senior vice president of marketing at HauteLook. It's that type of specific targeting and custom campaign that tends to be most successful on Facebook, he said.

"(Diane von Furstenberg) is a leader in its space," Bettinelli said. "They want to do something very different. Only fans of HauteLook or DVF could participate in the sale."

Gerten acknowledges that it's still early days. But he estimates there will be about $100 million in retail sales on Facebook this year.

8th Bridge also plans to soon release a new travel planning app for groups to plan trips together on Facebook. For example, three different family members in different cities could arrange a family trip to Disneyland and arrange flight times, hotel information and possibly other activities—and purchase tickets. This product—which uses the natural communication benefits of Facebook—sounds like an interesting use of ecommerce on Facebook.

For 1-800-Flowers.com, using 8thBridge is a way to draw people into buying flowers and others gifts for friends while they're already thinking about them on Facebook, said Kevin Ranford, vice president of online marketing, mobile & social media at the company.

"It's a great way to drive transactions and keep the user within that experience." Ranford said, "They're there updating their status, chatting with friends, posting pictures. To not drag them out of that engagement and get them into gift-giving mode is a huge win."

To Sell Or Not To Sell

But are people actually buying? And how wide is the uptake across categories?

"For the most part, there are pockets of opportunity." said Mulpuru, who interviewed 24 companies for the report. "Facebook is a communication tool and place for people to share their thoughts with one another. You have an impact, the same way as if you're chatting with friends."

Some products are inherently social such as books, DVDs, and movie and event tickets—and those have been successful because they are easy to buy and sell online and because those items are more inherently social. ("Did you see Inception?") But other products are not as inherently social, Mulpuru said.

"If I have a sweater I wear, would that persuade you to buy it?" Mulpuru said. "Not really. But if I saw a great movie and said you should see it, it'd probably have a much greater influence than the other myriad things I purchase. (Facebook's) not going to have an influence on the majority of things people buy because the majority of things people buy aren't about social activity."

However, Ranford says 1-800-Flowers believes e-commerce on Facebook is a big opportunity and the space is changing so quickly that to ignore it would be a mistake.

"We do firmly believe social communities are a winning place to be." Ranford said, "It's partly the category but it's just in general a great new evolution in how to market to shoppers. It's not a good move to ignore everything happening within social commerce to wait and see if shoppers are transacting or not. That's like waiting around to see if mobile will grow."

Cross-Store Shopping Carts

Payvment is another startup that provides online stores for companies to sell on Facebook—it now has 60,000 merchants using its technology. But Payvment's technology is self-serve and generally serves smaller clients than 8th Bridge—small and medium sized businesses.

The Payvment stores, which are installed on retailers' Facebook pages, are a big draw for those with large numbers of Facebook "fans". But those that are smaller or just starting out have not had as many purchases. Payvment responded in February by launching its Shopping Mall, which aggregates all merchants with Payvment stores. This surfaces merchants and has driven up sales, said Christian Taylor, chief executive of Payvment.

"They're not always putting their whole inventory on Facebook," Taylor said, "But it's select top-tier products they're giving deep discounts to, if you become a Facebook fan—as way to increase engagement and get closer to them."

A feature of Payvment's shopping cart technology is that a product does not disappear from a shopping cart when a user leaves a store. The product will still be there on a different Payvment store. People can check-out from multiple merchants at one time—something that can't be done with individual merchants. Merchants get paid immediately from consumers.

Interestingly unlike 8thBridge, Payvment doesn't charge for its Facebook stores. But it may eventually charge merchants for things like getting discovered easier by consumers.

"Our goal isn't to become an e-commerce company," Taylor said, "We want to become a discovery company. We're giving away the e-commerce part because we think it should be absolutely free."

Other Categories

Despite Mulpuru's critiques, she allows that a number of areas do sell well on Facebook. For one, small retailers whose only online presence is on Facebook—and may have once used Yahoo Merchant Solutions or eBay—have had success. Facebook is cheaper because there are few costs to setting up such a store.

And for some products like cell phones, consumer electronics, sporting goods or baby products, consumers especially want validation or advice for their choices, Mulpuru said. Also, high-volume popular products such as Pampers or Pop-tarts have fans that are eager to purchase new products or deals. Still the success of consumer packaged goods and other consumer products is mostly "top of the funnel" —meaning branding benefits, not direct sales, Mulpuru said.

Inherently social items like local and community products and services such as tickets are another area of success. These products are fundamentally about interaction with friends which make them a natural for Facebook. Online ticketing start-up Eventbrite says each Facebook share of an event ticket generates 11 visits to Eventbrite and $2.52 in revenue.

Selling for peer-to-peer marketplaces is also useful because people would more readily trust buying or selling from a friend or friend-of-a-friend than a stranger on Craigslist. Companies here include Yardsellr, Oodle and Facebook's own Facebook Marketplace. And of course a big source of sales is virtual goods, for which Facebook makes 30% through its Facebook Credits, though that is in a different category from the rest of e-commerce. Unlike with Credits, Facebook does not currently take any cut of sales that companies make of physical products on Facebook.

Ultimately, retailers seem eager to test out various methods of driving e-commerce on Facebook as part of a larger online sales and marketing strategy, not wanting to get left behind in relation to competitors. Advertising, promotions, deals, branding, and customer service are all part of the mix. And e-commerce is also an important piece of that puzzle.

(1763)

https://www.forbes.com/sites/tomiogeron/2011/04/12/what-is-facebooks-future-as-an-e-commerce-platform/#54eee13e4494

Part V Managing Financial Resources

Chapter 10 Principles of Accounting

Accounting or accountancy is the recording, classifying, summarizing, and interpreting of financial information about economic entities such as businesses and corporations to provide management and other interested parties the information they need to make decisions.

Financial accounting provides historical information to people outside the organization.	Managerial accounting provides forward-looking information to management on which they can base decisions.

Auditing
The job of reviewing and evaluating the information used to prepare a company's financial statements

Accountant

Private accountant	Public accountant
An accountant who works for a single organization	An accountant who provids accounting services to individuals or busineeses on a fee basis.

Certificate of accountant
The title of qualified accountants with a license to provide accounting services to the public, having passed relevant exams in the issuing countries.

Certified Public Accountant (CPA)	Certified Management Accountant (CMA)

There are many globally authentic accrediation associations issuing certificates for chartered accountants, e.g. CICPA (the Chinese Insitiue of Certified Public Accountants), AIA (The Association of International Accountants) ACCA (The Association Of Chartered Certified Accountants), AICPA (American Institute of Certified Public Accountants), ICAEW (Institute of Chartered Accountant in England and Wales), CGMA (Chartered Global Management Accountant)

Financial accounting Process

```
Analyze source documents → Record transactions in journals → Transfer posts/journal entries to ledger
                                                                      ↓
Take a trial balance ← Prepare financial statements ← Interpret financial statements
```

Bookkeeping The recording of business transactions in double entry system

Source documents: source of financial information recording business transactions, including invoices, sales and purchase orders, wage slips, credit notes, goods received notes, till rolls etc.

Journal: the record book or computer program where accounting data are first entered.

Ledger: a specialized accounting book or computer program in which information from accounting journals is accumulated into specific categories and posted so that managers can find all the information about one account in the same place.

Trial balance: a summary of all the financial data in the account ledgers that ensures the figures are correct and balanced.

Financial statements: (or financial report) is a formal record of the financial activities and position of a business, person, or other entity in a structured manner, typically including balance sheet, income statement and statement of cash flow.

Financial statements

① Balance sheet is a summary of the financial condition of a business on a specific date at the end of a specific reporting period, made up with assets, liabilities and owners' equity. The total of the left column is always equal to that of the right column, basically illustrated as follows:

②

Balance Sheet

As of December 12, 2018

Assets	Liabilities and owners' equity

Current assets
  Case
  Account/notes receivable
  Inventories
	Current liabilities
	  Account/notes payable
	  Accrued wages
	  Accrued taxes

Fixed assets
  Land
  Building
    Less: accumulated depreciation
  Machinery/equipment
    Less: accumulated depreciation
	Long-term liabilities
	  Mortgage payable
	  Long-term bonds

Intangible assets
  Good will
  R&D
  Intellectual rights
	Owners' equity
	  Stock/Capital
	  Retained earnings

Explanation for some key items:
- Cash includes currencies in hands and deposit at banks.
- Account receivable/payable: as accounting runs on the accruals concept, when credit loan occurs, i.e. delay of payment by the buyers, the amount earned or incurred should be recorded (when not actually received or paid). This concept also applies to accrued wages and taxes.
- Land is considered a fixed asset without depreciation in capitalist countries, while an intangible assets with amortization expense in China.
- Intangible assets, like good will and intellectual rights are only recorded when are bought or sold; and the expenses in research and development (R&D) can be taken as the value of the intellectual rights created by the company itself.
- Stock/capital for non-stock companies and sole proprietors, capital is used instead of stock.
- Retained earnings are earnings kept in the company after paying dividends to its stockholders.

The basic accounting equation derived from the statement of financial position can be expressed as:
$$\text{Assets} = \text{Liabilities} + \text{Owners' equity, or}$$
$$\text{Assets} - \text{Liabilities} = \text{Owners' equity}$$

Double-entry bookkeeping is the core of modern accounting system, in which every business transaction will be entered in two places, as debit and credit respectively. By adding up all entries in an account, the accountant can check its correctness against other relevant accounts.

Debit: bookkeeping entry that records increase in assets, or decrease in expenses, liabilities or owner's equity, etc., always enters in the left side in a T-account	Credit: bookkeeping entry in a T-account that records decrease in assets, or increase in expenses, liabilities or owner's equity, etc., always enters in the right side in a T-account

Assets	=	Liabilities	+	Owners' equity	
Debit for increase	Credit for decrease	Debit for decrease	Credit for increase	Debit for decrease	Credit for increase

③ Income Statement indicates the revenue, costs and earnings of a firm over a period of time, basically illustrated as follows:

Income Statement
For the year ended Dec. 31, 2018

Revenues

Less: Cost of goods sold
beginning inventory
    + purchase
    − ending inventory

Gross profit

Less: Expenses
selling expenses
    salaries and wages for sales persons
    advertising
    packaging expenses
administrative expenses
    salaries and wages for managerial persons
    rents
    utilities
    overheads
    depreciation

Net income before tax (or operating income)*
Less: income tax
Net income

* *Income can be a negative figure if the firm suffers losses; when it is a positive figure, we call it a "profit".*

Interpreting a company's performance with financial ratios:
- Liquidity ratios (Short-term position) measure the company's ability to repay its short-term debt with current assets or cash
- Current ratio = current assets/ current liabilities $\geqslant 2$
- Quick ratio = (current assets − inventories)/current liabilities $\geqslant 1$
- Leverage (debt) ratios (Long-term position) measure the company's ability to repay all its debt with all its assets, also a measurement of its capital structure.
- Debt-equity ratio = debt /equity $\leqslant 1$
- Profitability/performance ratios measure the company's use of its assets and control of its expenses to generate an acceptable rate of return
- Gross profit margin = Gross profit/ Net sales
- Net profit margin = Net income/ Net sales
- Return on Equity = Net income / Total owners' equity
- Activity/efficiency ratios measure the effectiveness of the firm's use of resources

- Inventory turnover = Cost of goods sold / Average inventory
- Accounts receivable turnover = Net sales / (average) Accounts receivable
- Market ratios measure investor response to owning a company's stock and also the cost of issuing stock. These are concerned with the return on investment for shareholders, and with the relationship between return and the value of an investment in company's shares.
- Earnings per share = net income/number of stock shares (+ stock options, preferred stock, convertible debt securities ...)

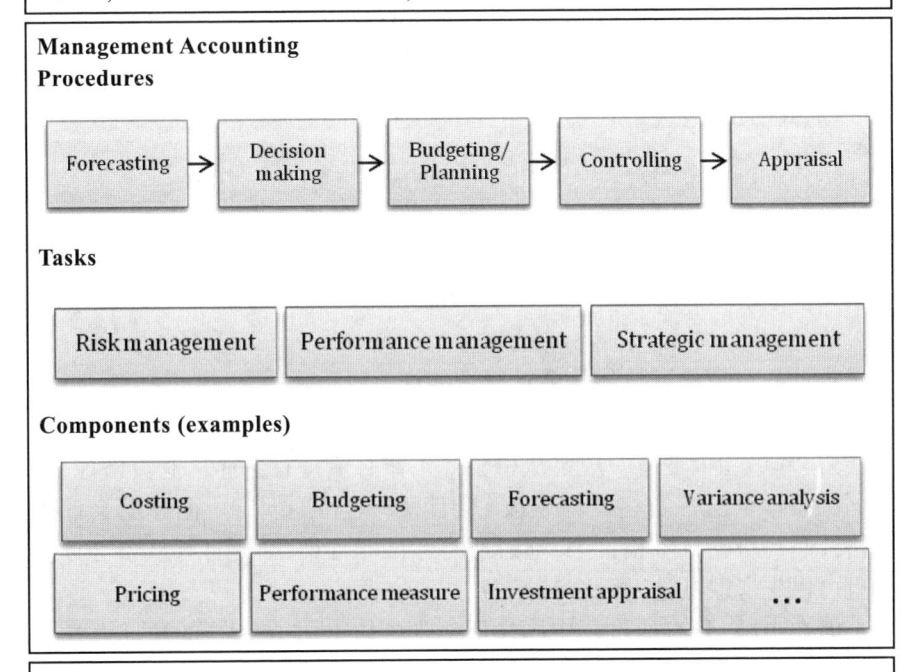

Management Accounting
Procedures

Forecasting → Decision making → Budgeting/Planning → Controlling → Appraisal

Tasks

Risk management | Performance management | Strategic management

Components (examples)

| Costing | Budgeting | Forecasting | Variance analysis |
| Pricing | Performance measure | Investment appraisal | ... |

Key Terms

financial accounting 财务会计	account receivable/payable 应收/应付账款
managerial accounting 管理会计	accruals concept 权责发生制
private accountant 专任会计师；私用会计师	double entry bookkeeping 复式记账法
public accountant 公共会计师	T-account T 形账户
auditing 审计	debit 借方
CPA 注册财务会计师	credit 贷方
CMA 注册管理会计师	revenues 收入
bookkeeping 簿记；记账	cost of goods sold 销售货物成本
source documents 原始凭证	beginning/ending inventory 期初/期末库存
journal 日记账	gross profit 毛利润
ledger 分类账	expenses 费用
trial balance 试平衡	net income 净损益；净收入

financial statements 财务报表	net profit 净利润
balance sheet 资产负债表	liquidity ratios 流动性比率
income statement 损益表	current ratio 流动比率
statement of cash flow 现金流量表	quick ratio 速动比率
assets 资产	leverage ratio 杠杆比
current assets 流动资产	debt/equity ratio 债务股本比
fixed assets 固定资产	profitability ratio 盈利能力比
intangible assets 无形资产	gross profit margin 毛利润率
liabilities 负债	net profit margin 净利润率
current liabilities 流动负债	return on equity 股本回报率
long-term liabilities 长期负债	activity/efficiency ratio 活动比/效率比
stock 股票	inventory turnover 库存周转率
capital 资本	accounts receivable turnover 应收账款周转率
owners' equity 所有者权益	market ratio 市场比率
retained earnings 留用利润	earnings per share 每股收益

在中国

会计从业资格证与注册会计师资格证

　　会计从业资格证是从事会计工作的基本证书，表示具有该职业的基本能力。原《会计法》中规定从事会计工作必须持有会计从业资格证，目前国家拟取消这一资格证并修改《会计法》的相关规定。而注册会计师资格证是高级会计资格证书，通过所有考试非常难，因此打算从事会计工作也可以先考取其他国际会计证书。

　　但在中国，只有通过了中国注册会计师协会（CICPA）的注册会计师资格证的所有考试取得证书，并且在会计事务所工作两年以上，才可以有对外的会计财务报告审计签字权，持有其他任何国际会计证书均不可拥有签字权。持有其他国际权威会计证书可以作为会计能力的证明，对进入会计师事务所或跨国公司从事财会工作是有利的。

Brainstorming

Think of common transactions and try to record them with double-entry bookkeeping method.

Find the figures of the assets and liabilities of a business at a specific time and the transactions during a year to work out a balance sheet and an income statement.

Summarize differences between financial accounting and management accounting. Predict their development trend.

Read More

Basic Accounting Principles and Guidelines

Since GAAP (Generally Accepted Accounting Principles) is founded on the basic accounting principles and guidelines, we can better understand GAAP if we understand those accounting principles. The following is a list of the ten main accounting principles and guidelines together with a highly condensed explanation of each.

1. Economic Entity Assumption

The accountant keeps all of the business transactions of a sole proprietorship separate from the business owner's personal transactions. For legal purposes, a sole proprietorship and its owner are considered to be one entity, but for accounting purposes they are considered to be two separate entities.

2. Monetary Unit Assumption

Economic activity is measured in U.S. dollars, and only transactions that can be expressed in U.S. dollars are recorded.

Because of this basic accounting principle, it is assumed that the dollar's purchasing power has not changed over time. As a result accountants ignore the effect of inflation on recorded amounts. For example, dollars from a 1960 transaction are combined (or shown) with dollars from a 2017 transaction.

3. Time Period Assumption

This accounting principle assumes that it is possible to report the complex and ongoing activities of a business in relatively short, distinct time intervals such as the five months ended May 31, 2017, or the 5 weeks ended May 1, 2017. The shorter the time interval is, the more likely the need for the accountant to estimate amounts relevant to that period. For example, the property tax bill is received on December 15 of each year. On the income statement for the year ended December 31, 2016, the amount is known, but for the income statement for the three months ended March 31, 2017, the amount was not known and an estimate had to be used.

It is imperative that the time interval (or period of time) be shown in the heading of each income statement, statement of stockholders' equity, and statement of cash flows. Labeling one of these financial statements with "December 31" is not good enough—the reader needs to know if the statement covers the one week ended December 31, 2017 the month ended December 31, 2017 the three months ended December 31, 2017 or the year ended December 31, 2017.

4. Cost Principle

From an accountant's point of view, the term "cost" refers to the amount spent (cash or the cash equivalent) when an item was originally obtained, whether that purchase happened last year or thirty years ago. For this reason, the amounts shown on financial statements are referred to as historical cost amounts.

Because of this accounting principle asset amounts are not adjusted upward for inflation. In fact, as a general rule, asset amounts are not adjusted to reflect any type of increase in value. Hence, an asset amount does not reflect the amount of money a company would receive if it were to sell the asset at today's market value. (An exception is certain investments in stocks and bonds that are actively traded on a stock exchange.) If you want to know the current value of a company's long-term assets, you will not get this information from a company's financial statements—you need to look elsewhere, perhaps to a third-party appraiser.

5. Full Disclosure Principle

If certain information is important to an investor or lender using the financial statements, that information should be disclosed within the statement or in the notes to the statement. It is because of this basic accounting principle that numerous pages of "footnotes" are often attached to financial statements.

As an example, let's say a company is named in a lawsuit that demands a significant amount of money. When the financial statements are prepared, it is not clear whether the company will be able to defend itself or whether it might lose the lawsuit. As a result of these conditions and because of the full disclosure principle the lawsuit will be described in the notes to the financial statements.

A company usually lists its significant accounting policies as the first note to its financial statements.

6. Going Concern Principle

This accounting principle assumes that a company will continue to exist long enough to carry out its objectives and commitments and will not liquidate in the foreseeable future. If the company's financial situation is such that the accountant believes the company will not be able to continue on, the accountant is required to disclose this assessment.

The going concern principle allows the company to defer some of its prepaid expenses until future accounting periods.

7. Matching Principle

This accounting principle requires companies to use the accrual basis of accounting. The matching principle requires that expenses be matched with revenues. For example, sales commissions expense should be reported in the period when the sales were made (and not reported in the period when the commissions were paid). Wages to employees are reported as an expense in the week when the employees worked and not in the week when the employees are paid. If a company agrees to give its employees 1% of its 2017 revenues as a bonus on January 15, 2018, the company should report the bonus as an expense in 2017 and the amount unpaid at December 31, 2017 as a liability. (The expense is occurring as the sales are occurring.)

Because we cannot measure the future economic benefit of things such as advertisements (and thereby we cannot match the ad expense with related future revenues), the accountant charges the ad amount to expense in the period that the ad is run.

(To learn more about adjusting entries, go to Explanation of Adjusting Entries and Quiz for Adjusting Entries.)

8. Revenue Recognition Principle

Under the accrual basis of accounting (as opposed to the cash basis of accounting), revenues are recognized as soon as a product has been sold or a service has been performed, regardless of when the money is actually received. Under this basic accounting principle, a company could earn and report $20,000 of revenue in its first month of operation but receive $0 in actual cash in that month.

For example, if ABC Consulting completes its service at an agreed price of $1,000, ABC should recognize $1,000 of revenue as soon as its work is done—it does not matter whether the client pays the $1,000 immediately or in 30 days. Do not confuse revenue with a cash receipt.

9. Materiality

Because of this basic accounting principle or guideline, an accountant might be allowed to violate another accounting principle if an amount is insignificant. Professional judgement is needed to decide whether an amount is insignificant or immaterial.

An example of an obviously immaterial item is the purchase of a $150 printer by a highly profitable multi-million dollar company. Because the printer will be used for five years, the matching principle directs the accountant to expense the cost over the five-year period. The materiality guideline allows this company to violate the matching principle and to expense the entire cost of $150 in the year it is purchased. The justification is that no one would consider it misleading if $150 is expensed in the first year instead of $30 being expensed in each of the five years that it is used.

Because of materiality, financial statements usually show amounts rounded to the nearest dollar, to the nearest thousand, or to the nearest million dollars depending on the size of the company.

10. Conservatism

If a situation arises where there are two acceptable alternatives for reporting an item, conservatism directs the accountant to choose the alternative that will result in less net income and/or less asset amount. Conservatism helps the accountant to "break a tie". It does not direct accountants to be conservative. Accountants are expected to be unbiased and objective.

The basic accounting principle of conservatism leads accountants to anticipate or disclose losses, but it does not allow a similar action for gains. For example, potential losses from lawsuits will be reported on the financial statements or in the notes, but potential gains will not be reported. Also, an accountant may write inventory down to an amount that is lower than the original cost, but will not write inventory up to an amount higher than the original cost.

What are principles of accounting?

Three meanings come to mind when you ask about principles of accounting...

Principles of accounting were often the title of the introductory course in accounting. They were also common for the textbook used in the course to be entitled Principles of Accounting.

Principles of accounting can also refer to the basic or fundamental accounting principles: cost principles, matching principles, full disclosure principles, materiality principles, going concern principles, economic entity principles, and so on. In this context, principles of accounting refer to the broad underlying concepts which guide accountants when preparing financial statements.

Principles of accounting can also mean Generally Accepted Accounting Principles (GAAP). When used in this context, principles of accounting will include both the underlying basic accounting principles and the official accounting pronouncements issued by the Financial Accounting Standards Board (FASB) and its predecessor organizations. The official pronouncements are detailed rules or standards for specific top.

Why are accounting principles important?

The purpose of having—and following—accounting principles is to be able to communicate economic information in a language that is acceptable and understandable from one business to another. Companies that release their financial information to the public are required to follow these principles in preparation of their statements.

Depending on the characteristics of a company or entity, the company law and other regulations determine which accounting principles they are required to apply. The standard accounting principles are collectively known as Generally Accepted Accounting Principles (GAAP). GAAP provides the framework foundation of accounting standards, concepts, objectives and conventions for companies, serving as a guide of how to prepare and present financial statements.

(1635)

www.accountingcoach.com

Key Components of Management Accounting

Management accounting, in accordance with the Chartered Institute of Management Accountants (CIMA), is the procedure of recognizing, gauging, gathering, studying, researching, analyzing and communicating of information utilized by the management to plan, evaluate and control within body and to ensure proper use of liability for its resources.

It also includes the preparation of financial reports for non-management groups such as tax authorities and regulatory agencies.

On the other hand, The American Institute of Certified Public Accountants (AICPA) says that management accounting, as a practice extends to three areas, such as:

• Risk Management contributes to practices and frameworks for determining, gauging, managing and reporting risks to the attainment of the objectives and goals of the organization.

• Performance Management develops the practice of decision-making and managing the organization's performance.

• Strategic Management advances the function of the management accountant as a tactical partner in the organization.

An excellent management accounting process also helps in tackling the four major aspects of a business, such as:

• Proper planning

• Directing

• Decision-making

• Controlling

The Objectives of Management Accounting

Management accounting has the following core objectives:

• To formulate effective strategies and techniques in reaching the company's goals quickly but surely

• To plan and construct business activities to ensure the business' sustained growth and profit

• To help the firm in making the right financial decision by making use of effective strategies

• To use resources optimally

• To support financial reports

• To safeguard asset

How Can Management Accounting Keep Your Business Afloat In Spite of the Recession and Competition?

It is said that the strength and sustainability of a business relies on management accounting. This is the reason why accountants who perform this job are paid higher than those who perform other accounting jobs. So, how can management accounting keep your business afloat in spite of the recession and competition? They are as follows:

• Management accounting provides factual information in relation to the actual and budgeted figures, therefore allowing the business owners and managers to take the right cost controlling measures.

• It gives timely feedback in relation to present operational activities, thus helping in re-evaluating the operational decisions and having better control over the business' activities.

• It also helps in gauging the performance of different departments and sub-units within a company or organization. This information can then be utilized to determine and reward the better performing employees and departments. For example, an employee might be the reason for the company's higher sales figures. As a result, you may prefer to promote him to manage the other staff.

• Management accounting helps business owners or managers to fully analyze the organization. In this regard, management accounts can give useful information when looking at the plans of an organization and when performing any SWOT analysis. This type of analysis is designed to analyze the strengths, weaknesses, opportunities and threats that a business is faced with.

• Management accounting also determines the profitable and non-profitable services or products. For instance, this can greatly help the company in speeding up the process of discontinuing a product that is making a huge loss. In turn, this will lead to great financial savings.

Management Accountants—What Do They Do?

Management accountants have a twice working relationship. As a tactical partner and provider of a decision-based operation and financial information, management accountants are obliged to manage the team and report responsibilities and relationships to the finance organization of the corporation.

They also break down the outflow or cost into processes and functions to make the process of cost control smooth at every prepared level in the business. They also suggest smart alternatives in order to enhance the business' productivity.

In management accounting, accountants also develop a high standard for all working areas in the business sector. They determine the areas of invisible losses, inefficiencies, leakages and wastages that the business has dealt with in the past few years.

Management accounting does not just cover financial records, but can be applied all over a company's or organization's activities to determine areas that require improvement. This is the reason why it is considered as a very crucial tool in helping a business achieve their goals and objectives.

According to experts, management accounting must not be seen as something that only large businesses should try.

Any business, no matter how large or small must prepare management accounting information, even though it is just written down or printed on a piece of paper.

Bear in mind that this is one of the most helpful tools for the success of your business. Without proper and excellent management accounting, your business will just be caught up in a snare the moment you least expect it. Thus, you need to entrust your business' accounting needs only to qualified and knowledgeable management accountants.

(793)

http://marketinghrdpresentation.com/apps25/2012/12/22/key-components-of-management-accounting/

Chapter 11 Money and Banking

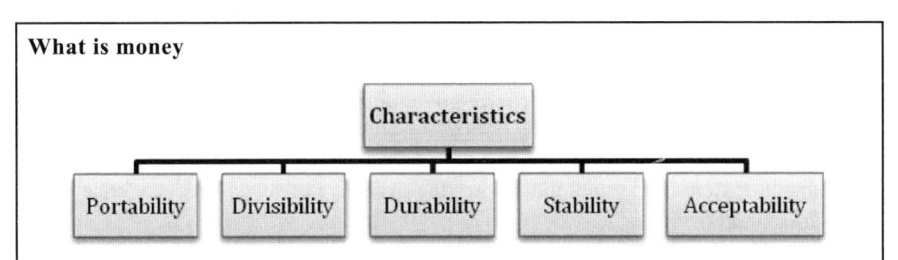

What is money

```
                    Characteristics
   ┌──────────┬──────────┬──────────┬──────────┐
Portability Divisibility Durability Stability Acceptability
```

Money must be easy to carry, easily divided into different denominations, standing wear the tear during transaction, stable in value and acceptable by the public. Among them, acceptability is the most important one, i.e. it must be made legal tender by the government.

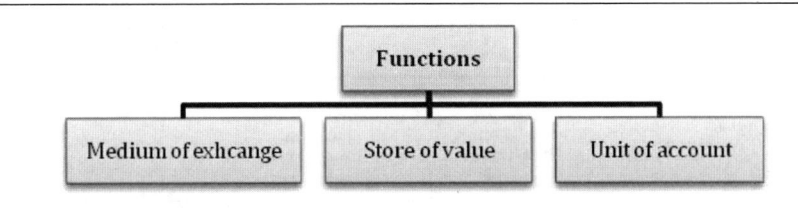

```
                Functions
   ┌──────────────┬──────────────┐
Medium of exhcange  Store of value  Unit of account
```

Money can be used to trade for things, stored for future use and measure the relative values of goods and services.

Types of money

In economy and finance, money has a much broader meaning than "currency". According to their liquidity, different forms of money can be divided into M0, M1, M2, M3... Larger figures indicate lower liquidity.

M0 is the most liquid form of money, currency, including paper money and coins.
M1 is the spendable money supply, also referred to as narrow money or transaction money.
M2 includes M1 and the convertible money supply, also referred to as broad money and near money.

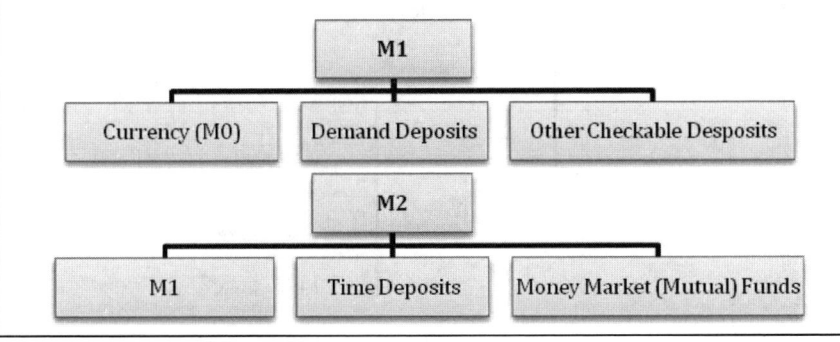

```
                    M1
      ┌─────────────┼──────────────────┐
 Currency (M0)  Demand Deposits  Other Checkable Desposits

                    M2
      ┌─────────────┼──────────────────┐
     M1         Time Deposits   Money Market (Mutual) Funds
```

Demand deposits are deposits can be drawn anytime at request, against which checks can be drawn. Besides this type of deposits, others against which checks can be written are also included in M1.

Time deposits bear higher interest rate and a fixed-term maturity, thus prior notice is required to draw before the maturity date and the holder may suffer interest loss.

(Mutual) funds are operated by investment companies that bring together money from many investors. Money market funds are only invested in a collection of short-term, low-risk securities, like short-term government bonds, central bank bills, etc.

Financial System

A financial system is a system that allows the exchange of funds between lenders, investors, and borrowers.

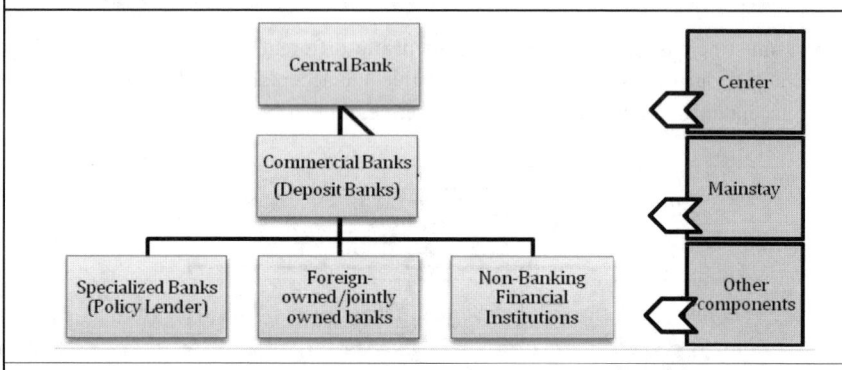

```
                    Central Bank ──────────▷ Center

                    Commercial Banks
                    (Deposit Banks) ───────▷ Mainstay

    Specialized Banks   Foreign-owned/    Non-Banking
    (Policy Lender)     jointly owned     Financial      ▷ Other
                        banks             Institutions      components
```

Central Bank is an institution that manages a state's currency, money supply and interest rates.

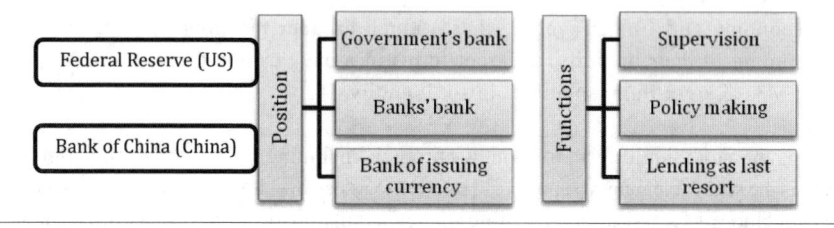

```
    Federal Reserve (US)              Government's bank      Supervision

                          Position    Banks' bank    Functions    Policy making

    Bank of China (China)             Bank of issuing           Lending as last
                                      currency                  resort
```

Commercial Bank is an institution that provides services such as accepting deposits, providing business loans, and offering basic investment products.

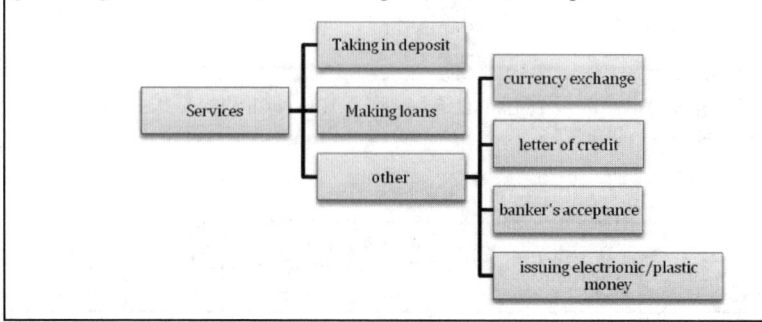

```
                    Taking in deposit
                                          currency exchange
    Services ─────  Making loans
                                          letter of credit
                    other
                                          banker's acceptance

                                          issuing electronic/plastic
                                          money
```

Specialized banks/policy lenders are non-commercial, non-profit banks funded by the government, aiming at providing funds in specialized fields based on economic policies.

> e.g. Agricultural Development Bank of China, Import and Export Bank of China, World Bank, Asia Development Bank, etc.

Non-banking Financial Institutions

> e.g. pension fund (social security), insurance company, financial company, financial leasing company, securities company, trust and investment company, etc.

Money supply

Money in circulation is issued by the central bank, and also created by the whole financial system. Financial institutions expand money supply through the fractional reserve banking system, as in modern economies, most of the money supply is in the form of bank deposits; this process is called money creation.

	Acquired reserves and deposits	Reserve (reserve ratio=0.1)	Excess reserve	Amount bank can lend = new money created
Bank 1	$10,000	$1,000	$9,000	$9,000
Bank 2	9,000	900	8,100	8,100
Bank 3	8,100	810	7,290	7,290
Bank N	...	...	...	...
	Total			$90,000

Money multiplier (m) = 1/required reserve ratio = 1/0.1 = 10
Maximum money creation = excess reserves × m = 9,000 × 10 = 90,000

Monetary policies

Instruments the central bank uses to monitor the total supply of money, i.e. the monetary aggregates, in the economy.

open-market operation	discount rate	reserve requirements
•buying or selling government bonds and other financial instruments to manage the money in circulation	•increasing or decreasing the interest rate it charges on loans to commercial banks	•the proportion of total liabilities that banks must keep on hand overnight, either in its vaults or at the central bank.

\multicolumn{4}{	l	}{How can central banks use the three monetary instruments to adjust money supply?}
money supply	open-market operation	discount rate	reserve requirements
increase	buy in	lower	lower
decrease	sell out	higher	lower

Note: Open-market operation is the most frequently used instrument, as it is easy to conduct and can change the money supply by a small or large amount on any day. Discount rate is the second to use and adjustment of reserve requirements should be used with great caution as it may cause too large and abrupt changes in policy.

在中国

支票

支票在发达国家是非常常见的支付手段,如美国,人们在进行大额支付时经常使用支票,但在中国,支票仅限于公司使用,个人支票业务大部分银行并未开通,因此个人支票也没有进入流通领域,我们通常使用银行卡或者手机支付。

Key Terms

portability 便携性	central bank 中央银行
divisibility 可分割性	commercial bank 商业银行
durability 耐用性	specialized bank 政策性银行
stability 稳定性	financial institutions 金融机构
acceptability 可接受性	federal reserve 美联储
legal tender 法定货币	money supply 货币供应
medium of exchange 交换媒介	money creation 货币创造
store of value 价值储存	required reserve 存款准备金
unit of discount 会计单位	reserve ratio 准备金率
currency 货币	excess reserve 准备金剩余
demand deposits 活期存款	money multiplier 货币乘数
checkable deposits 可开立支票账户	monetary policy 货币政策
time deposits 定期存款	open-market operation 公开市场操作
money market funds 货币市场基金	discount rate 贴现率
financial system 金融体系	reserve requirements 准备金要求

Brainstorming

How to understand payment with WeChat or Alipay? Mini Fund (Lingqiang Tong) in WeChat Wallet and Yu'E Bao in Alipay?

Read recent financial news and exchange your ideas with knowledge learnt in this chapter.

Read More

International Finance: The International Monetary System
The International Monetary System

The rules and procedures for exchanging national currencies are collectively known as the international monetary system. This system doesn't have a physical presence, like the Federal Reserve System, nor is it as codified as the Social Security system. Instead, it consists of interlocking rules and procedures and is subject to the foreign exchange market, and therefore to the judgments of currency traders about a currency.

Yet there are rules and procedures—exchange rate policies—which public finance officials of various nations have developed and from time to time modify. There are also physical institutions that oversee the international monetary system, and the most important of these being the International Monetary Fund.

Exchange Rate Policies

In July 1944, representatives from 45 nations met in Bretton Woods, New Hampshire to discuss the recovery of Europe from World War II and to resolve international trade and monetary issues. The resulting Bretton Woods Agreement established the International Bank for Reconstruction and Development (the World Bank) to provide long-term loans to assist Europe's recovery. It also established the International Monetary Fund (IMF) to manage the international monetary system of fixed exchange rates, which was also developed at the conference.

The new monetary system established more stable exchange rates than those of the 1930s, a decade characterized by restrictive trade policies. Under the Bretton Woods Agreement, IMF member nations agreed to a system of exchange rates that pegged the value of the dollar to the price of gold and pegged other currencies to the dollar. This system remained in place until 1972. In 1972, the Bretton Woods system of pegged exchange rates broke down forever and was replaced by the system of managed floating exchange rates that we have today.

The Bretton Woods system broke down because the dynamics of supply, demand, and prices in a nation affect the true value of its currency, regardless of fixed rate schemes or pegging policies. When those dynamics are not reflected in the foreign exchange value of the currency, the currency becomes overvalued or undervalued in terms of other currencies. Its price—fixed or otherwise—becomes too high or too low, given the economic fundamentals of the nation and the dynamics of supply, demand, and prices. When this occurs, the flows of international trade and payments are distorted.

In the 1960s, rising costs in the United States made U.S. exports uncompetitive. At the same time, western Europe and Japan emerged from the wreckage of World War II to become productive economies that could compete with the United States. As a result, the U.S. dollar became overvalued under the fixed exchange rate system. This caused a drain on the U.S. gold supply, because foreigners preferred to hold gold rather than overvalued dollars. By 1970, U.S. gold reserves decreased to about $10 billion, a drop of more than 50 percent from the peak of $24 billion in 1949.

In 1971, the U.S. decided to let the dollar float against other currencies so it could find its proper value and imbalances in trade and international funds flows could be corrected. This indeed occurred and evolved into the managed float system of today.

A nation manages the value of its currency by buying or selling it on the foreign exchange market. If a nation's central bank buys its currency, the supply of that currency decreases and the supply of other currencies increases relative to it. This increases the value of its currency.

On the other hand, if a nation's central bank sells its currency, the supply of that currency on the market increases, and the supply of other currencies decreases relative to it. This decreases the value of its currency.

The International Monetary Fund plays a key role in operations that help a nation manage the value of its currency.

The International Monetary Fund

The International Monetary Fund (www.imf.org) is like a central bank for the world's central banks. It is headquartered in Washington, D.C., has 184 member nations, and cooperates closely with the World Bank, which we discuss in The Global Market and Developing Nations. The IMF has a board of governors consisting of one representative from each member

Part V Managing Financial Resources

nation. The board of governors elects a 20-member executive board to conduct regular operations.

The goals of the IMF are to promote world trade, stable exchange rates, and orderly correction of balance of payments problems. One important part of this is preventing situations in which a nation devalues its currency purely to promote its exports. That kind of devaluation is often considered unfairly competitive if underlying issues, such as poor fiscal and monetary policies, are not addressed by the nation.

Member nations maintain funds in the form of currency reserve units called Special Drawing Rights (SDRs) on deposit with the IMF. (This is a bit like the federal funds that U.S. commercial banks keep on deposit with the Federal Reserve.) From 1974 to 1980, the value of SDRs was based on the currencies of 16 leading trading nations. Since 1980, it has been based on the currencies of the five largest exporting nations. From 1990 to 2000, these were the United States, Japan, Great Britain, Germany, and France. The value of SDRs is reassigned every five years.

SDRs are held in the accounts of IMF nations in proportion to their contribution to the fund. (The United States is the largest contributor, accounting for about 25 percent of the fund.) Participating nations agree to accept SDRs in exchange for reserve currencies—that is, foreign exchange currencies—in settling international accounts. All IMF accounting is done in SDRs, and commercial banks accept SDR-denominated deposits. By using SDRs as the unit of value, the IMF simplifies its own and its member nations' payment and accounting procedures.

In addition to maintaining the system of SDRs and promoting international liquidity, the IMF monitors worldwide economic developments, and provides policy advice, loans, and technical assistance in situations like the following:

After the collapse of the Soviet Union, the IMF helped Russia, the Baltic states, and other former Soviet countries set up treasury systems to assist them in moving from planning to market-based economies.

During the Asian financial crisis of 1997 and 1998, the IMF helped Korea to bolster its reserves. The IMF pledged $21 billion to help Korea reform its economy, restructure its financial and corporate sectors, and recover from recession.

In 2000, the IMF Executive Board urged the Japanese government to stimulate growth by keeping interest rates low, encouraging bank restructuring, and promoting deregulation.

In October 2000, the IMF approved a $52 million loan for Kenya to help it deal with severe drought. This was part of a three-year $193 million loan under an IMF lending program for low-income nations.

Most economists judge the current international monetary system a success. It permits market forces and national economic performance to determine the value of foreign currencies, yet enables nations to maintain orderly foreign exchange markets by cooperating through the IMF.

The EU and the Euro

The biggest news on the foreign currency front over the past few years is the adoption of the euro by the European Union (EU). Twelve member states of the EU use the euro instead of their old local currencies: Austria, Belgium, Finland, France, Germany, Greece, Ireland, Italy, Luxembourg, Netherlands, Portugal, and Spain.

Nations that adopt the euro participate in a single EU monetary policy and are subject to fiscal guidelines requiring them to keep deficits to a certain level and to balance their federal budgets by 2006. Although it will reconsider the matter again, Britain has refused to adopt the euro and has stuck with the pound sterling. This reflects England's traditional sense of "apartness" from continental Europe and its reluctance to give up sovereignty over its economic policies.

(1294)

https://www.infoplease.com/homework-help/social-studies/international-finance-international-monetary-system

Part VI Dealing with Crisis and Risks

Chapter 12 Financing and Investment

Sources of founds

Short-term financing
- trade credit
  - open account
  - promissory note
  - draft
- bank loans
  - secured
  - unsecured
- commercial paper
- factoring

Long-term financing
- Debt (external) financing
  - loans/mortgages
  - bonds
- Equity (internal) financing
  - stock
  - retained earnings
  - depreciation

Trade credit is the delay of payment provided by the seller to the buyer. (As mentioned in Chapter 9, in this case, though the payment has not been effected, this transaction should be recorded in the journal and other financial statements, as follows:

Seller		Buyer	
Debit	Credit	Debit	Credit
account receivable	inventory	inventory	account payable

Therefore, in both seller and buyer's accounting books, there exists an open account.)

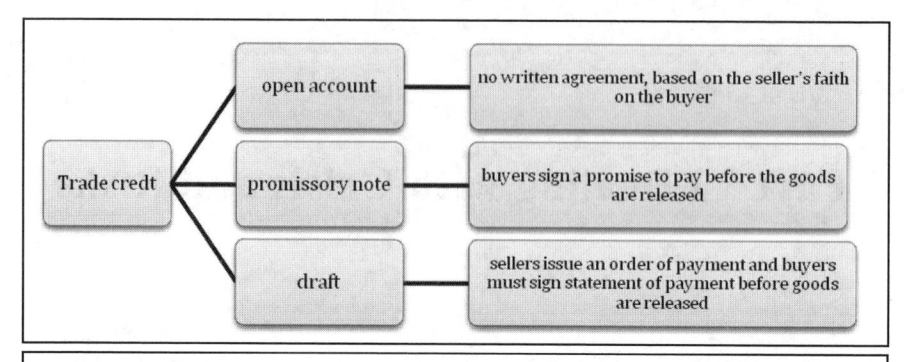

```
                                    ┌─ open account      → no written agreement, based on the seller's faith on the buyer
Trade credit ───────────┼─ promissory note  → buyers sign a promise to pay before the goods are released
                                    └─ draft                   → sellers issue an order of payment and buyers must sign statement of payment before goods are released
```

Bank loans can be granted secured or unsecured. Secured loans require the borrower to put up collateral-assets can be seized by the bank in case the borrower fails to repay. Loans can also be secured by asking a second party to sign the promissory note, who is responsible for the repayment if the borrower fails to.

*for short-term loans, collateral usually includes inventory, account receivables, securities. Unsecured loans are granted based on credit. Credit loans can be made one time only, or on the basis of lines of credit—the maximum amount the borrower is permitted to owe at any time. Line of credit can be arranged on a continual basis, i.e. revolving credit agreement, like the form of credit card.

Commercial papers are short-term, unsecured bonds issued by very credit-worthy companies.

Factoring means selling account receivables to factors, the collecting agents, under the face value to exchange for cash.

Debt vs. Equity Financing

Debt financing	Equity financing
• means borrowing money from outside sources and the borrower has to pay back the loan on time regardless of the firm's financial conditions. • is simpler to handle and less expensive. Owners can retain full ownership and control of the company. Too much debt, however, can impair the credit rating of the company, and if the company fails to pay, it may lose its assets and go bankrupt.	• is selling a part of your ownership as the source of funds by issuing stocks, and thus sharing the ownership interests with investors. • is safer as no pressure of regular repayment of the principal and interest. But it will dilute the ownership of the company and the original owners may even lose control of the company.

According to the basic accounting equation (refer to Chapter 9), debts plus equity equals assets. Therefore, debt and equity are both important sources of capital, and the mix of the two is called capital structure.

Debt Financing

> Long-term loans are often secured with fixed assets, and referred to as mortgage.

> Bonds are another typical example of debt financing; in nature, they are unsecured promissory notes, or OIUs.

Equity Financing

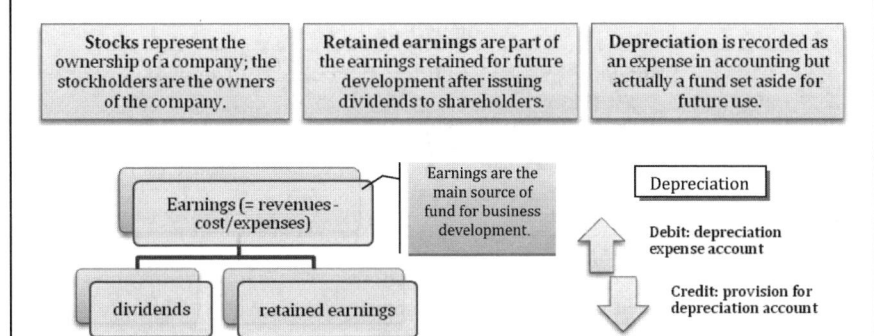

> Stocks represent the ownership of a company; the stockholders are the owners of the company.

> Retained earnings are part of the earnings retained for future development after issuing dividends to shareholders.

> Depreciation is recorded as an expense in accounting but actually a fund set aside for future use.

Earnings (= revenues - cost/expenses) → dividends, retained earnings

Earnings are the main source of fund for business development.

Depreciation
Debit: depreciation expense account
Credit: provision for depreciation account

Features of bonds

fixed: face value, interest rate, maturity date
fluctuating: selling price

As bonds carry fixed face value and interest rate, their earnings are fixed. Therefore, with the fluctuation of prevailing interest rate at the market, which represents investors' expectation for rate of return, the bonds prices will fluctuate.

> Prices of bonds fluctuate with the change of prevailing interest rate at the market in opposite direction.

An simplified solution (example):

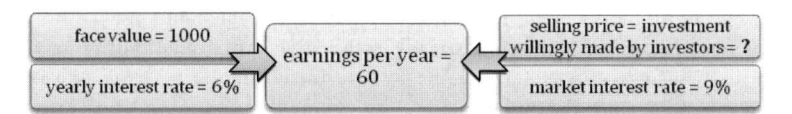

face value = 1000
yearly interest rate = 6%
earnings per year = 60
selling price = investment willingly made by investors = ?
market interest rate = 9%

As what pursued by the investors is the higher rate of return, the return rate of this bond mustn't be lower than 9% now. And if the return rate is higher than 9%, the demand will exceed the supply and thus force the price higher. Therefore, the equilibrium price of this bond is around 667 (= 60 ÷ 9%), when the return rate of this bond equals 9%.

Features of stocks

> Stock prices reflect the investors' sentiment about the current outlook of the company.

Stock prices are usually constantly moving. In addition to the company's fortunes, economic and world events can influence the prices of its shares.

As Investment

A Comparison

	Bonds	Preferred Stock	Common Stock
earnings	fixed payment (interest vs. dividend)		not fixed
payment rights	first payment over common stocks		last to be paid
voting rights	no voting rights		yes
callable	yes		no
maturity	fixed maturity	no maturity	
nature	debt	hybrid	equity
safety	the best	good	the least

Securities Market

Securities Market

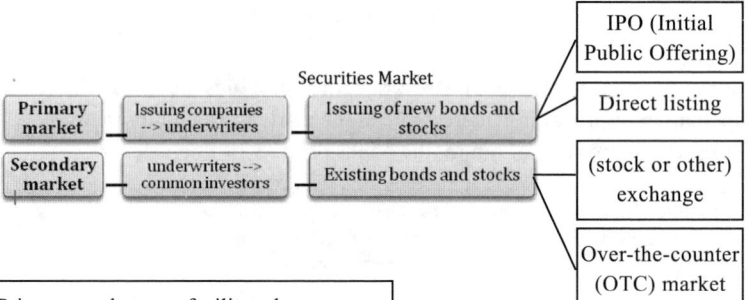

- Primary market: Issuing companies --> underwriters → Issuing of new bonds and stocks
- Secondary market: underwriters --> common investors → Existing bonds and stocks

- IPO (Initial Public Offering)
- Direct listing
- (stock or other) exchange
- Over-the-counter (OTC) market

Primary markets are facilitated by underwriting groups consisting of investment banks (or securities companies) that set a beginning price range for a given security and oversee its sale to investors. Once the initial sale is complete, further trading is conducted on the secondary market, where the bulk of exchange trading occurs each day.

The process of offering shares in a private corporation to the public for the first time is called an initial public offering (IPO). In an initial public offering, the issuer, or company raising capital, brings in underwriting firms or investment banks to help determine the best type of security to issue, offering price, amount of shares and time frame for the market offering.

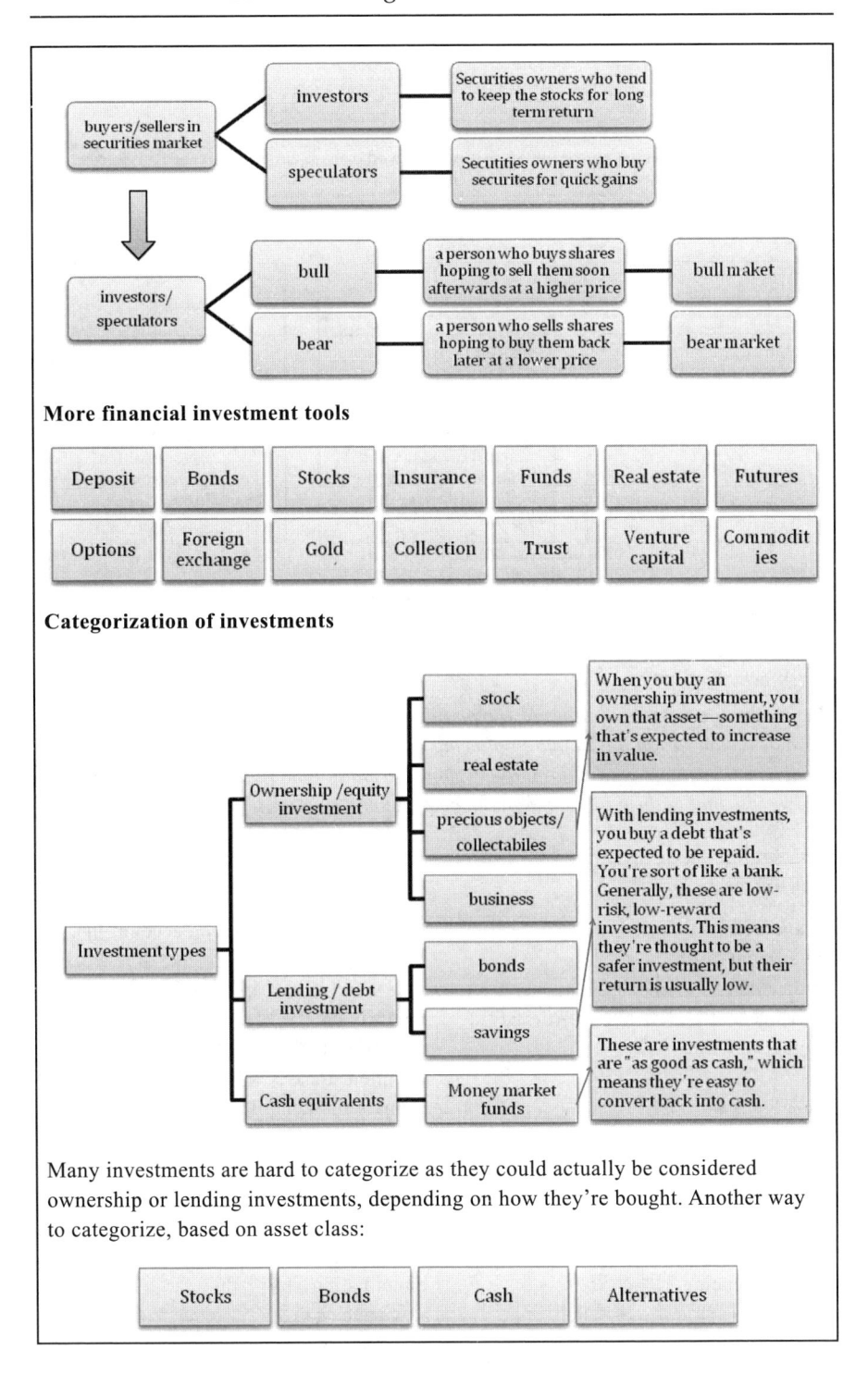

Part VI Dealing with Crisis and Risks

Buyers/sellers in securities market

- **investors**: Securities owners who tend to keep the stocks for long term return
- **speculators**: Secutities owners who buy securites for quick gains

Investors/speculators

- **bull**: a person who buys shares hoping to sell them soon afterwards at a higher price → **bull maket**
- **bear**: a person who sells shares hoping to buy them back later at a lower price → **bear market**

More financial investment tools

Deposit	Bonds	Stocks	Insurance	Funds	Real estate	Futures
Options	Foreign exchange	Gold	Collection	Trust	Venture capital	Commodities

Categorization of investments

Investment types

- **Ownership/equity investment**
  - stock
  - real estate
  - precious objects/collectabiles
  - business

  When you buy an ownership investment, you own that asset—something that's expected to increase in value.

- **Lending/debt investment**
  - bonds
  - savings

  With lending investments, you buy a debt that's expected to be repaid. You're sort of like a bank. Generally, these are low-risk, low-reward investments. This means they're thought to be a safer investment, but their return is usually low.

- **Cash equivalents**
  - Money market funds

  These are investments that are "as good as cash," which means they're easy to convert back into cash.

Many investments are hard to categorize as they could actually be considered ownership or lending investments, depending on how they're bought. Another way to categorize, based on asset class:

Stocks	Bonds	Cash	Alternatives

商务导论

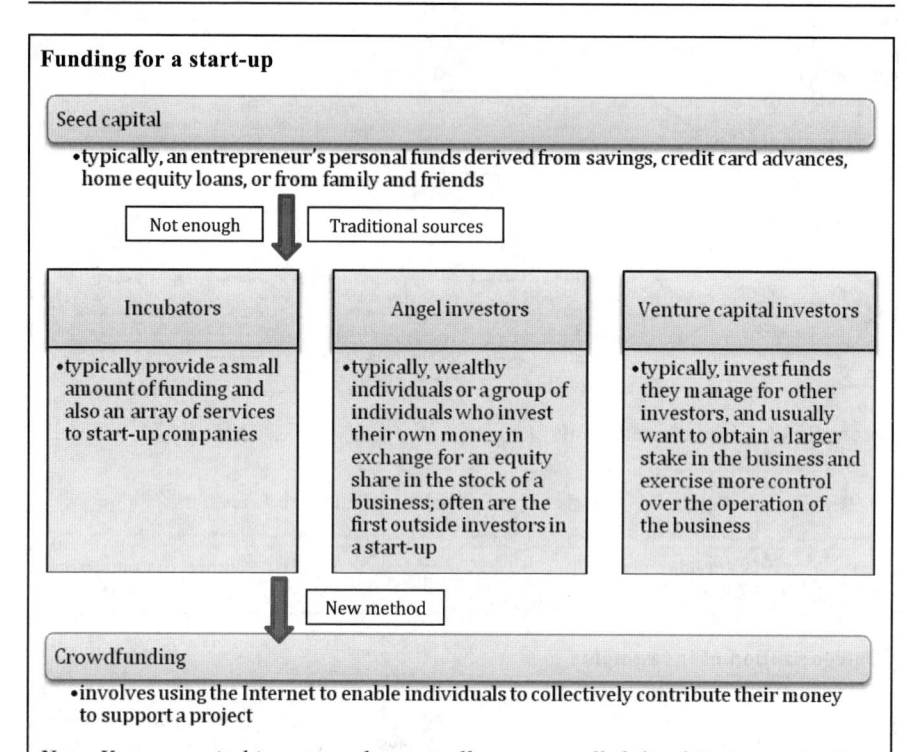

Funding for a start-up

Seed capital
- typically, an entrepreneur's personal funds derived from savings, credit card advances, home equity loans, or from family and friends

[Not enough] [Traditional sources]

Incubators
- typically provide a small amount of funding and also an array of services to start-up companies

Angel investors
- typically, wealthy individuals or a group of individuals who invest their own money in exchange for an equity share in the stock of a business; often are the first outside investors in a start-up

Venture capital investors
- typically, invest funds they manage for other investors, and usually want to obtain a larger stake in the business and exercise more control over the operation of the business

[New method]

Crowdfunding
- involves using the Internet to enable individuals to collectively contribute their money to support a project

Note: Venture capital investors also typically want a well-defined "exit strategy," such as a plan for an initial public offering or acquisition of the company by a more established business within a relatively short period of time (typically 3 to 7 years), which will enable them to obtain an adequate return on their investment.

Key Terms

financing 融资	provision for depreciation account 折旧准备账户
investment 投资	face value 票面价格（值）
trade credit 行业信用	maturity date 到期日
open account 往来账户；未结清账户	preferred stock 优先股
promissory note 本票	common stock 普通股
draft 汇票	primary market 一级市场
bank loans 银行贷款	secondary market 二级市场
secured loans 抵押贷款	underwriter 承销商
unsecured loans 无抵押贷款	investment bank 投资银行
commercial paper 商业票据	securities company 证券公司
factoring 贴现	IPO 首次公开募股
debt financing 债务融资	direct listing 直接上市
equity financing 股本融资	exchange 交易所
mortgage 抵押贷款；房屋抵押贷款	over-the-counter market 场外市场
bonds 债券	

Part VI Dealing with Crisis and Risks

stock 股票	speculator 投机者
retained earnings 留用利润	bull market 牛市
depreciation 折旧	bear market 熊市
debit 借方；借记	venture capital 风险投资
credit 贷方；贷记	seed capital 种子资本；原始资本
collateral 抵押物	incubator 孵化器
dividend 红利；股息	angel investor 天使投资人
depreciation expense account 折旧费账户	crowdfunding 众筹

在中国

IPO

中国IPO监管实行核准制，即对拟上市公司进行多方面的实质审核，这项工作主要由证监会发行审核委员会（下称发审委）负责。中国内地采用审批制，在内地IPO流程分为受理、反馈会、见面会、初审会、发审会、封卷、核准发行等主要环节。总体来看，整个审核流程充分反映了依法行政、公开透明、集体决策、分工制衡的要求。

而美国被普遍认为是注册制的代表性市场之一。什么是注册制？宽泛地讲，它要求拟上市公司按要求进行信息披露，而监管机构只负责监督其信息披露的充分真实性，而不对其信息内容做价值判断。而在核准制中，监管机构或交易所会根据拟上市公司提交的申请文件，对其是否适宜上市做出判断，然后批准或拒绝上市申请。

资本市场

在资本市场上，不同的投资者与融资者都有不同的规模大小与主体特征，存在着对资本市场金融服务的不同需求。投资者与融资者对投融资金融服务的多样化需求决定了资本市场应该是一个多层次的市场经济体系。

我国资本市场从20世纪90年代发展至今，已由场内市场和场外市场两部分构成。其中场内市场的主板（含中小板）、创业板（俗称二板）和场外市场的全国中小企业股份转让系统（俗称新三板）、区域性股权交易市场、证券公司主导的柜台市场共同组成了我国多层次资本市场体系（见图示）。

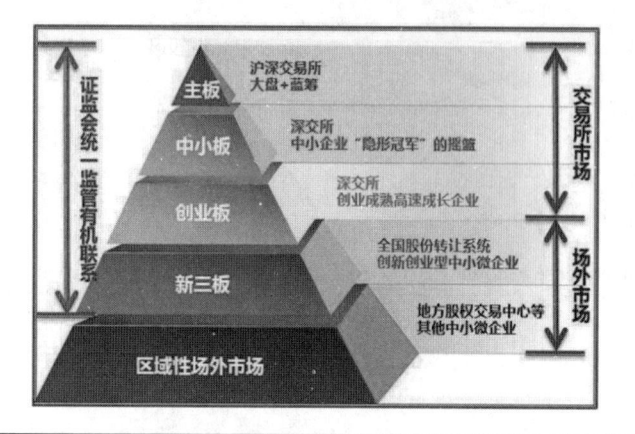

> **Brainstorming**
>
> What are possible motives of financing and investment?
> Read recent news about securities market and analyze with knowledge in this chapter.
> Talk about risks in investment with examples from personal experience or from news.

Read More

Small Business Financing: Debt Or Equity?

Small businesses often need money. This is especially true for companies in the beginning stages of development. Finding that money can be difficult, tighter lending standards and venture capitalists still recovering from the recessionary fallout are producing an environment in which funding is a challenge. There are two basic types of funding available to small businesses-debt financing and equity financing. As a small business owner, which is best for you?

Debt Financing

Purchasing a home, a car or using a credit card are all forms of debt financing. You are taking a loan from a person or business and making a pledge to pay it back with interest. Debt financing for your business works in a similar way. As a business owner, you can apply for a business loan from a bank or receive a personal loan from friends, family or other lenders, all of which you must pay back. Even if family members lend you money for your business, they must charge the minimum IRS interest rate in order to avoid the gift tax.

The advantages of debt financing are numerous. First, the lender has no control over your business. Once you pay the loan back, your relationship with the financier ends. Next, the interest you pay is tax deductible. Finally, it is easy to forecast expenses because loan payments do not fluctuate.

The downside to debt financing is very real to anybody who has debt. Debt is a bet on your future ability to pay back the loan. What if your company hits hard times or the economy, once again, experiences a meltdown? What if your business does not grow as fast or as well as you expected? Debt is an expense and you have to pay expenses on a regular schedule. This could put a damper on your company's ability to grow.

Finally, although you may be an LLC or other business entity that provides some separation between company and personal funds, the lender may still require you to guarantee the loan with your family's financial assets.

If you think debt financing is right for you, the U.S. Small Business Administration works with select banks to offer a guaranteed loan program that makes it easier for small businesses to secure funding.

Equity Financing

The public does not understand equity financing as well as debt financing, because equity financing involves investors. You could offer shares of your company to family, friends and other small investors, but equity financing often involves venture capitalists or angel investors. The popular ABC series, "Shark Tank," highlights entrepreneurs who present their business ideas to a group of investors in an attempt to secure equity financing.

The big advantage of equity financing is that the investor takes all of the risk. If your company fails, you do not have to pay the money back. You will also have more cash available because there are no loan payments. Finally, investors take a long-term view and understand that growing a business takes time.

The downside is large. In order to gain the funding, you will have to give the investor a percentage of your company. You will have to share your profits and consult with your new partners any time you make decisions affecting the company.

The only way to remove investors is to buy them out, but that will likely be more expensive than the money they originally gave you.

Which Funding Method Should I Choose?

Often you will not have a choice. Formal equity financing is difficult to secure especially for small, early-stage startups. Venture capitalists are looking for companies with global reach. Angel investors, those who fund on a smaller scale, are often looking to invest a minimum of $300,000 and possibly a 50% stake in the company, especially if it is in the very beginning stages, according to an article released by Entrepreneur.com. If your company is a startup serving a local market and does not need large-scale funding, debt financing is probably your best, and perhaps only, option.

Larger startups often combine debt and equity financing to reduce the downside of both types.

The Bottom Line

The type of financing you seek depends largely on your startup. If you are just getting started, consider a loan from family, friends or a bank.

As you grow and reach a larger market, equity funding may become a more viable option if you are willing to give up a portion of your company.

(747)

https://www.investopedia.com/financial-edge/1112/small-business-financing-debt-or-equity.aspx

What Is Stock Market Leverage?

A brokerage firm can deny an extension of time to fulfill a margin call.

More Articles

1. How to Borrow Against Your Investments
2. What Is Margin Equity?
3. What Are the Benefits of Portfolio Margin Accounts?

Leverage is often spoken of concerning the real estate market, but stock market leveraging is a practice often used by investors. The basic concept of leverage in the stock market, also called margin trading, involves borrowing capital to invest in more stock than what you can afford on your own. Stock market leverage can result in an increase in your return on investment, but you can lose more money than when buying stock using only your funds.

How Trading on Margin Works

Trading stock using margin starts with opening a margin account with your brokerage firm. This type of account differs from a regular cash account that you open with a financial institution. You must pay a deposit that acts as your margin, or initial equity in the account. Brokerage firms typically require an initial deposit of at least $2,000. In most cases, you can borrow up to 50 percent of your margin to invest in financial securities. You must also pay interest and fees for borrowing money.

SEC Requirements

After the purchase of the stock, you must keep a minimum amount of equity in your margin account. According to the Securities and Exchange Commission, you must maintain at least 25 percent of the value of your purchased equities in your margin account at all times. If the value of your securities drops substantially, the brokerage firm can issue a margin call, requiring that you repay all or a portion of your loan.

Rules

According to the Securities and Exchange Commission, the Federal Reserve Board, FINRA, the New York Stock Exchange and other self-regulatory exchanges determine the specific rules established to govern stock market leverage. Brokerage firms often establish their own rules regarding margin accounts. In the case of a margin call, the brokerage firm does not need your permission to sell a portion of the financial securities in your account. You also do not get to decide which assets the firm sells.

Potential

Stock market leverage offers investors the potential to earn a higher return on their investment because they are able to buy more shares than with using their own money alone. For example, if you buy a share of stock priced at $100 using your own money and the price increases to $150, you earn a 50 percent return on your investment. In contrast, if you use stock market leverage and buy the same stock on margin using $50 of your own money and borrow the other $50, your return is 100 percent if the stock price increases to $150.

Risk

The primary risk associated with margin trading is the ability to lose a substantial amount of money in a short period of time. The fact that you borrowed money to invest in stock results in the possibility of losing more money than you personally put up to buy shares. The sale of assets in your account by the brokerage firm can result in additional losses. Understanding the margin agreement given to you by your broker and the rules of margin trading can help minimize risk.

(551)

https://finance.zacks.com/stock-market-leverage-5622.html

Part VI Dealing with Crisis and Risks

Chapter 13 Risk Management

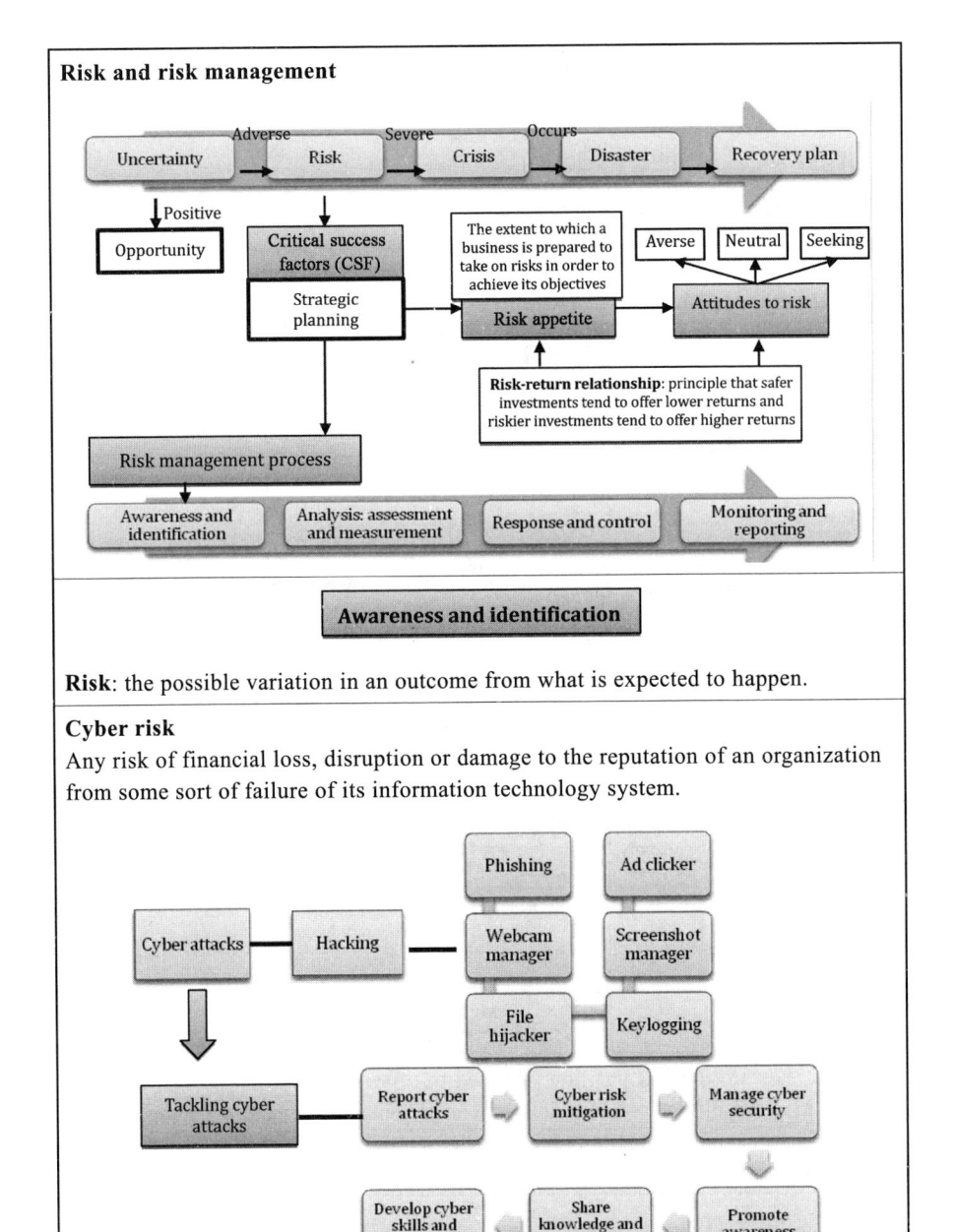

Risk and risk management

Uncertainty —Adverse→ Risk —Severe→ Crisis —Occurs→ Disaster → Recovery plan

↓ Positive
Opportunity

Critical success factors (CSF)
Strategic planning

Risk appetite: The extent to which a business is prepared to take on risks in order to achieve its objectives

Attitudes to risk: Averse | Neutral | Seeking

Risk-return relationship: principle that safer investments tend to offer lower returns and riskier investments tend to offer higher returns

Risk management process
- Awareness and identification
- Analysis: assessment and measurement
- Response and control
- Monitoring and reporting

Awareness and identification

Risk: the possible variation in an outcome from what is expected to happen.

Cyber risk
Any risk of financial loss, disruption or damage to the reputation of an organization from some sort of failure of its information technology system.

Cyber attacks — Hacking
- Phishing
- Ad clicker
- Webcam manager
- Screenshot manager
- File hijacker
- Keylogging

Tackling cyber attacks:
Report cyber attacks ⇒ Cyber risk mitigation ⇒ Manage cyber security
Develop cyber skills and awareness ⇐ Share knowledge and expertise ⇐ Promote awareness

Analysis: assessment and measurement

To measure the severity of the risk a business is facing in terms of exposure, volatility, impact and probability.

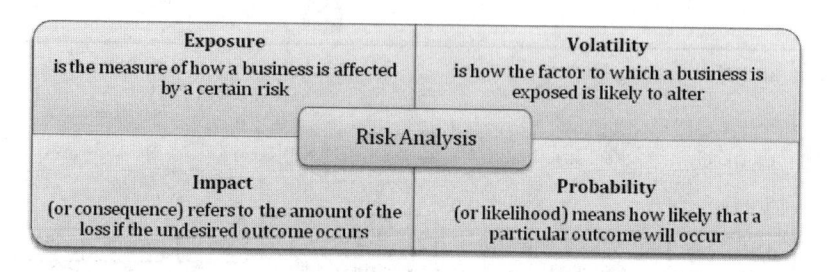

Risk Analysis

- **Exposure**: is the measure of how a business is affected by a certain risk
- **Volatility**: is how the factor to which a business is exposed is likely to alter
- **Impact** (or consequence): refers to the amount of the loss if the undesired outcome occurs
- **Probability** (or likelihood): means how likely that a particular outcome will occur

Gross risk = probability × Impact

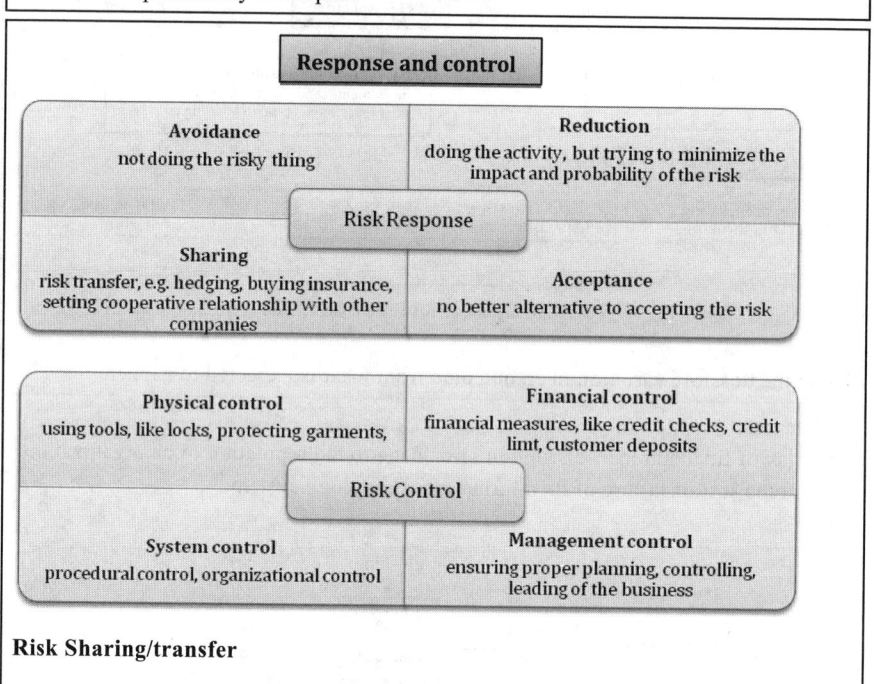

Response and control

Risk Response

- **Avoidance**: not doing the risky thing
- **Reduction**: doing the activity, but trying to minimize the impact and probability of the risk
- **Sharing**: risk transfer, e.g. hedging, buying insurance, setting cooperative relationship with other companies
- **Acceptance**: no better alternative to accepting the risk

Risk Control

- **Physical control**: using tools, like locks, protecting garments,
- **Financial control**: financial measures, like credit checks, credit limit, customer deposits
- **System control**: procedural control, organizational control
- **Management control**: ensuring proper planning, controlling, leading of the business

Risk Sharing/transfer

Hedging

A hedge is an investment position intended to offset potential losses or gains that may be incurred by a companion investment. In simple language, a hedge is a risk management technique used to reduce any substantial losses or gains suffered by an individual or an organization.

Part VI Dealing with Crisis and Risks

A hedge can be constructed from many types of financial instruments, including stocks, exchange-traded funds, insurance, forward contracts, swaps, options, gambles, many types of over-the-counter and derivative products, and futures contracts.

Insurance

Insurance is a risk-sharing mechanism whereby the insured pays a premium to an insurance company, who in return issues a policy, a formal agreement to pay the policyholder a specified amount in the event of losses.

Key Terms	
risk management 风险管理 uncertainty 不确定 risk 风险 crisis 危机 disaster 灾难 recovery plan（风险）补偿计划 critical success factors 关键成功要素 strategic planning 战略规划 risk appetite 风险偏好 risk-return relationship 风险回报关系 business risk 商业风险 strategy risk 战略风险 enterprise risk 企业风险 product risk 产品风险 financial risk 财务风险 operation risk 经营风险 process risk 过程风险 people risk 人员风险 system risk 系统风险 event risk 事件风险 disaster risk 灾难风险 regulatory risk 监管风险 reputation risk 声誉风险 systemic risk 系统性风险 cyber risk 网络风险 cyber attack 网络攻击 hacking 黑客 phishing 网络钓鱼 webcam 网络摄像头 file hijacker 文件黑客	risk volatility 风险波动 risk probability 风险概率 risk avoidance 风险规避 risk reduction 风险降低 risk sharing 风险分摊 risk acceptance 风险接受 hedge 套期保值 insurance 保险 insurable risk 可保风险 utmost good faith 最大诚信原则 indemnity 损失补偿原则 contribution 损失分摊 subrogation 担保取代 proximate 近因原则 property insurance 财产保险 liability insurance 责任保险 general liability 一般责任 life insurance 生命保险；寿险 term life insurance 定期寿险 straight life insurance 终身寿险 limited payment life insurance 有限缴费期限终身寿险 endowment life insurance 两全寿险；储蓄型寿险 health insurance 健康险 casualty insurance 意外险 critical illness 重大疾病 medical expense 医疗费 directors and officers liability insurance 公司董事及高级职员责任险

ad clicker 文件劫持者 keylogging 键盘侧录 risk exposure 风险暴露；风险敞口 risk impact 风险影响	employer's liability insurance 雇主责任险 key person insurance 关键人物险 group health/life insurance 集团健康险/寿险 credit insurance 信用保险 fidelity and surety bonds 忠实险和履约保证保险

在中国

五险一金（Insurance）

企业购买的保险包括政府强制要求购买的保险和企业自愿购买的保险。政府强制性保险各个国家要求的不同。在中国，政府规定的强制性保险、福利主要是五险一金，即养老保险、医疗保险、失业保险、工伤保险、生育保险及住房公积金。其中，工伤保险和生育保险是由用人单位完全缴纳的，剩余的三险一金（或四金）是由单位和个人共同缴纳的，是政府强制要求单位和个人购买的基本保险。

Brainstorming
Analyze your own risk appetite. How to understand the cost and benefit of buying insurance? Should business firms buy insurance for employees?

Read More

How to do a risk assessment: A case study

There's no shortage of consultants and authors to tell boards and senior leaders that risk assessment is something that should be done. Everyone knows that. But in the chronically short-staffed world of the charitable sector, who has time to do it well? It's too easy to cross your fingers and hope disaster won't happen to you!

If that's you crossing your fingers, the good news is that risk assessment isn't as complicated as it sounds, so don't be intimidated by it. It doesn't have to take a lot of time, and you can easily prioritize the risks and attack them a few at a time. I recently did a risk assessment for CCCC and the process of creating it was quite manageable while also being very thorough.

I'll share my experience of creating a risk assessment so you can see

Part VI Dealing with Crisis and Risks

how easy it is to do.

Step 1: Identify Risks

The first step is obvious—identify the risks you face. The trick is how you identify those risks. On your own, you might get locked into one way of thinking about risk, such as people suing you, so you become fixated on legal risk. But what about technological risks or funding risks or any other kind of risks?

I found a helpful way to identify the full range of risks is to address risk from three perspectives:

Mission Success—everything you do to fulfill your organizational purpose. Documents such as a Theory of Change or a Logic Model, a Strategy Map or a Strategic Plan, and a list of your programs, can help you think through your mission-related risk in an orderly way. You'll cover everything from risks dealing with vulnerable people and staff security on the front lines to foreign governments closing access to their countries and governance issues in your own ministry.

Two of the mission-related risks we identified at CCCC were 1) if we gave wrong information that a member relied upon to their detriment; and 2) if a Certified member had a public scandal.

Organizational Health—everything related to the sustainability of your ministry's health and viability over the longer term. Think in terms of financial, human, and physical resources, your operating (business) model, and organizational structure.

We listed several risks to organization health for CCCC. Among them were 1) a disaster that would shut down our operations at least temporarily, and 2) a major loss from an innovation that did not work.

Environmental—everything that is happening outside your organization that could affect either your mission success or organizational health. This includes a scan of the social, political, economic and other environments in which you operate.

We identified a risk related to the sociopolitical environment.

I began the risk assessment by reviewing CCCC from these three perspectives on my own. I scanned our theory of change, our strategy map, and our programs to identify potential risks. I then reviewed everything we had that related to organizational health, which included our Vision

2020 document (written to proactively address organizational health over the next five years), financial trends, a consultant's report on a member survey, and a review of our operations by an expert in Canadian associations. I also thought about our experience over the past few years and conversations I've had with people. Finally, I went over everything we know about our environments and did some Internet research to see what else was being said that might affect us.

With all of this information, I then answered questions such as the following:

What assumptions have I made about current or future conditions?

How valid are the assumptions?

What are my nightmare scenarios?

What do I avoid thinking about or just hope never happens?

What have I heard that went wrong with other organizations like ours?

What am I confident will never happen to us? Hubris is the downfall of many!

What is becoming more scarce or difficult for us?

At this point, I created a draft list of about ten major risks and distributed it to my leadership team for discussion. At that meeting we added three additional risks. Since the board had asked for a report from staff for them to review and discuss at the next board meeting, we did not involve them at this point.

Step 2: Probability/Impact Assessment

Once you have the risks identified, you need to assess how significant they are in order to prioritize how you deal with them. Risks are rated on two factors:

How likely they are to happen? (That is, their Probability)

How much of an effect could they have on your ministry?(Their anticipated Impact)

Each of these two factors can be rated High, Medium, or Low. Here's how I define those categories:

Probability

High: The risk either occurs regularly (such as hurricanes in Florida) or something specific is brewing and becoming more significant over time, such that it could affect your ministry in the next few years.

Part VI Dealing with Crisis and Risks

Medium: The risk happens from time to time each year, and someone will suffer from it (such as a fire or a burglary). You may have an elevated risk of suffering the problem or you might have just a general risk, such as everyone else has. There may also be a general trend that is not a particular problem at present but it could affect you over the longer term.

Low: It's possible that it could happen, but it rarely does. The risk is largely hypothetical.

Impact

High: If the risk happened, it would be a critical life or death situation for the ministry. At the least, if you survive it would change the future of the ministry and at its worst, the ministry may not be able to recover from the damage and closure would be the only option.

Medium: The risk would create a desperate situation requiring possibly radical solutions, but there would be a reasonable chance of recovering from the effects of the risk without long term damage.

Low: The risk would cause an unwelcome interruption of normal activity, but the damage could be overcome with fairly routine responses. There would be no question of what to do, and it would just be a matter of doing it.

I discussed my assessments of the risks with staff and then listed them in the agreed-upon priority order in six Probability/Impact combinations:

High/High – 2 risks
High/Medium – 1 risk
Medium/High – 2 risks
Medium/Medium – 3 risks
Low/High – 3 risks
Low/Medium – 2 risks

I felt that the combinations High/Low, Medium/Low, and Low/Low weren't significant enough to include in the assessment. The point of prioritizing is to help you be a good steward as you allocate time and money to address the significant risks. With only thirteen risks, CCCC can address them all, but we know which ones need attention most urgently.

Step 3: Manage Risk

After you have assessed the risks your ministry faces (steps 1 and 2), you arrive at the point where you can start managing the risks. The options for managing boil down to three strategies:

Prevent: The risk might be avoided by changing how you do things. It may mean purchasing additional equipment or redesigning a program. In most cases, though, you probably won't actually be able to prevent the risk from ever happening. More likely you will only be able to mitigate the risk.

Mitigate: Mitigate means to make less severe, serious, or painful. There are two ways to mitigate risk: 1) find ways to make it less likely to happen; and 2) lessen the impact of the risk if it happens. Finding ways to mitigate risk and then implementing the plan will take up most of the time you spend on risk assessment and management. This is where you need to think creatively about possible strategies and action steps. You will also document the mitigating steps you have already taken.

Transfer or Eliminate: If you can't prevent the risk from happening or mitigate the likelihood or impact of the risk, you are left with either transferring the risk to someone else (such as by purchasing insurance) or getting rid of whatever is causing the risk so that the risk is no longer applicable. For example, a church with a rock climbing wall might purchase insurance to cover the risk or it might simply take the wall down so that the risk no longer exists.

Step 4: Final Assessment

Armed with all this information, it's time to prepare a risk report for final review by management and then the board. I've included a download in this post to help you write the report. It is a template document with an executive summary and then a detailed report. They are partially filled out so you can see how it is used.

After preparing your report, review it and consider whether or not the mitigating steps and recommendations are sufficient. Do you really want to eliminate some aspect of your ministry to avoid risk? Do you believe that whatever action has been recommended is satisfactory and in keeping with the ministry's mission and values? Are there any other ways to get the same goal achieved or purpose fulfilled without attracting risk?

Finally, after all the risk assessment and risk management work has been done, the ministry is left with two choices:

Accept whatever risk is left and get on with the ministry's work.

Reject the remaining risk and eliminate it by getting rid of the source of the risk.

Step 5: Ongoing Risk Management

On a regular basis, in keeping with the type of risk and its threat, the risk assessment and risk management plan should be reviewed to see if it is still valid. Have circumstances changed? Are the plans working? Review the plan and adjust as necessary.

Key Thought: You have to deal with risk to be a good steward, and it is not hard to do.

(1650)

Part VII Doing Business Globally

Chapter 14 Intercultural Communication

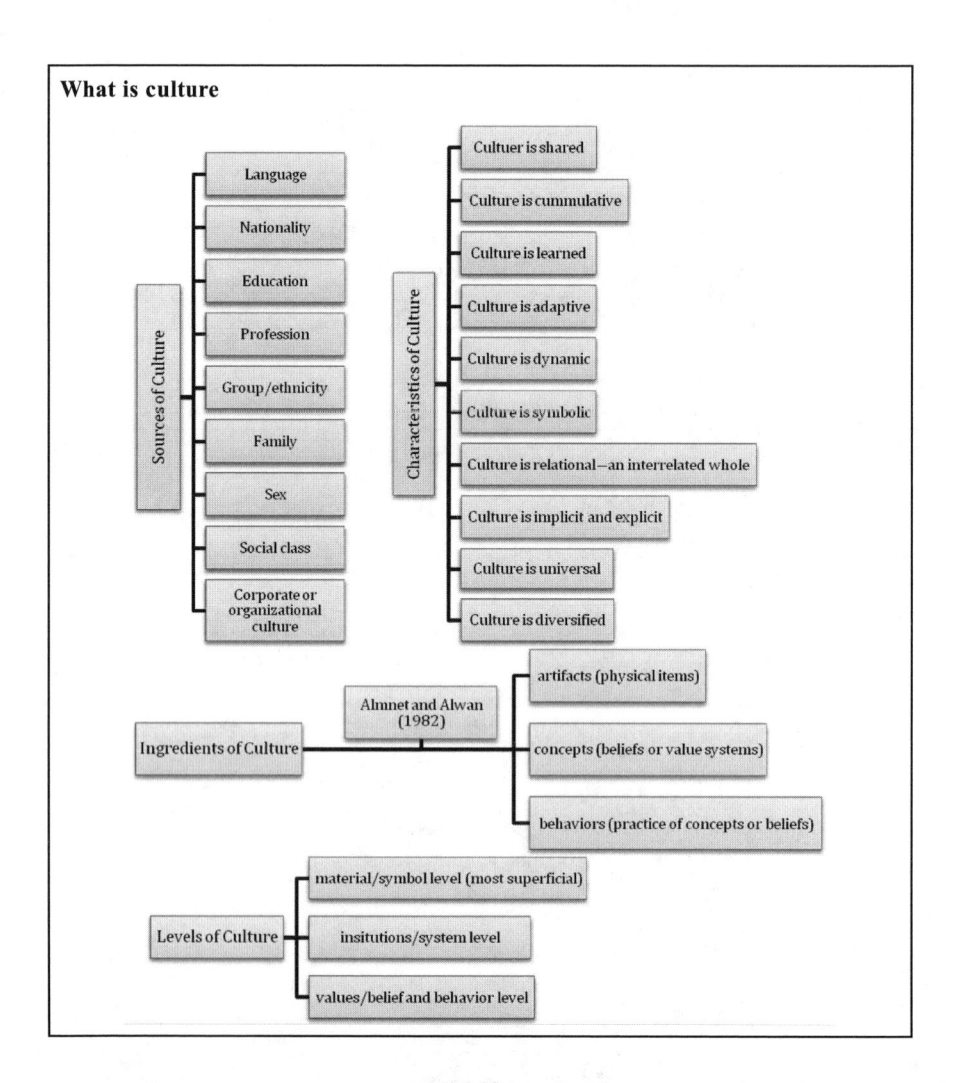

What is culture

Sources of Culture
- Language
- Nationality
- Education
- Profession
- Group/ethnicity
- Family
- Sex
- Social class
- Corporate or organizational culture

Characteristics of Culture
- Cultuer is shared
- Culture is cummulative
- Culture is learned
- Culture is adaptive
- Culture is dynamic
- Culture is symbolic
- Culture is relational—an interrelated whole
- Culture is implicit and explicit
- Culture is universal
- Culture is diversified

Ingredients of Culture — Almnet and Alwan (1982)
- artifacts (physical items)
- concepts (beliefs or value systems)
- behaviors (practice of concepts or beliefs)

Levels of Culture
- material/symbol level (most superficial)
- insitutions/system level
- values/belief and behavior level

· 148 ·

Intercultural Theories

- Intercultural Theories
  - Kluckhohn and Strodtbeck's Value Orientation and Basic Values
  - Hofstede-bond Value Dimensions
  - Hall's High-and Low-Context Orientation
  - Hall's Monochronic vs. Polychronic Culture
  - Trompenaars and Hampden-Turner's Cultural Factors
  - Triandis' Individualism and Collectivism

Kluckhohn and Strodtbeck's Value Orientation and Basic Values

Orientation	Basic Values		
Human nature	Basically evil	Mixture	Basically good
Relationship to nature	Subordinate to nature/ Nature controls human	Harmony with nature	Dominant over nature/ Humans control nature
Sense of time	Past-oriented	Present-oriented	Future-oriented
Activity	Being—who you are	Growing—becoming	Doing—what you're doing
Social relationships	Hierarchy	Group	Individual

Hofstede-bond Value Dimensions

Dimension	Basic Value
Power distance	Power is distributed unequally in situations and organizations.
Individualism/ collectivism	Individualism means everyone centers on individual interest, such as his own or his family. Collectivism focuses on the common interest of a group.
Masculinity/Femininity	Masculinity refers to a clear distinction between social roles played by men and women. Femininity does not distinguish social roles so distinctly.
Uncertainty Avoidance	Different cultures will differ from each other in the avoidance of uncertain situations.
Long-term/short-term orientation	Long-term orientation looks into the future. Short-term orientation stresses past and present.

Hall's High-and Low-Context Orientation

Low Context	High Context
Tends to prefer direct verbal interaction	Tends to prefer indirect verbal interaction
Tends to understand meaning at one level only	Tends to understand meanings embedded at many socio-cultural levels
Is generally less proficient in reading nonverbal cues	Is generally more proficient in reading nonverbal cues
Values individualism	Values group membership
Relies more on logic	Relies more on context and feeling
Employs linear logic	Employs spiral logic
Says "no" directly	Talks around point, avoids saying "no"
Communicates in highly structured messages, provides details, stresses literal meanings, gives authority to written information	Communicates in simple, ambiguous, noncontexted messages; understands visual messages readily

Hall's Monochronic vs. Polychronic Culture

Monochronic people	Polychronic people
Do one thing at a time	Do many things at once
Concentrate on the job	Are highly distractible and subject to interruptions
Take time commitments seriously	Consider time commitments an objective to be achieved, if possible
Are low-context and need information	Are high-context and already have information
Are committed to the job	Are committed to people and human relationship
Adhere religiously to plans	Change plan often and easily
Are concerned about not disturbing others; follow rules of privacy and consideration	Are more concerned with those who are closely related than with privacy
Show great respect for private property; seldom borrow or lend	Borrow and lend things often and easily
Emphasize promptness	Base promptness on the relationship
Are accustomed to short-term relationships	Have strong tendency to build lifetime relationships

Trompenaars and Hampden-Turner's Cultural Factors

Orientation	Basic Value
Universalism vs. Particularism	attaches great importance to rules means finding exceptions; modifications are allowed
Neutral vs. Emotional	emotions will not show too much emotions are overt and naturally shown
Communitarianism vs. Individualism	collectivism, emphases rights of the group or society concerned with rights of individuals
Inner-directed vs. Outer-directed	emphasizes thinking and personal judgement seeks data or information in the outer world
Time as sequence vs. Time as synchronization	one activity at a time, one after another several activities at the same time
Achieved status vs. Ascribed status	gaining status or rewards through performance relies more on seniority; status is acquired by right
Specific vs. Diffuse	a larger public space (compared with private space) to let others in; direct and extroverted public and private space are similar in size, guarded carefully; indirect and introverted

Triandis' Individualism and Collectivism

Individualism	Collectivism
Independence and individual achievement	Interdependence and group success
Self-expression, individual thinking and personal choice	Norms, authority/elders, group consensus
Egalitarian relationships and flexibility in roles	Stable, hierarchical roles
Private property, individual ownership	Shared property, group ownership
Understands the physical world apart from human life	Understands the physical world in the context of its meaning for human life

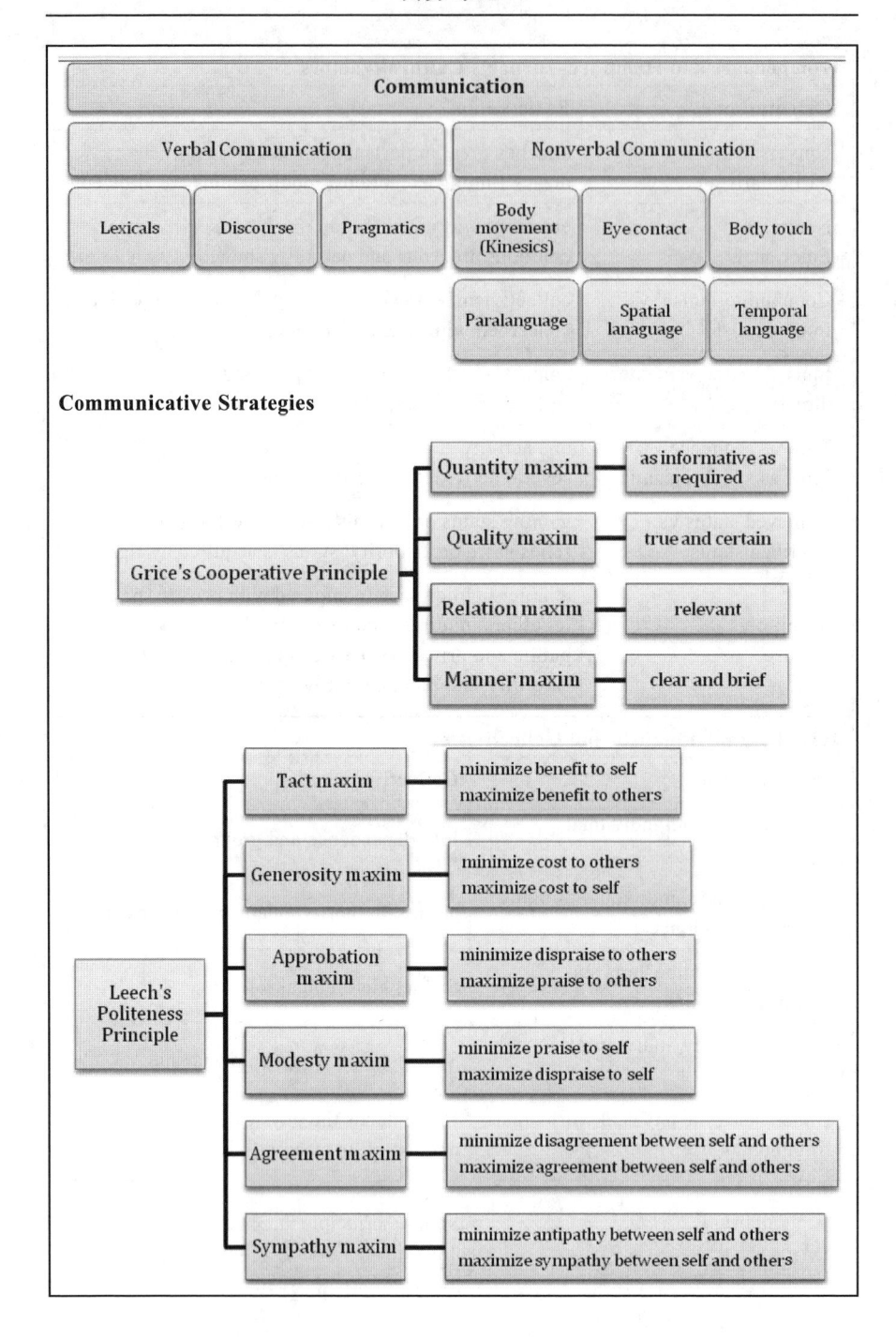

Communication

- **Verbal Communication**
  - Lexicals
  - Discourse
  - Pragmatics
- **Nonverbal Communication**
  - Body movement (Kinesics)
  - Eye contact
  - Body touch
  - Paralanguage
  - Spatial lanaguage
  - Temporal language

Communicative Strategies

- **Grice's Cooperative Principle**
  - Quantity maxim — as informative as required
  - Quality maxim — true and certain
  - Relation maxim — relevant
  - Manner maxim — clear and brief

- **Leech's Politeness Principle**
  - Tact maxim — minimize benefit to self / maximize benefit to others
  - Generosity maxim — minimize cost to others / maximize cost to self
  - Approbation maxim — minimize dispraise to others / maximize praise to others
  - Modesty maxim — minimize praise to self / maximize dispraise to self
  - Agreement maxim — minimize disagreement between self and others / maximize agreement between self and others
  - Sympathy maxim — minimize antipathy between self and others / maximize sympathy between self and others

Part VII Doing Business Globally

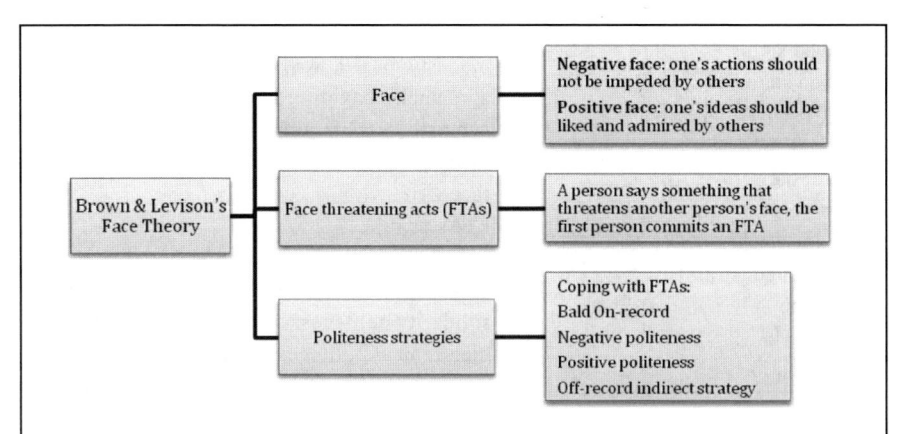

```
Brown & Levison's Face Theory
├── Face
│   ├── Negative face: one's actions should not be impeded by others
│   └── Positive face: one's ideas should be liked and admired by others
├── Face threatening acts (FTAs)
│   └── A person says something that threatens another person's face, the first person commits an FTA
└── Politeness strategies
    └── Coping with FTAs:
        Bald On-record
        Negative politeness
        Positive politeness
        Off-record indirect strategy
```

Face refers to fundamental cultural ideas about the nature of the social persona, honor and virtue, shame and redemption and how these are expressed, protected and threatened in social interaction.

Key Terms

corporate/organizational culture 企业／组织文化	ethnocentrism 民族优越感
artifacts 物品	culture shock 文化冲击
concepts 观念	taboo 禁忌语
behaviors 行为	personal attributes 个人特征
value orientation 价值取向	communication skills 沟通技巧
value dimension 价值维度	psychological adaptation 心理适应
power distance 权力距离	cultural awareness 文化意识
individualism 个人主义	verbal communication 言语沟通
collectivism 集体主义	nonverbal communication 非言语沟通
masculinity 阳性文化	lexical 词汇
femininity 阴性文化	discourse 话语
uncertainty avoidance 不确定性规避	pragmatics 语用
long-term/short-term orientation 远／近期导向	kinesics 身势语
	paralanguage 副语言
low context 低语境	spatial language 空间语言
high context 高语境	temporal language 时间语言
monochronic 单一时间模式的	cooperative principle 合作原则
polychronic 多元时间模式的	quantity maxim 数量最大化；量准则
universalism 普遍主义；普世主义	quality maxim 质量最大化；质准则
particularism 特殊主义；个别主义	relation maxim 关系最大化；关系准则
communitarianism 社群主义	manner maxim 方式准则
inner-directed 内部指向的	politeness principle 礼貌原则
outer-directed 外部指向的	tact maxim 得体准则
synchronization 同步；同时性	generosity maxim 慷慨准则
	approbation maxim 赞扬准则

achieved status 获得身份 ascribed status 赋予身份 specific 专门空间 diffuse 扩散空间 cultural barriers 文化障碍 cognitive constraints 认知限制 behavior constraints 行为限制 emotional constraints 情绪限制 stereotype 成见；定式化思维 prejudice 偏见 discrimination 歧视	modesty maxim 谦逊准则 agreement maxim 一致准则；赞同准则 sympathy maxim 共情准则 face theory 面子理论 face 面子 FTAs 面子威胁行为 politeness strategies 礼貌策略 deference politeness system 顺从礼貌体系 solidarity politeness system 团结礼貌体系 hierarchical politeness system 等级礼貌体系

在中国

西方交际理论中的 face theory 来源于中国文化中的"面子"观，中国人爱面子是根深蒂固的文化传统。我们有很多关于"面子"的表达，如"丢面子""给面子""争面子"，有时候也可以用"脸"，如"丢脸""不要脸"，都反映了中国人的面子观。"面子"和"脸"的影响之深，在英文中经常直接用拼音译为"mianzi"和"lian"。

Brainstorming

Cite examples at different levels to demonstrate Chinese culture.
Compare Chinese culture with that of another country with the theories mentioned in this chapter.
Compare the difference between western "face" with Chinese "mianzi".

Read More

Cultural differences in business—are you aware of them?

A key to being successful in business internationally is to understand the role of culture in international business. Whatever sector you are operating in, cultural differences will have a direct impact on your profitability. Improving your level of knowledge of international cultural difference in business can aid in building international competencies as well as enabling you to gain a competitive advantage.

However, on one hand, where it is important to be aware of cultural differences of different countries, on the other hand, it is also hard to be aware of every single aspect of each country's organisational culture.

Therefore, you should be aware of the key factors that have a direct impact on business. These are:

Communication is the key to success for any business, whether you are operating nationally or internationally, but when operating internationally it becomes even more important due to language barriers.

Being aware of basic customer needs is an important aspect as this will give the advantage of conveying your message. In simple terms, if you are aware of the customer's cultural background, then you will be able to adopt better and more suitable advertising methods.

Body language is another key factor in cultural difference. As different countries have different ways to convey or share their message, for instance, in Germany people tend to speak loudly when sharing ideas, whereas in Japan people speak softly, it is very important to know what your body language should be when interacting with people whether it's your business partner or an interviewer.

Before launching a marketing campaign, always conduct research to become aware of your target audience since customer demand, decision making, gender views and ideologies greatly vary in cultures.

(290)

https://businessculture.org/business-culture/cultural-differences-in-business/

How cultural differences impact international business

As companies continue to expand across borders and the global marketplace becomes increasingly more accessible for small and large businesses alike, 2017 brings ever more opportunities to work internationally.

Multinational and cross-cultural teams are likewise becoming ever more common, meaning businesses can benefit from an increasingly diverse knowledge base and new, insightful approaches to business problems. However, along with the benefits of insight and expertise, global organizations also face potential stumbling blocks when it comes to culture and international business.

While there are a number of ways to define culture, put simply it is a set of common and accepted norms shared by a society. But in an international business context, what is common and accepted for a professional from one country, could be very different for a colleague from overseas. Recognizing and understanding how culture affects international business in three core areas: communication, etiquette, and organizational hierarchy can help you to avoid misunderstandings with colleagues and clients from abroad and excel in a globalized business environment.

1. Communication

Effective communication is essential to the success of any business venture, but it is particularly critical when there is a real risk of your message getting "lost in translation". In many international companies, English is the de facto language of business. But more than just the language you speak, it's how you convey your message that's important. For instance, while the Finns may value directness and brevity, professionals from India can be more indirect and nuanced in their communication. Moreover, while fluent English might give you a professional boost globally, understanding the importance of subtle non-verbal communication between cultures can be equally crucial in international business.

What might be commonplace in your culture—be it a firm handshake, making direct eye contact, or kiss on the cheek—could be unusual or even offensive to a foreign colleague or client. Where possible, do your research in advance of professional interactions with individuals from a different culture. Remember to be perceptive to body language, and when in doubt, ask. While navigating cross-cultural communication can be a challenge, approaching cultural differences with sensitivity, openness, and curiosity can help to put everyone at ease.

2. Workplace etiquette

Different approaches to professional communication are just one of the innumerable differences in workplace norms from around the world. CT Business Travel has put together a useful infographic for a quick reference of cultural differences in business etiquette globally.

For instance, the formality of address is a big consideration when dealing with colleagues and business partners from different countries. Do they prefer titles and surnames or is being on the first-name basis acceptable? While it can vary across organizations, Asian countries such as South Korea, China, and Singapore tend to use formal "Mr./Ms. Surname". while Americans and Canadians tend to use first names. When in doubt, erring on the side of formality is generally safest.

The concept of punctuality can also differ between cultures in an international business environment. Different ideas of what constitutes being "on time" can often lead to misunderstandings or negative cultural perceptions. For example, where an American may arrive at a meeting a few minutes early, an Italian or Mexican colleague may arrive several minutes—or more—after the scheduled start-time (and still be considered "on time").

Along with differences in etiquette, come differences in attitude, particularly towards things like workplace confrontation, rules and regulations, and assumed working hours. While some may consider working long hours a sign of commitment and achievement, others may consider these extra hours a demonstration of a lack of efficiency or the deprioritization of essential family or personal time.

3. Organizational hierarchy

Organizational hierarchy and attitudes towards management roles can also vary widely between cultures. Whether or not those in junior or middle-management positions feel comfortable speaking up in meetings, questioning senior decisions, or expressing a differing opinion can be dictated by cultural norms. Often these attitudes can be a reflection of a country's societal values or level of social equality. For instance, a country such as Japan, which traditionally values social hierarchy, relative status, and respect for seniority, brings this approach into the workplace. This hierarchy helps to define roles and responsibilities across the organization. This also means that those in senior management positions command respect and expect a certain level of formality and deference from junior team members.

However, Scandinavian countries, such as Norway, which emphasize societal equality, tend to have a comparatively flat organizational hierarchy. In turn, this can mean relatively informal communication and an emphasis on cooperation across the organization. When defining roles in multinational teams with diverse attitudes and expectations of organizational hierarchy, it can be easy to see why these cultural differences can present a challenge.

(783)

http://www.hult.edu/blog/cultural-differences-impact-international-business/

Part VII Doing Business Globally

Chapter 15 International Business Practices

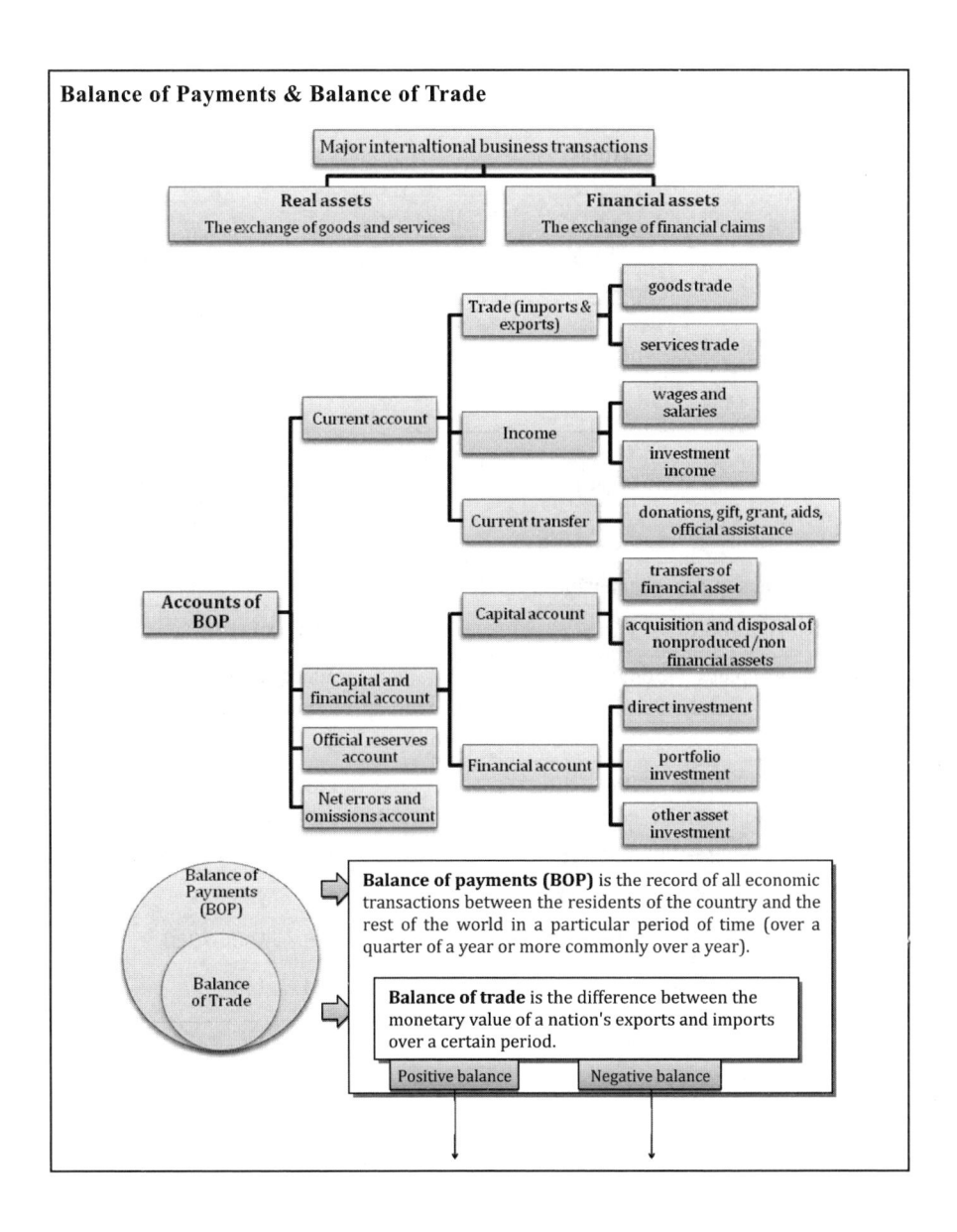

Balance of Payments & Balance of Trade

```
                    Major international business transactions
                   ┌────────────────────┴────────────────────┐
              Real assets                              Financial assets
     The exchange of goods and services          The exchange of financial claims
```

Accounts of BOP:
- Current account
  - Trade (imports & exports)
    - goods trade
    - services trade
  - Income
    - wages and salaries
    - investment income
  - Current transfer
    - donations, gift, grant, aids, official assistance
- Capital and financial account
  - Capital account
    - transfers of financial asset
    - acquisition and disposal of nonproduced/non financial assets
  - Financial account
    - direct investment
    - portfolio investment
    - other asset investment
- Official reserves account
- Net errors and omissions account

Balance of payments (BOP) is the record of all economic transactions between the residents of the country and the rest of the world in a particular period of time (over a quarter of a year or more commonly over a year).

Balance of trade is the difference between the monetary value of a nation's exports and imports over a certain period.

| Positive balance | Negative balance |

· 159 ·

Any transaction will be recorded as a positive entry in one account and a negative entry in another account; therefore, the balance of one account may be negative or positive, while the total payments are always balanced, i.e. the BOP is always in balance in theory.

e.g. import of $50,000 worth of goods:
Debit: $50,000 goods imported (current account)
　　Credit: $50,000 capital outflow (capital account)

Forms of International Business

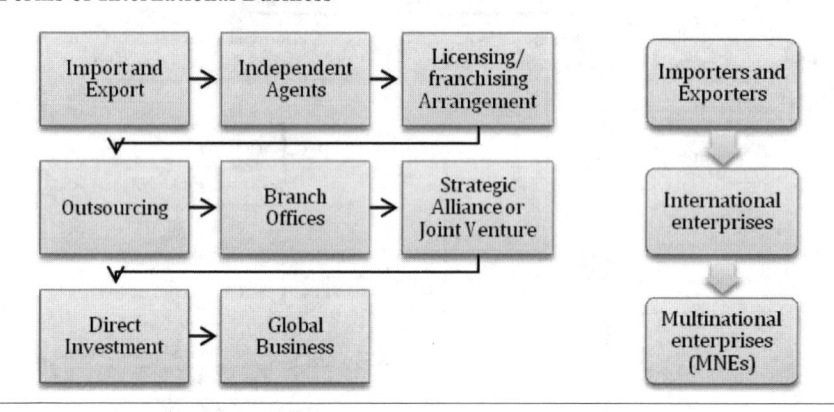

Import and Export → Independent Agents → Licensing/franchising Arrangement

Importers and Exporters ↓

Outsourcing → Branch Offices → Strategic Alliance or Joint Venture

International enterprises ↓

Direct Investment → Global Business

Multinational enterprises (MNEs)

Economic Reason for international trade

Absolute Advantages					Comparative Advantages				
A country produces a product more cheaply or efficiently than another country					A country produces a product more cheaply or efficiently than another product				
	Production cost before specialization		Production cost after specialization			Production cost before specialization		Production cost after specialization	
	x	y	x	x		x	y	x	y
Country A	120	150	240	110	Country A	110	130	220	-
Country B	140	110	-	170	Country B	170	150	-	300

Import and Export

Importer/exporter is a firm that buys / makes products in one country and imports/sells them from /in other countries.

Advantages	Disadvantages
· Easy to start · Excellent way to learn about global business	· Lowest level of involvement · Hard to expand

Independent Agent

A foreign individual or an organization who agrees to represent an exporter's interest.

Advantages	Disadvantages
· Easy to start and server the relationship · Low cost and low risk	· Agents may not be responsible · Firms represented are invisible

Licensing/franchising

License is a permission given to another company to manufacture or sell a product, or to use a brand name. Franchise is the most common form of licensing arrangement, which involves an annual fee plus a minimum order for goods.

Advantages	Disadvantages
· Inexpensive to develop · More reliable than agents	· Limited participation in the business · May develop potential rivals

Outsourcing

Outsourcing is an agreement in which one company hires another company to be responsible for an existing internal activity, such as manufacturing, facility management, call support, accounting service, etc.

Advantages	Disadvantages
· Way to handle short-term labor shortage · Help to concentrate on core operations · Save capital, energy and time · Lower risk	· May have problem in quality control · May develop potential rivals

Branch Offices

A branch office is an outlet of a company or, more generally, an organization that – unlike a subsidiary – does not constitute a separate legal entity, while being physically separated from the organization's main office. (Refer to Chapter 1 for more about "branches")

Advantages	Disadvantages
· More tangible presence · Better control	· Limited scale · Limited understanding of local surroundings

Strategic Alliance vs. Joint Venture

Joint venture is a separate business with two or more businesses taking a financial stake (usually, but not always, as shareholders) and management as agreed.

Advantages	Disadvantages
· Shared investment and risk · Reduced competition · Combined advantages of all parties	· Internal disputes · Potential rivals if the relationship breaks down

Strategic alliance is an informal or weak contractual agreement between parties or a minority cross-shareholding arrangement.

Advantages	Disadvantages
· Similar to joint venture · More flexible	· Looser arrangement, is easier to break · May become illegal cartel · Less commitment

Portfolio Investment

The investment represents a non-controlling interest in a company or ownership of a loan to another party. Portfolio investments are passive investments, as they do not entail active management or control of the issuing company. Rather, the purpose of the investment is solely financial gain, in contrast to foreign direct investment (FDI), which allows an investor to exercise a certain degree of managerial control over a company.

Advantages	Disadvantages
· Flexible investment · Easy to get involved and withdraw	· Short-term interest · No controlling power to the business

Note: *For international transactions, equity investments where the owner holds less than 10% of a company's shares are classified as portfolio investments. These transactions are also referred to as "portfolio flows" and are recorded in the financial account of a country's balance of payments.*

·Direct Investment

Arrangement involves more substantial investment as buying or establishing tangible assets, e.g. manufacturing plant, R&D center, in another country.

Advantages	Disadvantages
· Most tangible presence · Direct control · More resources available as a member of local business communities	· Expensive · Large input in manpower · Highly risky · Lack of local experience

Part VII Doing Business Globally

•Global Business

A multinational firm uses whatever approach seems best suited to a particular situation in its worldwide business.

Note: *all the above forms of business (except import and export) can be domestic or international contracting.*

Barriers to international business

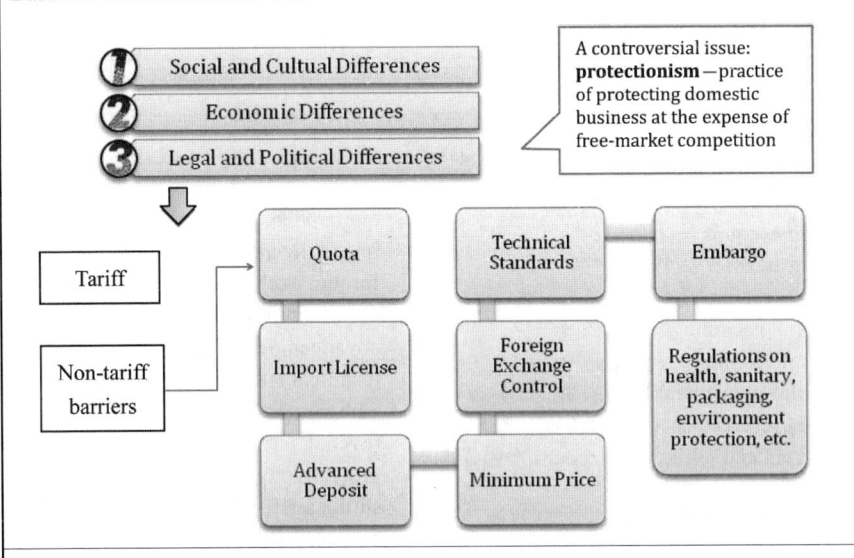

1. Social and Cultural Differences
2. Economic Differences
3. Legal and Political Differences

A controversial issue: **protectionism** — practice of protecting domestic business at the expense of free-market competition

- Tariff
- Non-tariff barriers:
  - Quota
  - Import License
  - Advanced Deposit
  - Technical Standards
  - Foreign Exchange Control
  - Minimum Price
  - Embargo
  - Regulations on health, sanitary, packaging, environment protection, etc.

Tariffs

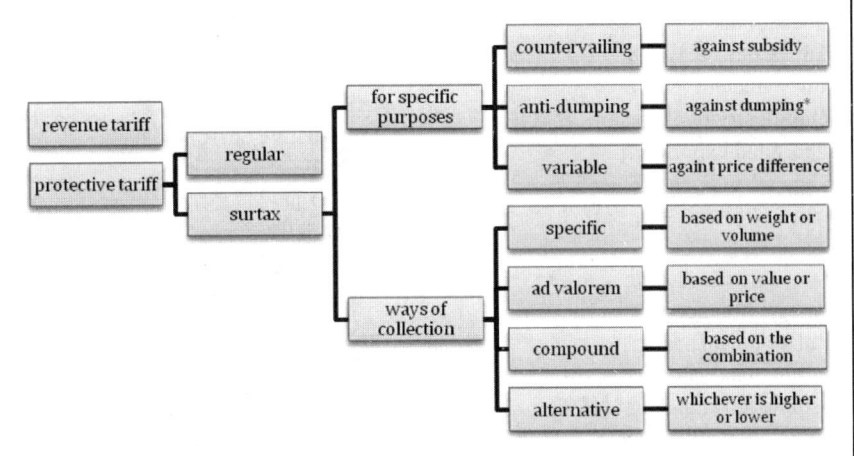

- revenue tariff
- protective tariff
  - regular
  - surtax
    - for specific purposes
      - countervailing — against subsidy
      - anti-dumping — against dumping*
      - variable — against price difference
    - ways of collection
      - specific — based on weight or volume
      - ad valorem — based on value or price
      - compound — based on the combination
      - alternative — whichever is higher or lower

*Dumping: practice of selling a product abroad for less than the comparable price charged at home. (As some countries do not recognize China as a market economy, the price or value of a product on a third market will be referred to when they decide whether the Chinese product is dumped.)

商务导论

International Trade/Economic Agreement (with China)

United Nations (UN)	World Trade Organization (WTO)	World Bank (WB)	Asian-Pacific Economic Cooperation (APEC)	Boao Forum for Asia (BFA)
Association of Southeast Asian Nations (ASEAN)	Shanghai Cooperation Organizaiton (SCO)	BRICS (Brazil, Russia, India, China, South Africa)	Forum on China-Africa Cooperation (FOCAC)	The Group of 20 (G20)

Key Terms

real asset 实物资产
financial asset 金融资产
Balance of Payments (BOP) 国际收支平衡表
current account 往来账户；经常账户
current transfer 经常性转移
capital account 资本账户
financial account 金融账户
direct investment 直接投资
portfolio investment 间接投资；证券投资
official reserves account 官方储备账户
net errors and omissions account 净错误与遗漏账户
balance of trade 贸易收支；贸易差额
positive balance 正差额
negative balance 负差额
trade surplus 贸易顺差
trade deficit 贸易逆差
flow statement 流量表
double-entry bookkeeping 复式记账
import and export 进出口
independent agents 独立代理
licensing/franchising 授权经营；特许经营
outsourcing 外包
branch offices 办事处
strategic alliance 战略合作
joint venture 合资企业
multinational enterprises (MNEs) 多国公司
absolute advantage 绝对优势
comparative advantage 相对优势
protectionism（贸易）保护主义

tariff 关税
Non-tariff barriers 非关税壁垒
quota 配额
import license 进口许可证
foreign exchange control 外汇管制
minimum price 最低价格
advanced deposit 预付款
technical standards 技术标准
embargo 禁令
revenue tariff 财政关税
protective tariff 保护性关税
surtax tariff 附加税
countervailing tariff 反补贴税
anti-dumping tariff 反倾销税
variable tariff 差价税
specific tariff 从量税
ad valorem tariff 从价税
compound tariff 混合税
alternative tariff 选择税
UN 联合国
WTO 世界贸易组织
WB 世界银行
APEC 亚太经济合作组织
BFA 博鳌亚洲论坛
ASEAN 东南亚洲国家联盟
SCO 上海合作组织
BRICS 金砖国家
FOCAC 中非合作论坛
G20 二十国集团

Brainstorming
Search for facts of China's BOP and try to analyze them. Read recent news about trade barriers against China. Discuss them. What is the significance of joining in WTO?

Read More

Four Types of International Business Strategies
International

Using an international strategy means focusing on exporting products and services to foreign markets, or conversely, importing goods and resources from other countries for domestic use. Companies that employ such strategy are often headquartered exclusively in their country of origin, allowing them to circumvent the need to invest in staff and facilities overseas. Businesses that follow these strategies often include small local manufacturers that export key resources to larger companies in neighboring countries. However, this model is not without significant business challenges, like legally establishing local sales and administrative offices in major cities internationally; managing global logistics involving the import, export, and manufacture of products; and ensuring compliance with foreign manufacturing and trade regulations.

Despite its relative challenges, the international strategy may be the most common, because on average, it requires the least amount of overhead. Companies striving to expand internationally may try a combination of strategies to see which works the best for them in terms of logistics and profits. For example, a company may start off using the international strategy—exporting its products overseas as a way to test the international market—and gauge how successfully its products sell. Subsequently, the company may need to adjust its strategy and create a multi-domestic platform through which it can manufacture and sell its goods more efficiently.

Multi-domestic

In order for a business to adopt a multi-domestic business strategy, it must invest in establishing its presence in a foreign market and tailor its products or services to the local customer base. As opposed to marketing foreign products to customers who may not initially recognize or understand them, companies modify their offerings and reposition their marketing strategies to engage with foreign customs, cultural traits and traditions. Multi-domestic businesses often keep their company headquarters in their country of origin, but they usually establish overseas headquarters, called subsidiaries, which are better equipped to offer foreign consumers region-specific versions of their products and services. These companies also frequently lease buildings abroad to serve as sales offices, manufacturing facilities or storage for housing service operations.

Multi-domestic strategies are largely adopted by food and beverage companies. For example, the Kraft Heinz Company makes a specialized version of its ketchup for customers in India—featuring a different blend of spices—to help match the nation's culinary preferences. However, these adjustments are often expensive and can incur a certain level of financial risk when launching unproven products in a new market. As such, companies usually only utilize this expansion strategy in a limited number of countries.

Global

In an effort to expand their customer base and sell products in more foreign markets, companies following a global strategy leverage economies of scale as much as possible to boost their reach and revenue. Global companies attempt to homogenize their products and services in order to minimize costs and reach as broad an international audience as possible. These companies tend to maintain a central office or headquarters, usually in their country of origin, while also establishing dozens of operations in countries all over the world.

Even when keeping essential aspects of their goods and services intact, companies adhering to the global strategy typically have to make some practical small-scale adjustments in order to break into international markets. For example, software companies need to adjust the language used in their products, while fast-food companies may add, remove or change the name of certain menu items in order to better suit local markets, while keeping their core items and global message intact.

Transnational

The transnational business strategy is one of the most intricate

Part VII Doing Business Globally

methods that businesses can employ when expanding internationally, and can be seen as a combination of the global and multi-domestic strategies. While this strategy keeps a business's headquarters and core technologies in its country of origin, it also allows a company to establish full-scale operations in foreign markets. The decision-making, production and sales responsibilities are evenly distributed to individual facilities in these different markets, allowing companies to have separate marketing, research and development departments aimed at responding to the needs of the local consumers.

A company that employs this strategy has the challenge of identifying the best management tactics for achieving positive economies of scale and increased efficiency. Having many inter-organizational entities collaborating in dozens of foreign markets requires a significant startup investment. Costs are driven by foreign legal and regulatory concerns, hiring new employees and buying or renting offices and production spaces. Therefore, this strategy is more complex than others because pressures to reduce costs are combined with establishing value-added activities to optimize adjustments that are necessary to gain leverage and be competitive in each local market. Given these challenges, larger corporations—such as General Electric and Toyota—typically employ a transnational strategy as they are able to invest in research and development in foreign markets, as well as establish production, manufacturing, sales and marketing divisions in these regions.

(816)

International Trade Organizations

The International Trade Organization (ITO) was the proposed name for an international institution for the regulation of trade.

Led by the United States in collaboration with allies, the effort to form the organization from 1945 to 1948, with the successful passing of the Havana Charter, eventually failed due to lack of approval by the US Congress. Until the creation of the World Trade Organization in 1994, international trade was managed through the General Agreement on Tariffs and Trade (GATT).

Proposal of an international trade institution

The Bretton Woods Conference of 1944, which established an international institution for monetary policy, recognized the need for a comparable international institution for trade to complement the International Monetary Fund and the World Bank. Bretton Woods was attended by representatives of finance ministries and not by representatives of trade ministries, the proposed reason why a trade agreement was not negotiated at that time.

In early December 1945, the United States invited its war-time allies to enter into negotiations to conclude a multilateral agreement for the reciprocal reduction of tariffs on trade in goods. In July 1945, the US Congress had granted President Harry S. Truman the authority to negotiate and conclude such an agreement. At the proposal of the United States, the United Nations Economic and Social Committee adopted a resolution, in February 1946, calling for a conference to draft a charter for an International Trade Organization.

A Preparatory Committee was established in February 1946, and met for the first time in London in October 1946 to work on the charter of an international organization for trade; the work was continued from April to November 1947.

General Agreement on Tariffs and Trade

At the same time, the negotiations on the General Agreement on Tariffs and Trade (GATT) in Geneva advanced well, and by October 1947 an agreement was reached: on October 30, 1947 eight of the twenty-three countries that had negotiated the GATT signed the "Protocol of Provisional Application of the General Agreement on Tariffs and Trade". Those eight countries were the United States, the United Kingdom, Canada, Australia, France, Belgium, the Netherlands, and Luxembourg.

Havana Charter

In March 1948, the negotiations on the ITO Charter were successfully completed in Havana Charter. The Havana Charter (formally the "Final Act of the United Nations Conference on Trade and Employment") provided for the establishment of the ITO, and set out the basic rules for international trade and other international economic matters. It was signed by 56 countries on March 24, 1948. It allowed for international cooperation and rules against anti-competitive business practices.

The Charter, proposed by John Maynard Keynes, was to establish the ITO and a financial institution called the International Clearing Union (ICU), and an international currency; the bancor. The Havana Charter institutions were to stabilize trade by encouraging nations to "net zero", with trade surplus and trade deficit both discouraged. This negative feedback was to be accomplished by allowing nations overdraft equal to half the average value of the country's trade over the preceding five years, with interest charged on both surplus and deficit.

Failure in United States Congress

The Charter never came into force, in part because in 1950 the United States government announced that it would not submit the treaty to the United States Senate for ratification. While repeatedly submitted to the US Congress, the charter was never approved. The most usual argument against the new organization was that it would be involved into internal economic issues. On December 6, 1950 President Truman announced that he would no longer seek Congressional approval of the ITO Charter. Because of the American rejection of the Charter, no other state ratified the treaty. Elements of the Charter would later become part of the General Agreement on Tariffs and Trade (GATT).

Individual trade agreements and World Trade Organization

In the absence of an international organization for trade, countries turned, from the early 1950s, to the only existing multilateral international institution for trade, the "GATT 1947", to handle problems concerning their trade relations. Therefore, the GATT would over the years "transform itself" into a de facto international organization. It was contemplated that the GATT would be applied for several years until the ITO came into force. However, since the ITO was never brought into being, the GATT gradually became the focus for international governmental cooperation on trade matters.

Seven rounds of negotiations occurred under GATT before the eighth round—the Uruguay Round—concluded in 1994 with the establishment of the World Trade Organization (WTO) as the GATT's replacement. The

GATT principles and agreements were adopted by the WTO, which was charged with administering and extending them.

(773)

https://en.wikipedia.org/wiki/International_Trade_Organization

Part VIII Understanding Principles of Economy

Chapter 16 Micro Economics

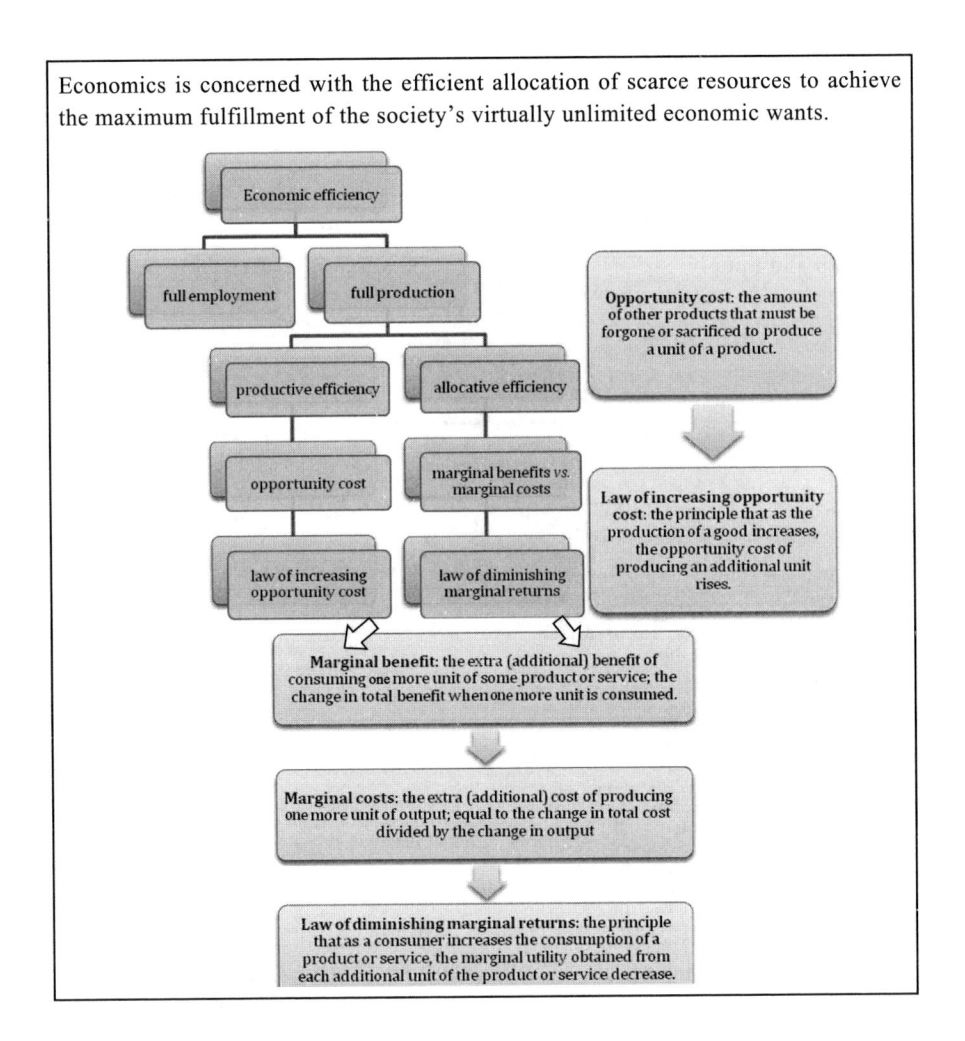

Economics is concerned with the efficient allocation of scarce resources to achieve the maximum fulfillment of the society's virtually unlimited economic wants.

- Economic efficiency
  - full employment
  - full production
    - productive efficiency
      - opportunity cost
        - law of increasing opportunity cost
    - allocative efficiency
      - marginal benefits vs. marginal costs
        - law of diminishing marginal returns

Opportunity cost: the amount of other products that must be forgone or sacrificed to produce a unit of a product.

Law of increasing opportunity cost: the principle that as the production of a good increases, the opportunity cost of producing an additional unit rises.

Marginal benefit: the extra (additional) benefit of consuming one more unit of some product or service; the change in total benefit when one more unit is consumed.

Marginal costs: the extra (additional) cost of producing one more unit of output; equal to the change in total cost divided by the change in output

Law of diminishing marginal returns: the principle that as a consumer increases the consumption of a product or service, the marginal utility obtained from each additional unit of the product or service decrease.

商务导论

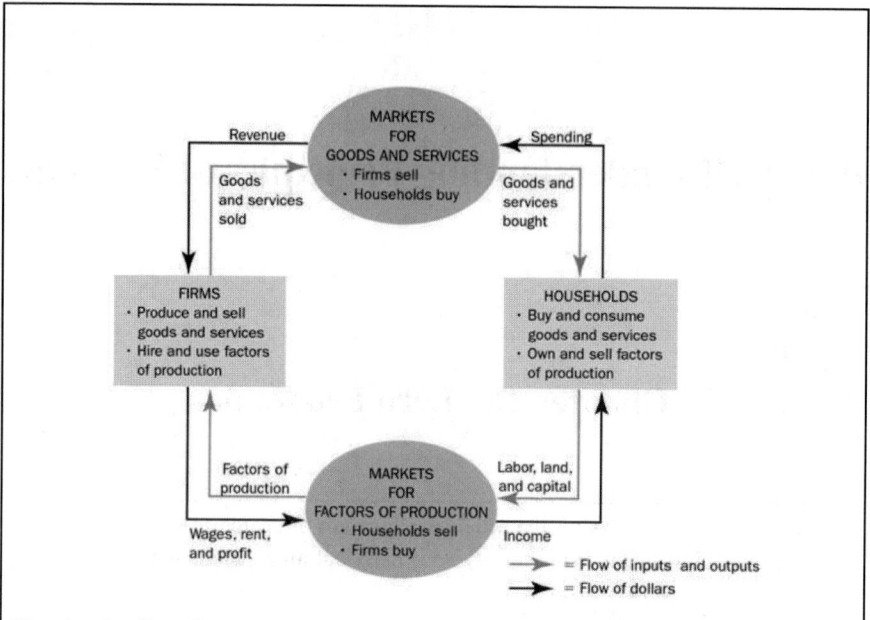

```
                    MARKETS
        Revenue      FOR        Spending
                GOODS AND SERVICES
         Goods   · Firms sell   Goods and
         and services · Households buy  services
         sold                    bought

    FIRMS                      HOUSEHOLDS
  · Produce and sell          · Buy and consume
    goods and services          goods and services
  · Hire and use factors      · Own and sell factors
    of production               of production

         Factors of   MARKETS    Labor, land,
         production    FOR       and capital
                  FACTORS OF PRODUCTION
         Wages, rent, · Households sell  Income
         and profit   · Firms buy

                    ⟶ = Flow of inputs and outputs
                    ➡ = Flow of dollars
```

The circular flow diagram suggests a complex, interrelated web of decision making and economic activity involving businesses and households.

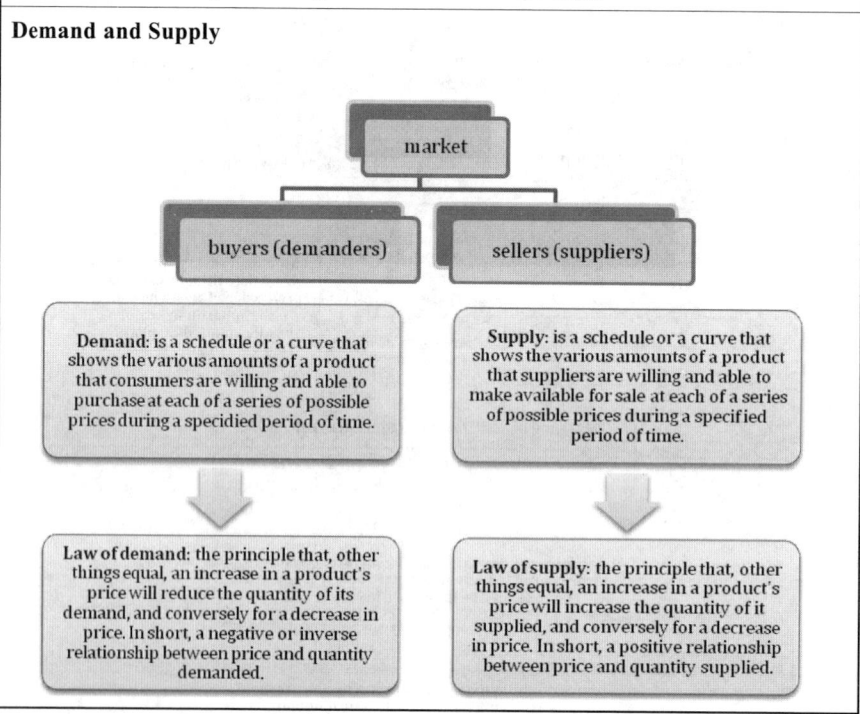

Demand and Supply

```
                market
               /      \
    buyers (demanders)  sellers (suppliers)
```

Demand: is a schedule or a curve that shows the various amounts of a product that consumers are willing and able to purchase at each of a series of possible prices during a specidied period of time.

⬇

Law of demand: the principle that, other things equal, an increase in a product's price will reduce the quantity of its demand, and conversely for a decrease in price. In short, a negative or inverse relationship between price and quantity demanded.

Supply: is a schedule or a curve that shows the various amounts of a product that suppliers are willing and able to make available for sale at each of a series of possible prices during a specified period of time.

⬇

Law of supply: the principle that, other things equal, an increase in a product's price will increase the quantity of it supplied, and conversely for a decrease in price. In short, a positive relationship between price and quantity supplied.

Part VIII Understanding Principles of Economy

Demand Curve

Supply Curve

Outward shift of demand/supply curve, shows an increase in demand/supply at each market price.

Inward shift of demand/supply curve, shows an decrease in demand/supply at each market price.

Determinants of demand	Determinants of supply
Tastes	Resource prices
Number of buyers	Number of sellers
Income	Taxes and subsidies
Expectations about prices and incomes	Price expectations
Prices of related goods: substitute goods complementary goods	Prices of other goods Technology

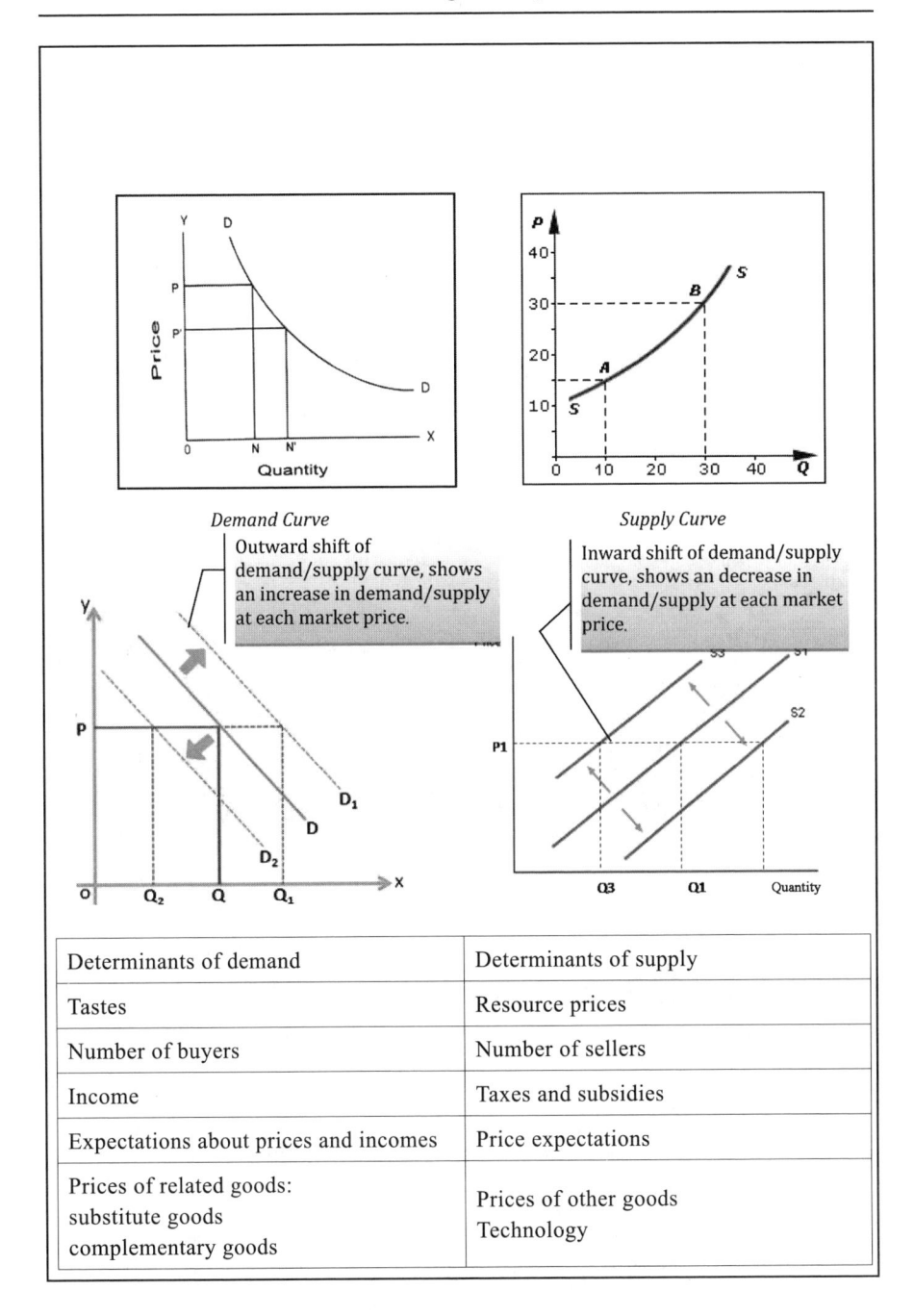

Price Elasticity of Demand

The responsiveness (or sensitivity) of consumers to a price change is measured by a product's **price elasticity of demand**: the ratio of the percentage change in quantity demanded of a product or reource to the percentage change in its price

Elastic Demand
Demand is elastic if a specific percentage change in price results in a larger percentage change in quantity demanded.

Inelastic Demand
Demand is inelastic, if a specific percentage change in price produces a smaller percentage change in quantity demanded.

Unit Elasticity
The percentage change in price and the resulting percentage change in quantity demanded are the same.

Perfectly Elastic
Quantity demanded can be of any amount at a particular price; graphs as a horizontal demand curve.

Perfectly Inelastic
Price change results in no change whatsoever in the quantity demanded; graphs as a vertical demand curve.

Total Revenue (TR) Test
The total revenue is the total amount the seller receives from the sale of a product in a particular time period. TP= P * Q. TP is releated to the price elasticity.

Elastic Demand
If demand is elastic, a decrease in price will increase total revenue, i.e. TR changes in the opposite direction from price.

Inelastic Demand
If demand is inelastic, a price decrease will reduce total revenue, i.e. TR changes in the same direction as price.

Substitutability
The larger the number of substitute goods that are available, the greater the price elasticity of demand.

Proportion of Income
Other things equal, the higher the price of a good relative to consumers' incomes, the greater the price elasticity of demand.

Determinants of price elasticity of demand

Luxuries vs. Necessities
The more that a good is considered to be a "luxury" rather than a "necessity", the greater is the price elasticity of the demand.

Time
Product demand is more elastic the longer the time period under consideration, as consumers often need time to adjust to changes in prices.

Price Elasticity of Supply

The responsiveness (or sensitivity) of suppliers to a price change is measured by a product's **price elasticity of supply**: the ratio of the percentage change in quantity supplied of a product or resource to the percentage change in its price.

Market Period
The time immediately after price change, which is too short for producers to respond with a change in quantity supplied; therefore, the supply is inelastic in this period of time.

Short run
In the short run, the production capacity of individual suppliers and the entire industry is fixed, but they can make more intensive production to increase the supply; thus the supply is elastic in the short run.

Long run
The long run is a time period long enough for firms to adjust their capacity and for new firms to enter the industry; therefore, the supply is more elastic in the long run.

Part VIII Understanding Principles of Economy

Note: there is no total-revenue test for elasticity of supply, as price and TR always move together regardless of the degree of elasticity or inelasticity.

Key Terms	
micro economics 微观经济学 economic efficiency 经济效率 full employment 完全就业 full production 完全生产 productive efficiency 生产效率 opportunity cost 机会成本 law of increasing opportunity cost 机会成本增加定律 allocative efficiency 分配效率 marginal benefits 边际利益 marginal costs 边际成本 law of diminishing marginal returns 边际回报递减定律 circular flow 经济循环 demand 需求 supply 供应 law of demand 需求定律 law of supply 供给定律 demand curve 需求曲线 supply curve 供给曲线	outward shift 向外移动 inward shift 向内移动 substitute goods 替代产品 complementary goods 互补产品 equilibrium price 均衡价格 surplus 剩余 shortage 短缺 price elasticity 价格弹性 elastic demand 弹性需求 inelastic demand 非弹性需求 unit elasticity 单位弹性 perfectly elastic 完全弹性 perfectly inelastic 完全非弹性 total revenue test 总收入测试 substitutability 可替代性 luxuries 奢侈品 necessities 必需品 market period 市场周期 cross elasticity 交叉弹性 independent goods 独立商品

Brainstorming

Find examples from your daily life to explain "opportunity cost".
Take apartment-rent as example. Explain the law of demand and supply and how the equilibrium price is reached.
Analyze the elasticity of some products you are familiar with.

Read More

Differences between Macroeconomics and Microeconomics

The heading says it all and I guess you already have an idea about it. Nevertheless for those who don't have much of an idea, Microeconomics and Macroeconomics (herein micro and macro economics) are the two broad branches in the vast field of "Economics" and I say "vast" because together, both the branches include policy, development, agriculture, politics, governance, labour and what not! Adam Smith is considered the "Father of Economics" especially as the "Father of Microeconomics" and John Maynard Keynes (Keynes is pronounced like Cairns) is arguably considered the "Father of Macroeconomics"—perhaps two of the greatest economists of our generation.

What is Macroeconomics?

In short, Macroeconomics is a "top-down" approach and is in a way, a helicopter view of the economy as a whole. It aims at studying various phenomena like the country's GDP (Gross Domestic Product) growth; inflation and inflation expectations; the government's spending, receipts and borrowings (fiscal policies); unemployment rates; monetary policy etc. to ultimately help understand the state of the economy, formulate policies at a higher level and conduct macro research for academic purposes. For example, Central Banks of all the countries majorly look at the macroeconomic situation of the country and also the globe in order to make crucial decisions like setting the country's policy interest rates. But it is worth mentioning that they look at micro aspects also.

Example: If you have been following recent global financial and economic events, the most talked about is the topic of the USA Federal Reserve's course of interest rate hikes. In a year, the Federal Reserve holds eight scheduled meetings for two consecutive days to decide and convey their policy stance known as "FOMC meetings" (Federal Open Market Committee meetings). The meeting majorly focuses on macro policy and stability based on data analysis and research, the conclusion being whether they should hike their policy interest rate or not. This meeting is part of a macroeconomic policy given that it looks at the economy as a whole and the outcome is a macro event.

What is Microeconomics?

Microeconomics in short, is a "bottom-up" approach. Detailed, it comprises the basic components that make up the economy which includes the factors of production (Land, Labour, Capital and Organization/Entrepreneurship). The three sectors of the economy—Agriculture, Manufacturing, and Services/Tertiary sectors and the components thereof understandably come up because of the factors of production. Microeconomics largely studies supply and demand behaviours in different markets that make up the economy, consumer behaviour and spending patterns, wage-price behaviour, corporate policies, impact on companies due to regulations etc.

Part VIII Understanding Principles of Economy

Example: For those who have been following the Indian growth story, you would be aware of the fact that the monsoon could have an impact on inflation especially food inflation. A bad monsoon could increase inflation given that the supply of fodder, vegetables etc. doesn't match the demand and a good monsoon could decrease/stabilize inflation due to obvious reasons. This affects the spending behaviour of individual consumers, agrarian based corporates and their like. (More on supply and demand coming up!)

Yes, you saw it coming—macro and micro economics are two sides of the same coin i.e., they have several things in common despite looking like seemingly different topics. Though there's no thin line of difference between the two, they are interrelated. So let's see what they have in common.

Macroeconomics vs Microeconomics—Commonalities

The following section will surely help you appreciate economics a lot more with many interesting concepts that one comes across, than just know the commonalities between the two.

Of course, the basics—Demand and Supply Relationship

The basic rationale is that "assuming all other factors remaining the same/equal," the quantity demanded decreases as price increases and the quantity demanded increases as price decreases (inverse relationship). All other factors remaining the same, the quantity supplied increases as price increases and the quantity supplied decreases as price decreases (direct relationship). This relationship between demand and supply attains the "state of equilibrium" or the optimal relationship when the quantity demanded and quantity supplied are equal. When they aren't equal, what arises is either a shortage or excess which gets adjusted to achieve equilibrium again?

A higher price set by sellers would cause a surplus of stock (Surplus/ Excess Quantity supplied) forcing them to lower prices (from Surplus Prices to the Equilibrium Price) to match the corresponding demand. A lower price set by sellers would cause a shortage of stock (Shortage of Quantity supplied) forcing prices to go up (from the Shortage Price to the Equilibrium Price) to keep pace with the corresponding demand.

(*Note*: By "higher" and "lower" prices, we mean the price relative to *the "Equilibrium Price" —that which a buyer should ideally bid/buy for (OR) the price relative to that which a seller should ideally ask/offer.*)

(879)

https://www.wallstreetmojo.com/macroeconomics-vs-microeconomics/

Part VIII Understanding Principles of Economy

Chapter 17 Macro Economy

This part overlaps with Chapters 2 and 10 with more details to some concepts

GDP
GDP includes only the market value of final goods and ignores intermediate goods altogether to avoid multiple counting. Alternatively, we could avoid multiple counting by measuring and cumulating only the value added at each stage.
Calculation of GDP should also exclude nonproduction transactions, because they have nothing to do with the generation of final goods.

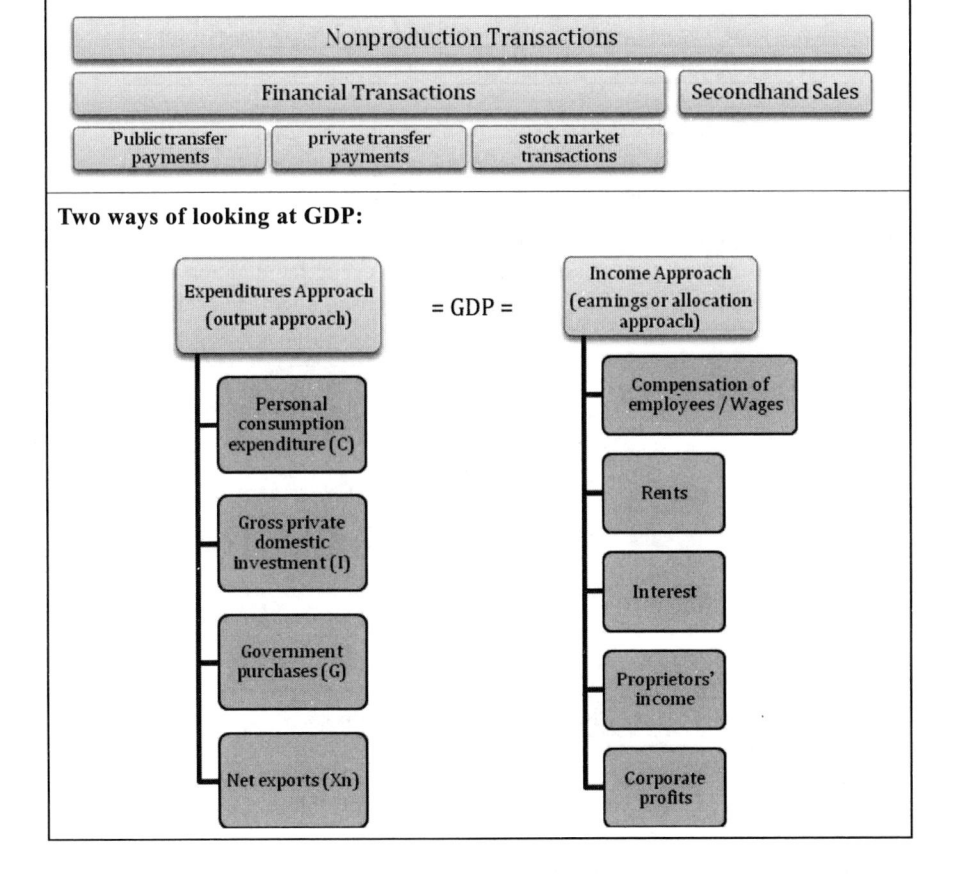

```
                    Nonproduction Transactions
         Financial Transactions              Secondhand Sales
  Public transfer    private transfer    stock market
    payments           payments          transactions
```

Two ways of looking at GDP:

```
Expenditures Approach              Income Approach
  (output approach)    = GDP =   (earnings or allocation
                                       approach)
    │                                       │
    ├─ Personal                             ├─ Compensation of
    │  consumption                          │  employees / Wages
    │  expenditure (C)                      │
    │                                       ├─ Rents
    ├─ Gross private                        │
    │  domestic                             ├─ Interest
    │  investment (I)                       │
    │                                       ├─ Proprietors'
    ├─ Government                           │  income
    │  purchases (G)                        │
    │                                       └─ Corporate
    └─ Net exports (Xn)                        profits
```

Other national accounts

- **Net domestic product (NDP)**: NDP = GDP - consumption of fixed capital (depreciation)
- **National income (NI)**: NI = NDP - net foreign factor income - indirect business taxes
- **Personal income (PI)**: PI = NI - social security contributions - corporate income taxes - undistributed corporate profits - transfer payments
- **Disposable income (DI)**: DI = PI - personal taxes = consumption + saving

Nominal GDP vs. Real GDP

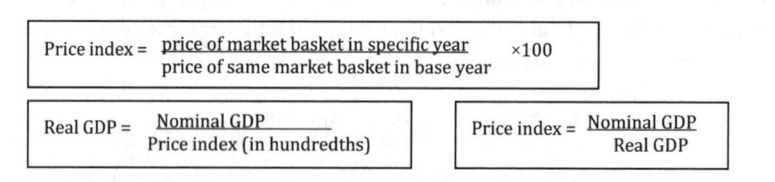

$$\text{Price index} = \frac{\text{price of market basket in specific year}}{\text{price of same market basket in base year}} \times 100$$

$$\text{Real GDP} = \frac{\text{Nominal GDP}}{\text{Price index (in hundredths)}} \qquad \text{Price index} = \frac{\text{Nominal GDP}}{\text{Real GDP}}$$

The Consumer Price Index (CPI)
The CPI reports the price of a market basket of some 300 consumer goods and services that presumably are purchased by a typical urban consumer.

The Business Cycle / Economic Cycle

Economists distinguish four phases of the business cycle; the duration and strength of each phase may vary; thus some prefer "fluctuations" rather than cycles.

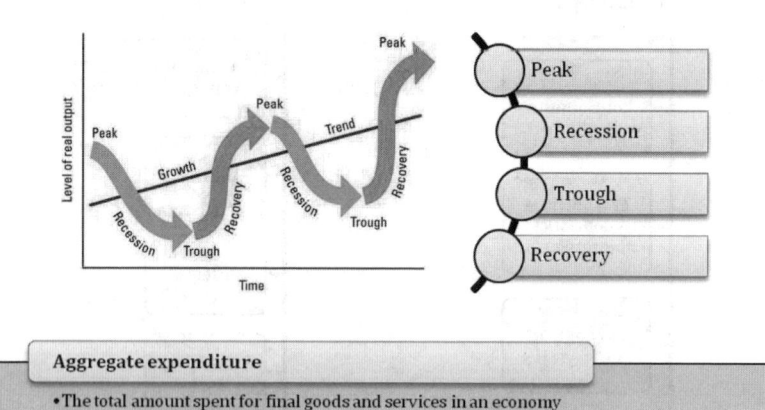

- Peak
- Recession
- Trough
- Recovery

Aggregate expenditure
- The total amount spent for final goods and services in an economy

Consumption and Saving

Consumption is the largest component of aggregate expenditure.
Saving = Disposable Income (DI) − Consumption (C)
Non-income determinants of consumption and saving

Part VIII Understanding Principles of Economy

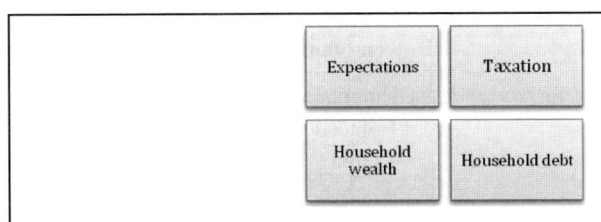

- Expectations
- Taxation
- Household wealth
- Household debt

Investment
Investment is the second component of private spending
Two basic determinates of investment spending

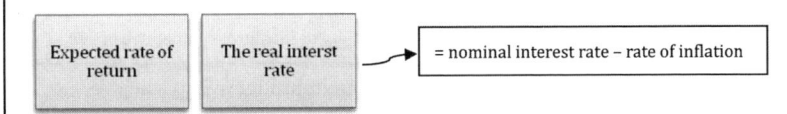

- Expected rate of return
- The real interst rate → = nominal interest rate – rate of inflation

Equilibrium GDP
In a closed private economy, where there is neither a government nor foreign sector, aggregate expenditures are equal to consumption expenditures plus planned gross investment expenditures. The equilibrium output of such an economy is that level of output at which the total amount of spending is just equal to the amount produced, or GDP.
That is

$$\text{Equilibrium GDP} = C + I_g$$

Consumption expenditures rise with GDP while planned gross investment expenditures are independent of the level of GDP. The aggregate expenditures schedule shows the amount of desired spending at each possible output level and can be used to determine the equilibrium level of output.

The Multiplier Effect
A change in a component of aggregate expenditures leads to a larger change in equilibrium GDP.

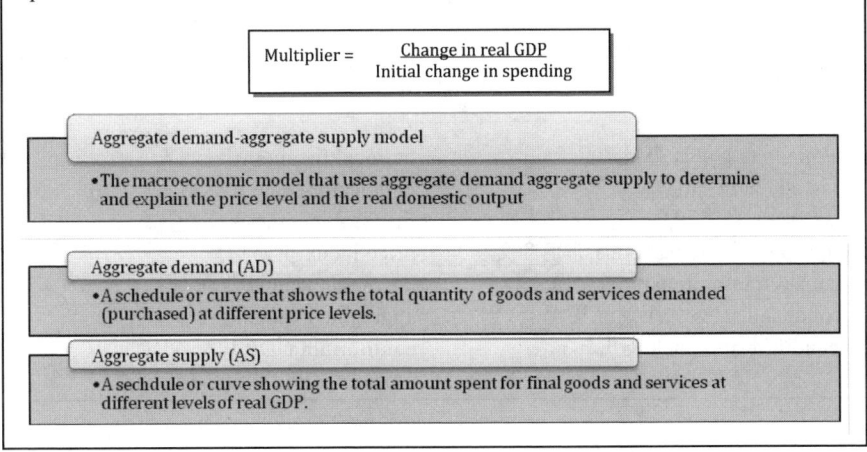

$$\text{Multiplier} = \frac{\text{Change in real GDP}}{\text{Initial change in spending}}$$

Aggregate demand-aggregate supply model
- The macroeconomic model that uses aggregate demand aggregate supply to determine and explain the price level and the real domestic output

Aggregate demand (AD)
- A schedule or curve that shows the total quantity of goods and services demanded (purchased) at different price levels.

Aggregate supply (AS)
- A sechdule or curve showing the total amount spent for final goods and services at different levels of real GDP.

Determinants of AD	Determinants of AS

1. Change in consumer spending
  a. Consumer wealth
  b. Consumer expectations
  c. Household indebtedness
  d. Taxes
2. Change in investment spending
  a. Interest rates
  b. Expected returns
    - Expected future business conditions
    - Technology
    - Degree of excess capacity
    - Business taxes
3. Change in government spending
4. Change in net export spending
  a. National income abroad
  b. Exchange rates
	1. Change in input prices
	  a. Domestic resource availability
	    - Land
	    - Labor
	    - Capital
	    - Entrepreneurial ability
	  b. Prices of imported resources
	  c. Market power
	    The ability to set above-competitive prices
	2. Change in productivity
	3. Change in legal-institutional environment
	  a. Business taxes and subsidies
	  b. Government regulations

Equilibrium price level
- The price level at which the aggregate demand curve intersects the aggregate supply curve

Equilibrium real domestic output
- The gross domestic product at which the total quantity of final goods and services purchased (aggregate expenditures) is euqal to the total quantity of final goods and services produces (the real domestic output); the real domestic output at which the aggregate demand curve intersects the aggregate supply curve

Changes in equilibrium

| Increases in AD: Demand-pull inflation | Decreases in AD: Recession and cyclical unemployment | Increases in AS: Full employment with price-level stability | Decreases in AS: Cost-push inflation |

Key Terms

intermediate goods 直接产品
value added 增加值
final goods 最终产品
nonproduction transactions 非生产交易
financial transactions 金融交易
secondhand sales 二手商品买卖
expenditure approach 支出计算法

national income 国民收入
personal income 个人收入
disposal income 可支配收入
price index 价格指数
business cycle 商业周期
aggregate expenditure 总开支
equilibrium GDP 均衡 GDP

personal consumption expenditure 个人消费支出	multiplier effect 扩大效应
gross private domestic investment 总私有国内投资	aggregate demand 总需求
	aggregate supply 总供给
government purchases 政府购买	equilibrium price level 均衡点价格水平
net exports 净出口	equilibrium real domestic output 均衡点真实国内生产
income approach 收入方法	demand-pull inflation 需求拉动型通货膨胀
compensation 报酬	
rents 房租	cost-push inflation 成本推动型通货膨胀
interest 利息	expansionary fiscal policy 扩张性财政政策
proprietors' income 所有者收入	
corporate profits 公司利润	contractionary fiscal policy 紧缩性财政政策
net domestic product 净国内产品	
	crowding-out effect 挤出效应
	impounding 扣押

Brainstorming

Think of a product whose demand or supply has increased or decreased in recent years. Analyze the reasons of its increase/decrease.

Search and compare the following data on the internet: GDP, GNP, CPI and per capita income of China in recent years.

Read More

Differences between Macroeconomics and Microeconomic
(continued)

How does Macro affect Micro?

Let's assume the nation's Central Bank cuts the policy interest rate (a macro impact) by 100 basis points (100 bps = 1%). This should ideally lower the borrowing costs of commercial banks with the Central Bank, helping lower their deposit rate, thus giving room to lower the rate on the loans they make to individuals and corporate. This is expected to cause a rise in borrowings aka "credit growth" given cheaper access to credit and therefore greater investment helping corporate invest in new assets, projects, expansion plans etc. which are developments on the micro front. This is just one of several examples where macro policies and decisions affect the micro economy. Additional examples can include:

Income tax changes;

Changes in subsidies;

Currency related policies (ex: China depegging the Yuan/Renminbi to the US Dollar) amongst others;

Unemployment rates in the economy could help understand how many jobs a company might create amongst other factors.

How does Micro affect Macro?

One of the multiple factors that set macro policies is the condition of the micro economy. To continue with the earlier example of the Central Bank given that they have lowered their policy rates, they observe the borrowing and investment patterns of corporates, individuals and households. These behavioural patterns can help determine whether the Central Bank should cut rates further if the outlook is weak, keep rates on hold or increase them if the outlook is picking up or shooting up. Additional examples include the following:

The Consumer Price Index (CPI) is determined by taking surveys of individuals and retailers based on their spending patterns where the outcome results in a certain "percentage figure" which is indicative of the rate of inflation. This figure is considered a key determinant for the Central Bank to set policy interest rates. The spending behaviour of individuals is a microeconomic variable.

Taking a deep dive into the US Federal Reserve and in particular the US economy, news would tell us that a major factor influencing their policy decisions is the payroll numbers or the wage growth which is part of the micro economy.

A key concept in Microeconomics is that of "Opportunity Cost" i.e., the cost incurred by not choosing the second best alternative given the choices are mutually exclusive (one choice eliminates the others). In other words, it is the marginal benefit one could derive by choosing the second best comparable alternative to achieve the same purpose given that the choices are mutually exclusive. On a more philosophical note, this has some roots in the concept of .

Example: You are a 5-year-old kid and have $5 with you to choose between an ice-cream and Swiss chocolate which cost $5 and $4 respectively (Would a 5-year-old kid really care if it were a Swiss chocolate or an ice-cream? I doubt he'd know its specialty. Who knows?). Let's say that the kid chooses the chocolate over the ice-cream just to spoil our clichéd

Part VIII Understanding Principles of Economy

assumption that a kid would always choose the ice-cream! He relishes the chocolate until he sees his friend relishing the ice-cream. The kid then tries to weigh the costs of his decision to go for the chocolate.

Macroeconomics vs Microeconomics—Key Differences

"The difference" is, of course, that micro gives the picture from the smaller parts of the economy while macro looks at the economy at large.

Other Differences

Remember the "Supply-Demand" graph shown earlier? Although the supply-demand behaviour applies to both fields of economics, it is believed that Microeconomics is based on the premise of buyers and sellers achieving equilibrium before long, if disequilibrium exists. Macroeconomics focuses on different cycles of the economy like the short and long term debt cycle, business cycles, super-cycles etc. ultimately leading us to believe that the economy could stay in a state of "disequilibrium" for longer than expected before everything adjusts to equilibrium. Just to introduce you to one of the harder concepts to master in economics without delving into it too much, Macroeconomics lends its roots to the "Theory of General Equilibrium."

A less significant distinction would be the different "Schools" of economics. There are multiple schools of Macroeconomics like Keynesian Economics, Monetary Economics, Chicagoan Economics and Austrian Economics to name a few. Some of those in Microeconomics are Classical Economics, Neo-Classical Economics and Islamic Economics to name a few.

A Tinge of Important History

There's more history apart from the fact that Adam Smith and J.M. Keynes were the so called "fathers" of micro and macro-economics. It is believed that Macroeconomics majorly evolved from an economic crisis, the infamous "Great Depression" from 1929 to the late 1930s where J.M. Keynes and Milton Friedman played a major role in explaining and understanding the event. J.M. Keynes wrote a book titled *"The General Theory of Employment, Interest and Money"* where he sought to explain the Great Depression through aggregate expenditures, income levels, employment levels and government spending—Keynesian Economics. Milton Friedman, a highly regarded economist explained the Great

Depression by a banking crisis, deflation, higher interest rates and restrictive Monetary Policy—School of Monetary Economics.

If you understood the above paragraph and its various inter linkages, you are on the verge of becoming an upcoming economist and a good economic thinker. If you didn't totally understand it, you are going to start thinking more about economics and the more you think about it, the more you would appreciate it.

Macroeconomics vs Microeconomics—Conclusion

Firstly, to be honest, if you have absorbed all the material above, you have possibly gone through the best crash course in Micro and Macro economics and a bit of Finance—there's no doubt about that. You probably know much more than you may actually have to. Well…if you have not lasted till the conclusion and are directly coming to it seeking a recap, you are going to be disappointed. Why? Simply because you have to read everything above to really appreciate the subject. After all, there is nothing greater than learning, understanding and appreciating the beauty of a subject, especially a subject as broad as Economics.

Secondly, you would have or at least should have observed the particularity in the language used to explain different concepts. Oftentimes, loose or not so precise language could either cast doubts or not explain the influencing items. For example, to explain the principle of "Opportunity Costs" you would have come across the word "mutually exclusive". To help understand the importance attached to these words, they have been marked them in Italics.

The next time you bargain with a dealer or a seller, be sure to keep in mind that some fundamental economic principles are in place; that your transactions are part of the micro economy and, that a whole lot of people like you who are buying stuff (material or immaterial) are actually impacting the macro economy at large. Hope you have learnt a lot of new concepts. That's enough of economics for now!!!

(1158)

https://www.wallstreetmojo.com/macroeconomics-vs-microeconomics/

Reference

[1] 陈准民. 工商导论(第二版)[M]. 北京:高等教育出版社,2009.

[2] 邓国清. 工商导论(英文版)[M]. 北京:对外经济贸易大学出版社,2014.

[3] 窦卫霖. 跨文化交际基础[M]. 北京:对外经济贸易大学出版社,2007.

[4]Andrew Gillespie. 商务专业英语基础(图示教程)[M]. 上海:上海外语教育出版社,2000.

[5]Campbell R. McConnell. 经济学[M]. 北京:高等教育出版社,2002.

[6]Gareth R. Jones. 工商导论——如何为人创造价值[M]. 北京:人民邮电出版社,2007.

[7]Jeff Madura. 商学导论[M]. 北京,人民邮电出版社,2008.

[8]William G. Nickels, James M. McHugh, and Susan M. MCHugh. 商务学导论[M]. 北京:清华大学出版社,2012.

[9]Ricky W. Griffin & Ronald J. Ebert. *Business* (Fifth Edition)[M]. New Jersey, Prentice Hall, 1998.

[10]The Institute of Chartered Accountants in England and Wales, *Business, Technology and Finance* (Study Manual 2018), 2017.

[11]The Institute of Chartered Accountants in England and Wales, *Business Strategy and Technology* (Study Manual 2018), 2017.